GREAT ESTATES

GREAT ESTATES

THE LIFESTYLES AND HOMES
OF AMERICAN MAGNATES

WILLIAM G. SCHELLER

UNIVERSE

(PAGE 1)

The Lower Loggia at The Breakers, Newport, Rhode Island.

PHOTO © RICHARD CHEEK FOR THE PRESERVATION SOCIETY OF NEWPORT COUNTY.

(PAGE 2)

The Breakers main gate mid-winter.

PHOTO © THE PRESERVATION SOCIETY OF NEWPORT COUNTY.

(PAGE 5)

A garden view of Rockefeller's Kykuit.

USED WITH PERMISSION OF NATIONAL TRUST FOR HISTORIC PRESERVATION. PHOTO © EZRA STOLLER, ESTO PHOTOGRAPHICS.

(PAGE 6)

Malcolm Forbes with one of his Harley-Davidsons.

PHOTO COURTESY THE FORBES ARCHIVES. © 2002 ALL RIGHTS RESERVED. PHOTO BY GLEN A. DAVIS.

Published by:

Universe Publishing
A Division of Rizzoli International Publications, Inc.
300 Park Avenue South
New York, NY 10010
www.rizzoliusa.com

© 2009 Universe Publishing

Editor: Leslie Conron Carola
Copy Editor: Deborah Teipel Zindell
Designer: Kevin Osborn, Research & Design, Ltd.,
                 Arlington, Virginia

2009 2010 2011 2012 / 10 9 8 7 6 5 4 3 2 1

Printed in China

ISBN-13: 978-0-7893-9959-5

Library of Congress Catalog Control Number: 2008933174

Contents

Introduction

*L*ONG before the principles of egalitarianism were enshrined in the Declaration of Independence and the Constitution, the settlers of British North America had set a course of social and political development in which hereditary aristocracy would play no significant role. There would be royal charters and land grants, to the likes of the Duke of York and Lord Baltimore; and land itself became something of a patent of nobility in places where it was practical to plant thousands of acres in tobacco or cotton. But the grandees of Spanish America, and the *seigneurs* of New France, would never provide a model for Virginia or New England.

But it wasn't very long before America had an aristocracy, the aristocracy it wanted, the aristocracy its religion (at least in New England) and its system of commerce told it it must have. It wasn't possible for a Puritan to ever know for sure if he or she were one of the elect, predestined for salvation, but worldly success—as long as it wasn't accompanied by prideful extravagance—might be a very good sign that God was smiling upon a person in a spiritual as well as material sense. And the rise of American trade soon made the existence of a wealthy mercantile class inevitable.

As the nineteenth century progressed, the money earned was invested in manufacturing, and then in railroads. Revolutions in printing technology and mass literacy enabled publishing empires to flourish, while urbanization and mass production of consumer goods made retailing a pathway to great riches. New developments in lighting and transportation made oil standard. In the twentieth century, motion pictures and broadcasting, followed by high technology and its information-age applications, created more immense fortunes.

America had its aristocracy, sustained not by looking after bloodlines but by looking out for the main chance. It wasn't hereditary—well, usually for no more than a few generations—but it was as much a part of the national furniture as the House of Lords in Great Britain.

(ABOVE)

The gazebo in the gardens at Lyndhurst.

PHOTO LYNDHURST ARCHIVES, A NATIONAL TRUST HISTORIC SITE.
© LYNDHURST 1999-2002.

(OPPOSITE)

A festive dining table at Skibo Castle, Scotland, home of Andrew Carnegie.

PHOTO SKIBO CASTLE, SCOTLAND.

Britain's Lords have kept their titles, but lost their power. The New World aristocracy had no titles to lose, but its power has never been in doubt. That includes its power to fascinate the rest of us, a power made more tantalizing by the thought of all the main chances that are still out there.

❋ ❋ ❋ ❋ ❋ ❋ ❋ ❋ ❋ ❋ ❋ ❋ ❋ ❋ ❋ ❋ ❋

If there has been a sea change in the ways in which great fortunes are made, it has been more than matched by the style in which they have been spent. This isn't just a matter of the things that money can buy—the difference, say, between a private railroad car and a private jet. It's a matter of how inconspicuously so many of the very rich now consume. This is especially true of individuals who owe their fortunes to business success, as opposed, say, to entertainment or sports celebrity. (That much-ridiculed but nonetheless quite successful 1980s television program "Lifestyles of the Rich and Famous" didn't usually focus on CEOs.) If we look back on '80s binge chronicled in Tom Wolfe's *The Bonfire of the Vanities,* what we recall of most media reportage had to do not with the indulgences of individual magnificoes but with the sudden extravagances of a middle class gotten rich on the cheap: we weren't reading about plutocrats' racehorses, but about the BMW next door.

It has almost gotten to the point where we would like to hear about a tycoon who had furnished his Gulfstream like a private railroad car, in rosewood and velvet—although, puritans that they are, Wall Street's analysts would probably devalue his stock on the grounds that such anachronistic and recherché frivolity probably meant there was a loose nut on the corporate tiller. It's hard to say, though. Some moguls are granted a lot of latitude when it comes to tossing around pots of gold in a less than sobersided fashion. For some reason, balloons often figure into this scheme of indulgence: think of Richard Branson, master of the Virgin empire, who is always trying to set some lighter-than-air flight record; or the late Malcolm Forbes, a balloonist who wasn't interested in records unless it was the record for how much fun a man could have. Nevertheless, both these high fliers always made sure to flaunt the names of their business enterprises on the sides of their big billowing toys. Not only did this put them above the ranks of mere millionaire sportsmen, who have to plaster their balloons with the names of somebody else's watches or champagne; it showed that they could mix business with pleasure.

Why have things changed so completely, over such a relatively short span of years? For one thing, rich people —at least, people who get rich from exercising a genius for business—are better educated, more sophisticated, and simply have better taste. There are no modern counterparts of "Bet-a-Million" Gates, the Gilded-Age sport who brought forty changes of clothes to a Saratoga resort and wore them all in one day.

That's one reason. Another is, quite logically, a desire for privacy, which is inseparable from security. But perhaps the biggest reason of all has to do with the democratization of taste. At one time the only things money could buy, apart from land, were exaggerated versions of the things that most people had—essentially,

clothing, shelter, and transportation. If you were rich, you built a bigger house, filled it with expensive furniture and art, and hired a platoon of servants. You wore elaborate outfits—colorful outfits even if you were a man, at least until 19th-century style-setters decided that black was most becoming. You bought the best horses, and the most ostentatious carriage, that you could afford. And when you were done spending your money, there was no way on earth you could be mistaken for one of the people who worked for you.

This state of affairs persisted until some time in the latter half of the 20th century. Then the old arrangements seemed somehow to be stood on end: instead of factory workers buying suits so they could at least dress like an off-the-rack version of the boss on weekends, we began to see Sam Walton in a pickup truck, Steven Spielberg in a ball cap and sneakers, and Ted Turner pulling a plug of chewing tobacco out of his jeans. More than top hats have gone out of style—the top hat mentality has vanished as well.

With the exception of a few ascetics, the rich still have their houses and cars—but they are no longer on display. A freestanding mansion on Fifth Avenue would be unthinkable today, even if it weren't out of reach of all but a half-dozen super-moguls. Too many people would stare in the windows, or worse. Now we do our looking from a somewhat greater distance, and we treasure our few wealthy exhibitionists more than ever. They give us the enjoyment we once had watching Cornelius Vanderbilt careen along behind a pair of fast trotters, or squinting seaward as *Cleopatra's Barge*, the Crowninshield yacht, wafted into Salem harbor.

The Yankee Ships
Were Everywhere

NORTH American civilization came into existence at a turning point in the history of moneymaking. For centuries, land ownership had been the foundation of wealth, with trade—financed by the system of investment banking pioneered in late medieval Italy—only beginning to create a class of magnificoes to rival the landholding, and usually titled, classes. Industrial capitalism loomed on the horizon, but it was a horizon yet to be blurred by coal smoke and steam.

The European colonies in North America clustered tightly along the seacoasts, and along great rivers such as the Hudson and the St. Lawrence. Where the land was fertile, and where it was easy for crops to be siphoned toward the sea lanes, colonists ventured farther from the ocean. The great plantations of tidewater Maryland and Virginia, the Dutch patroonships of the Hudson valley, and the French seigneuries along the St. Lawrence all helped to create the first great North American fortunes, although in many cases these vast landholdings were granted to men who were already secure members of the European aristocracies. In the American South, plantation agriculture created its own small aristocracy—but one which, fertile as it was in yielding brainpower and military genius for the Revolution, provided no business model for the busy centuries to come. The true barons of American business first appeared in that corner of the continent where breaking out into broad agricultural hinterlands was most difficult, and where money had to be made in commerce if it was to be made at all.

To this day, the coast of New England is graced with the handsome 18th-century homes of shipowners and sea captains who took risks upon the North Atlantic and beyond, and who turned their profits into fine architecture, exquisite furniture, and old Madeira. Walk the streets of Portsmouth, New Hampshire, or Newburyport, Massachusetts—to name just two of the towns that bred the race of

(ABOVE)
The Salem vessel Friendship, *depicted on a plate typical of c. 1800 China Trade goods.*

THE PEABODY-ESSEX MUSEUM, SALEM. IMAGE #E62500.
PHOTO MARK SEXTON.

(OPPOSITE)
Elias Hasket Derby, America's first millionaire. Oil portrait by James Frothingham.

THE PEABODY-ESSEX MUSEUM, SALEM. NEG. #1201.
PHOTO MARK SEXTON.

Yankee traders—and the style of the era and the
opportunities it afforded are impossible to ignore.

THE HANCOCKS

In the largest of those seaports of colonial New
England, on the slopes of the highest hill, stood one of
the grandest of all those princely merchants' homes.
It isn't there any longer—the 19th century didn't share
today's passion for historic preservation—but the
surname of the man who built it looms large, in both the
literal and figurative sense, in the history of the United
States. Thomas Hancock was the son of a respected
pastor in Cambridge, Massachusetts, across the Charles
River from Boston. The path that led to his Beacon
Hill mansion began with the decision that he would not
follow his father into the ministry, as his brother John
would, but instead would cross the river to Boston and
apprentice to a bookseller. This was in 1717, when
Thomas was 14 years of age. John was already at
Harvard, and tuition for two was possibly too much
of a drain on a pastor's salary. Reverend Hancock might
also have seen that his second son's talents had a
worldly rather than a spiritual bent.

Thomas Hancock served his bookseller master for
seven years, learning everything from printing to
binding to retail sales. At the end of his apprenticeship
he opened his own shop, but the book business was too
narrow to contain him. By 1727, he was dabbling in
the long-distance transport and sale of general
merchandise; the next year, he and several partners
built a paper mill just south of Boston. In 1731,
Hancock married Lydia Henchman, the daughter of

one of his paper mill associates. To his native ambition—which by now included his first dabblings in politics—Thomas Hancock now added a matrimonial connection to a well-to-do family.

Bookselling became less and less of a factor in the Hancock enterprises, as the entrepreneur moved into land speculation and importing. In the Boston of the mid-1730s—a town barely a century old, but already a far cry from the cramped little theocracy of its early days—the name Hancock was one that was recognized on the docks and in the counting houses. Thomas Hancock needed a residence to match his station, and in 1736 he began building it on Beacon Hill.

For the past two centuries, a Beacon Hill address has been the *ne plus ultra* of social standing in Boston. But the brick row houses built along Beacon Street ("the sunny street that holds the sifted few," as the first Oliver Wendell Holmes called it) and adjacent streets came along later than Thomas Hancock's day; these were part of the development that followed the removal of the hill's steep summit and the building of Charles Bulfinch's magnificent Massachusetts State House in the late 1790s. The Beacon Hill on which Thomas Hancock bought property and built his mansion was very much the Boston outskirts in the 1730s; off on his own, surrounded by orchards and gardens that trailed down the hill's south slope to Boston Common, Hancock could enjoy town and harbor views yet at the same time feel as if he were living out in the countryside.

The house was Georgian, with the cool symmetry and gambrel roof characteristic of the style, and it was

sumptuously large for its era. Its two and a half stories contained a dozen or more principal rooms, with smaller chambers serving as quarters for servants and slaves (slavery was still legal in the Massachusetts of that era) and for such necessities as the storage of china. Fine porcelain, along with silver (the French Huguenot émigré Apollos Revere and his son, Paul, did lovely custom work in 18th-century Boston) and polished mahogany were prime tokens of success among the merchant princes of the day.

And so were fine carriages. Here Thomas Hancock really went over the top, ordering a coach that took its London manufacturer three years to build and ship. Hancock went into great detail about everything from size (it had to be big enough to accommodate his wife, a tall, heavy woman) to upholstery (scarlet or a light color, "whichever is most fashionable") to windows designed to incorporate sliding panels of both glass and canvas. Even the harnesses and bells were custom made, as befit Hancock's station.

Thomas Hancock died in 1764. His principal heir was his nephew, the son of Thomas's late brother. Like his father and grandfather, the young man's name was John. Educated at Harvard and polished with a tour of England at his uncle's expense, taught the intricacies of commerce and the ways of a gentleman, John Hancock became at age 27 heir to a fortune estimated at half a million dollars. Over the next 30 years, he would rule Boston society from the house on Beacon Hill, eventually serving as governor of Massachusetts. Along the way, he would become that rare thing among the rich and privileged — at least those who do not renounce their fortunes, as John Hancock

assuredly did not. He would become famous as a political revolutionary, a man whose grand signature would scream defiance at the British crown.

But John Hancock's career as a revolutionary and patriot was still 10 years in the future at the time he came into his inheritance. Throughout the 1760s and early 1770s, Hancock was busy with his role as a Boston selectman — and, later, a member of the Massachusetts legislature — and with keeping his business solvent in the face of an economic downturn made worse by the Sugar and Stamp acts imposed by the British upon the colonies. As with most of the future revolutionaries, independence was the furthest thing from Hancock's mind as he threaded his way through the tangle of growing injustices, most connected with taxes and restrictions on trade, that ultimately led to the outbreak of rebellion. By the time the die was cast, and Hancock was ready to affix that famous signature to the Declaration of Independence, he perhaps more than any of the other Founders gave the American Revolution its character as essentially a bourgeois, rather than a radical insurrection.

John Hancock might be a political bedfellow of the populist Sam Adams, but his aristocratic style didn't suffer at all. In fact — and the 1960s term "limousine liberal" might occur to us at this juncture — he seamlessly merged his image as a magnifico with that of the friend of the common man. He wheeled through the streets of Boston in Uncle Thomas's coach, impeccably attired in the best wigs and waistcoats, jeweled or even solid gold buttons gleaming; to keep his frequent entertainments lubricated, he might order 400 gallons of the best Madeira at a time to stock the Beacon Street cellars.

And yet he could stand before a gathering and denounce "the glare of wealth" and extol the virtues of poverty. Few seemed to mind, because John Hancock was a generous man. His ample bequests to Harvard College included a thousand books; he gave the city of Boston a fire engine, provided furnishings for churches, and donated firewood to the poor.

John Hancock's fortune survived the Revolution, but in the 10 years of life he had left after the conflict was over—years that included his terms as governor of Massachusetts—his profligate spending continued until he had worked his way nearly to the bottom of his inheritance and whatever money he had made on his own. When he died in 1793, Boston society was astounded to learn that "King Hancock" had not even left a will. What remained of his fortune was largely in land, including the Beacon Hill mansion. It was a sad postscript to John Hancock's short, showy life that the mansion his Uncle Thomas had built was demolished in 1863, when the property was taken for back taxes. If it had been spared, it would stand today just to the left of the State House, where, with its memories of flowing Madeira and the clatter of that regal carriage, it might have provided a vivid contrast with later gubernatorial preferences. Michael Dukakis, remember, used to ride the subways.

So it was with John Hancock, and with the other merchant princes of early New England. Their ostentation mostly came down to homes and furniture, food and drink, and fine apparel. As for that last item, remember that the 18th century was not the era of casual Fridays; nor were dress clothes limited to a palette of grays and blues. Take a look at Nicholas Boylston, Boston's premier importer of luxury goods, as painted in 1767 by John Singleton Copley. Lounging in his study, his arm resting on a ledger and a painting of a merchant ship behind him, his expression an odd mixture of impatience and nonchalance, the mogul wears a blue waistcoat, a brown damask dressing gown, and a red velvet turban to keep the chill off his shaven head (it's early morning, no doubt, and his valet hasn't

yet helped him with his wig). Such displays of male sartorial gorgeousness were *de rigeuer* among Boylston's set. John Hancock, as we saw, always made sure to cut a fine figure; and Harrison Gray Otis, a nabob of the next generation, wore gold lace in his hats.

HARRISON GRAY OTIS

Otis's is a name to be reckoned with when it comes to that other hallmark of high early American society, fine architecture. He had three houses built for himself, on and around Beacon Hill, within eight years beginning in 1796. Each was designed by the incomparable Charles Bulfinch in the chastely elegant Federal style, that miracle of proportioning and exquisite yet restrained detailing whereby an ostensible square box becomes a thing of lightness and loveliness. The first Otis house is on Cambridge Street, and is now the headquarters of the Society for the Preservation of New England Antiquities; its interior is resplendent in the bright, striking colors of the Federal era. The second—the only free-standing mansion surviving on Beacon Hill—is still a private home on Mt. Vernon Street. The last of

*Salem's Custom House and Derby Wharf, nerve
centers of the first great era of American trade.*
THE PEABODY-ESSEX MUSEUM, SALEM. NEG. #14.524.

the three, where the land speculator and congressman lived from 1804 until his death in 1848, stands on Beacon Street. It is the headquarters of the American Meteorological Society. Unlike Harrison Gray Otis, the meteorologists do not keep a perpetually filled Lowestoft porcelain punch bowl at the foot of the stairs. That might make the weather altogether too agreeable, all of the time.

Speaking of Otis, and of food and drink, we should note that he ate not three but four meals a day—and the first was generally a breakfast that included paté de foie gras.

✳ ✳ ✳ ✳ ✳ ✳ ✳ ✳ ✳ ✳ ✳ ✳ ✳ ✳ ✳ ✳ ✳

Boston may have remained the political capital of Massachusetts, but in the decades immediately following the winning of American independence, the port of Salem, some 15 miles north of Boston, became the mercantile center of the American universe. Poor Salem—it's ironic that when we think of it today, we tend to concentrate on the least savory part of its history, the 1690s witch trials that centered upon what is today part of the nearby town of Danvers. This is partly Salem's own fault, as it plays up its witch connections for the sake of tourism in what must be the world's only example of a successful attempt to lure visitors by recalling an instance of cruel persecution. But Salem's real fame ought to rest on its one-time status as a fabulously wealthy port—a mercantile hive so successful that there were Chinese traders, accustomed to dealing with their Yankee counterparts from Salem, who thought that the city must be a great

nation all its own. Indeed, on one Chinese map drawn 200 years ago, the word "Salem" sprawls across the entire eastern portion of the United States.

These were the days when "the Yankee ships were everywhere." So wrote Esther Forbes in her biography, *Paul Revere and the World He Lived In*. Forbes was referring to the fact that by the time of Revere's death, in 1818, bells made at his foundry in Canton, Massachusetts, might be heard not only in New England steeples, but on board ships "under the strange shadow of Java Head or in the cruel Straits of Sunda." The very ubiquity of Revere's bells suggests that the old patriot had struck upon a far more lucrative career than custom silversmithing, and had fallen into step with the way great fortunes would be made during the century just beginning. But between the end of the American Revolution and the 1820s—with a hiatus during the unpopular embargo leading up to the War of 1812 and the war itself—shipping was the path to American riches, and Salem was the place where that path most promisingly began.

ELIAS HASKET DERBY

Salem's wharves begat Thomas Handasyd Perkins, who turned down George Washington's offer to make him secretary of the Navy on the grounds that he was already in command of a larger fleet of ships. And Salem was the first American city to produce a millionaire. That was one Elias Hasket Derby, known in his day as "King" Derby. (Americans in those days were glad to get rid of a real king, but they clung to the sobriquet when it came to their Hancocks and Derbys.)

The 1727 Crowninshield-Bentley House, a
Georgian-style home reflecting the modest
circumstances of its builder, John Grouncell—or
Crowninshield, as his descendants spelled the name.

Like Hancock, Derby stood on another man's
shoulders when it came to acquiring his fortune—in
this case his father, Richard Derby, a prosperous pre-
Revolutionary merchant whose 1762 home, the oldest
brick house in Salem, survives on the grounds of the
Salem Maritime National Historic Site (the site also
includes Derby Wharf, and the 1819 Custom House
made famous by Nathaniel Hawthorne in *The Scarlet
Letter*). With its trim dormers, finely dentiled cornice,
and 12-over-12 windows, the Derby House is classic
Georgian, very much along the lines of the lost
Hancock mansion in Boston if not as large. From
those windows, Richard Derby could enjoy the finest
harbor views imaginable: his own ships, coming and
going, and unloading their lucrative cargoes at his
namesake wharf.

With the coming of the Revolution, more than a few
of those ships were privateers. Elias Hasket Derby
was by this time fully engaged in his father's business,
and he himself became one of America's most effective
carriers of letters of marque. Once the war was over,
he lost not a moment in converting to peacetime
commerce. In 1785 he sent his one-time privateer
Grand Turk into the East India trade, launching a series
of voyages so profitable it was said the younger Derby
was regularly accustomed to a 100 percent return.

Lord help anyone, in fact, who worked for King
Derby and failed to step lively enough to facilitate such
enormous profits. Derby was not the sort of man you
would want to present with a sloppy expense
account—or, for that matter, with any expense account
at all. He regularly required his ships' captains to

engage in enough side business to cover all expenses, so that his profits would be pure and unencumbered.

Elias Hasket Derby was a tall, dour man with formal, old-fashioned manners and a presence that combined stateliness with swagger. He carried a gold-headed cane and wore buckles studded with diamonds. He built what might have been the finest house in Salem—judging from the Federal-era architectural treasures that city still possesses, that would have been quite the superlative—but he built it primarily to please his wife, Elizabeth Crowninshield. One of the quirks of this particular Derby mansion was its black marble staircase, seven feet wide. It seems that Elizabeth Crowninshield Derby was chilled by the thought of her coffin someday being carried down the stairs at an unseemly angle, either head or feet first. So she specified a staircase wide enough to accommodate her remains at level broadside.

Elias Hasket Derby's real love (apart from his ships and Elizabeth, likely in that order) was his farm in suburban Danvers, where his greenhouses were planted in strawberries and lemons. Here he kept a curious artifact. It was a wooden effigy of a hermit, seated in a bark hut with a hermit's scant portion of bread and water before it. In the statue's hands was an open book inscribed, "Give me neither poverty or riches." Elias Hasket Derby, of course, had swerved radically toward one of those options rather than the other. His descendants swerved just as radically in the other direction: King Derby died in 1799, his million-dollar-plus fortune intact (Elizabeth had already taken her last dignified trip downstairs); but his sons were profligates who quickly ran through their inheritance. In 1810, the Derby mansion in Salem was demolished, for want of anyone who cared or could afford to keep it up.

THE CROWNINSHIELDS

The Crowninshields, the family that had produced Elizabeth Crowninshield Derby of the seven-foot-wide black marble staircase, were another Salem merchant family of legend. The first Crowninshield of any consequence was named John, who usually spelled his name "Grouncell" in the odd orthography of the 18th century. He was the son of a mysterious Doctor Johann von Kronenscheldt, who had turned up in Boston in 1684—he claimed to be a German nobleman, but no one has ever known for sure just who he was, where he came from, or whether he was an actual doctor even by the standards of the day—and settled in the town of Lynn, located midway between Boston and Salem.

John Grouncell was no merchant prince. He was primarily a fisherman and a smuggler, and he is remembered in Salem today as the builder of the 1727 Crowninshield-Bentley House, a modest early jewel in a Peabody-Essex Museum collection crowned by the great Federal mansions designed by Samuel McIntire for later shipping magnates. Grouncell/Crowninshield's son, George, started out modestly enough. He worked as a captain on ships belonging to King Derby, whose sister he had married. (His own sister was Elizabeth, Derby's wife.)

But by the 1790s, George Crowninshield was a shipowner himself. His favored cargo was pepper, which he and his captains bought along the west coast

of Sumatra in what is now Indonesia. The pepper trade was a tricky business, requiring the Yankee captains to employ all their wits against wily Malay suppliers, British competitors, and each other. But George Crowninshield was up to the challenge. In 1801, two of his ships brought more than a million pounds of pepper into Salem harbor. During the decade that followed, he and his sons came to think of Sumatra as "our pepper gardens." A lucrative coffee trade with India followed, and by 1810 the family had supplanted the Derbys as the lords of Salem's commerce.

George's sons were all agents of the family firm. One, Jacob, became a U.S. congressman to whom Thomas

Jefferson in 1804 offered the post of secretary of the Navy. He declined — the second Salem shipping tycoon to place his private seafaring concerns above responsibility for those of the nation. (His brother, Benjamin, took the job under James Madison in 1814.) The Crowninshields, as it turned out, had a navy of their own: during the War of 1812, six of the family's privateer vessels captured or sank more than 80 British ships.

Ultimately, it was neither a merchant ship nor a naval vessel that gave those early Crowninshields a unique place in the history of American seafaring. It was a yacht — the first ship in the nation built purely for pleasure.

George Crowninshield, Jr., was George Crowninshield's eldest son. A lifelong bachelor, he stayed home and helped run the Salem end of the family's far-flung operations, specializing in outfitting ships. With the development of his inner life hampered by the fact that he was nearly illiterate, he indulged a love of outward display. He drove a bright yellow carriage around Salem; he wore high tasseled boots, splashy waistcoats, and a powdered pigtail.

The career of the younger George Crowninshield offers one of America's first examples of wealth and industry ripening into eccentricity and decadence. By the time George, Sr., died in 1815, the family fortune was secure and, with three surviving brothers to help run things, there really wasn't much for the younger George to do. His legacy thus became not that of a firm hand on the levers of business, but on the tiller of his one spectacular indulgence—the yacht called *Cleopatra's Barge*.

Along with ceremony and display, George Crowninshield, Jr., loved the glamour of celebrity—especially titled celebrity. He had a particular fascination with Napoleon, and with Charlotte, Princess of Wales. Accordingly he hatched the idea of building a pleasure yacht and sailing it to Europe, hoping to attract visits from as many royal or at least noble

A replica of the main cabin of Cleopatra's
Barge, *as displayed in Salem's Peabody-Essex*
Museum.

THE PEABODY-ESSEX MUSEUM, SALEM.
PHOTO MARK SEXTON.

personages as possible. Perhaps, if the princess or someone equally glamorous were sufficiently impressed, he or she might be persuaded to accompany the yachtsman back to Salem. (Napoleon was unavailable, having already been exiled to St. Helena.)

Cleopatra's Barge was launched at Salem in October of 1816. She was a hermaphroditic brigantine (the name applies to a ship square-rigged on the foremast and rigged with a triangular fore-and-aft sail on the mainmast). She was the size of a small warship—83 feet long at the waterline, nearly 23 feet across at the beam, and weighing almost 200 tons. Her hull was a riot of color: one side was painted in horizontal bands, the other in a herringbone pattern, and there was gold leaf everywhere. The cabins and salons of the *Barge* would have done credit to a McIntire mansion: no expense was spared on carpets, on settees upholstered in velvet, on gilt mirrors, or on maple and mahogany paneling. The ceiling beams were edged in gilt beading; velvet ropes bound with gold cord were slung along the bulkheads to provide a grip for passengers in rough seas. The best porcelain, crystal, silver, and linen graced the dining salon.

Outfitted with a liveried crew, captained by George's cousin Benjamin Crowninshield, *Cleopatra's Barge* slipped out of Salem harbor on March 30, 1817, carrying her strange owner on a strange, glamour-seeking voyage.

It was a voyage of disappointment. A German baron and a British lord were entertained on board at Genoa, and Crowninshield did get to meet the mother, sister, brother, and uncle of Napoleon. At Elba, the deposed French emperor's erstwhile place of exile, the hero-worshiper from Salem even managed to buy a few of Napoleon's abandoned possessions, including a pair of his boots. But there had been no luck in contacting Marie Louise, Napoleon's estranged empress, nor the princess of Wales. And as a final insult, the supposed "adopted son" of Bonaparte, invited to sail to America on *Cleopatra's Barge*, turned out to be an impostor.

The *Barge* dropped anchor in Salem harbor in early October. George Crowninshield almost immediately began planning another cruise, but it never got under way. A little more than a month after his return, the pixilated scion of the House of Crowninshield dropped dead in the galley of his folly of a yacht.

Cleopatra's Barge did not long survive her master. By 1820 she was the property of Kamehameha, king of Hawaii, and she was lost on a reef (the king was not aboard) four years later. But a tribute to her splendor may be seen in her home port: replicas of the main cabin, and the master stateroom with its canopied bed, are on display at Salem's Peabody-Essex Museum.

THE BROWN BROTHERS

The Rhode Island cities of Providence and Newport were also bastions of trade in the 18th and early 19th centuries. In Providence, the name to conjure with was Brown—a name associated with the city to this day, through the family's role in creating and supporting Brown University.

Four Brown brothers came to maturity in the Providence of the mid- to late 1700s, sons of a merchant who had also dabbled in whaling, distilling, farming,

and slave trading. After the father's death, the four
boys—John, Moses, Joseph, and Nicholas (a fifth,
James, died as a very young man)—worked for an
uncle, Obadiah Brown, whose activities included
shipping and candlemaking. Eventually, Obadiah
and his nephews would become colonial America's
largest manufacturers of candles.

The Brown brothers prospered mightily in the
shipping and candlemaking enterprises, which they
inherited and managed with considerable harmony
following their uncle's death in 1762. But as the years
progressed, their individual personalities asserted
themselves . . . most significantly, around the issue
of slavery.

At first, all of the Brown brothers had benefited from
the slave trade. Just three years after coming
into their inheritance, Moses, Joseph, and John
collaborated in fitting out a brig for a slaving voyage. In
the years that followed, slaving loomed ever larger
as a component of John Brown's income. Around the
same time, Nicholas dabbled in the trade, but later
became a firm opponent. Joseph, as he grew older, took
less and less interest in business, preferring scientific
pursuits and architecture. Moses, meanwhile, came to
have the strongest misgivings of all regarding the
commerce in human lives: he taught his own slaves to
read and write, and gave them their freedom following
his midlife conversion to Quakerism. Thereafter he
became a leader in the anti-slavery movement, a position
that put him in dire opposition to his brother, John.
John Brown wasn't a reticent slaver, content to bank his
profits while keeping quiet about their source; he was an

active opponent of anti-slavery legislation. The wonder is that the brothers kept talking to each other. Moses and John remained quite close in the years prior to John's death in 1803. (Moses outlived all of his brothers, dying in 1836 at age 97.)

Aside from Brown University, the greatest tangible reminder of the years of the Brown brothers' ascendancy in Providence is the house that Joseph Brown designed for his brother, John, in 1786. John Quincy Adams called it "the most magnificent and elegant private mansion that I have ever seen on this continent." Adams was not given to exaggeration, and his words might well stand today: even though many a larger home has been built in North America over the past two centuries, few if any are more "magnificent and elegant."

The three-story, 12-room Brown house brings the classical regularity of high Georgian architecture to its pinnacle in this hemisphere. The central block of the building projects outwards, enhancing the imposing doorway and the lovely Palladian window on the second floor; above, the building's height is accentuated by a balustrade surrounding the roof. Inside, amid exquisite paneling and pedimented doorways, is a superb collection of 18th-century furniture and Chinese porcelain—a reminder that, in addition to slave trading, John Brown's fortune was built on his pioneering of the immensely lucrative China trade.

The proprietor of all this magnificence must have been a little rough on the furniture. John Brown was an immense specimen. He was so big that he took up the entire seat in his chaise; when his grandchildren rode with him, they had to sit on the floor between his legs.

JOHN JACOB ASTOR

The subway stop at Astor Place, across from Cooper Union in New York's East Village, is one of those old stations that still preserves the cool white tile walls of a century ago. Set amid the tiles in one of those walls is a curious plaque, which appears to have nothing to do with either subways or the world upstairs. It depicts a beaver gnawing on a stick. Its reference is to a tough little German immigrant, and to one of the greatest American fortunes.

Drop one "l", and the name of the village where John Jacob Astor was born in 1763 has a decided New York ring. Walldorf is in the province of Baden, and it was there that Astor's father, John Jacob, Sr., ran a butcher shop that might well have turned out to be the younger man's livelihood as well. Instead of cattle and pigs, though, there were beaver pelts in John Jacob Astor's future—beaver pelts, and an immense amount of real estate.

Astor came to the United States in 1784 by way of London, where he had worked for an older brother in the musical instrument business. He brought a consignment of flutes across the Atlantic, and sold them on the side while he worked for a fur dealer. Soon the two businesses intertwined, as Astor invested profits from importing and selling instruments in his first fur-buying trip to upstate New York.

Astor made connections in Montreal, capital of the North American fur trade, and expanded his business exporting pelts to the lucrative London market. In the late 1700s, the three dollars a beaver pelt fetched could

*John Jacob Astor's fur-trading enterprise led to
the establishment of the first American fur
monopoly in the United States.*

PHOTO COURTESY THE OREGON HISTORICAL SOCIETY, PORTLAND.

buy a musket, which could be traded to the Indians for
10 more pelts. With that rate of return working in his
favor, Astor entered the China trade around 1800—a
year when, after 16 years in America, he was already
worth $100,000. Furs went to China; tea and silk came
back. The exchange brought the coarse, crafty German
immigrant an enormous profit, $300,000 of which he
promptly sunk into what was by no means considered a
prudent investment in that first decade of the 1800s:
Manhattan real estate.

Buying and selling acreage in the yet-to-be-settled

parts of New York City was an amusing pastime—later,
Astor would hold his property and sublet it for
development—but furs were still the main event. The
American acquisition of the Louisiana Territory, and its
exploration by Lewis and Clark, paved the way for
Astor's creation of a string of fur-trading posts on the
Columbia River and the creation of the port called
Astoria where that river empties into the Pacific.

John Jacob Astor, through his American Fur
Company, became America's first monopolist and its
first multimillionaire. But he sold his interest in

American Fur in 1834, and from then on it was real estate all the way. Just how much money stood to be made from investing in the land the burgeoning metropolis stood on is apparent from a simple set of figures: in 1832, the assessed value of the city's property was $104 million. In 1836, the figure was $253 million. Astor bought land all over the city; and he was not averse to adding to his holdings through foreclosure. He didn't build on his property, but leased to others who did. The only building he constructed, aside from his own residence, was the Astor House Hotel. (Both the old and the present Waldorf-Astoria hotels, which commemorate both his name and his hometown, were built long after his death.)

Few people ever praised John Jacob Astor for his generosity, or made note of his self-indulgence. Cited by biographer Virginia Cowles as being "so niggardly it was almost pathological," he kept an eye on every dime. His only personal indulgence seems to have been the theater; he became part owner of the Park Theater in 1806, and rebuilt it when it burned in 1820. Presumably, he liked the idea of being able to enjoy a play now and then while saving money on his own tickets and charging others for theirs. His other pastimes didn't extend much beyond an after-dinner pipe and glass of beer, listening to music, an occasional game of checkers, and riding his horse around town. Aside from the fact that those rides often had the ulterior purpose of scouting out real estate, Astor's modest amusements might easily have been those of the middle-class butcher he had originally apprenticed to be.

John Jacob Astor IV, great-grandson of John Jacob and son of William Backhouse Astor, Jr., and Caroline Schermerhorn Astor, the Mrs. Astor who devised the famous "400"—a list of families and individuals whose lineage could be traced back at least three generations.
PHOTO LIBRARY OF CONGRESS.

Things weren't much different when it came to spending money on others. Astor provided well for his family, including a son and namesake who suffered from a lifelong mental condition, and he kept a comfortable household and ample table. But he was tightfisted with business associates and strangers. He once refused to pay $500 for a chronometer—a timekeeping device crucial for establishing longitude—for one of his ships, saying it was the captain's responsibility. The captain quit. An oft-repeated story has it that a petitioner for charity, disappointed with the five dollars Astor gave

him, pointed out that Astor's son, William Backhouse Astor, had given him ten dollars. "He can afford to," the old man replied. "He has a rich father." Astor even felt the need to comment on others' spendthrift habits: he once predicted a new hotel would fail because the management provided lumps of sugar that were too large.

In the end, the squat old tycoon—his once-wiry frame had filled out so that he looked the part of the beefy, aging butcher—did manage a bequest of nearly a half-million dollars to found the Astor Library (since incorporated into the New York Public Library), along with smaller sums for lesser institutions for his hometown of Walldorf. His legacy of between $20 and $30 million dollars left his family so well provided for that Astor remains to this day a synonym for inherited wealth. But when he was near death, at the age of 84 in 1848, he was still insisting that his agents pursue tenants for overdue rents.

THE DU PONTS OF DELAWARE

Another European immigrant, a man of much more substantial means than the young John Jacob Astor, arrived in the United States in 1800. In fact, Eleuthère Irénée du Pont de Nemours was perhaps alone among the aristocrats of American business in actually having *been* an aristocrat: his family belonged to the minor French nobility, and his father, Pierre, had been a distinguished diplomat who was involved in the secret negotiations that led to British acknowledgment of American independence in 1783.

Pierre du Pont brought his family to America to seek refuge from the excesses of the French Revolution, whose leaders of the moment he and his son Eleuthère had offended by publishing politically moderate tracts. The younger du Pont (he was 29 when he emigrated) did know his way around a printing press, but he was primarily a scientist. He listed his occupation as "botanist" on his immigration papers, and he did in fact bring along a number of young chestnut trees (he continued to import chestnuts, hybridized them, and planted them

throughout New Jersey and Delaware). But Eleuthère Irénée du Pont was first and foremost a chemist. His particular expertise was with gunpowder, the manufacture of which he had studied with the great French scientist Antoine Lavoisier.

On a cold, damp day in the winter of 1801, E. I. du Pont was hunting in the woodlands around the Pennsylvania–Delaware border. His rifle continually misfired because of the moist air, and his day's sport was ruined. But he didn't blame the weather. He blamed his powder, which absorbed the dampness, and he decided he could use his French training to create a better product.

Using waterpower from Delaware's Brandywine River, E. I. du Pont set up his first black powder mill near Wilmington in 1802 and started selling his product two years later. The venture was well timed: the War of 1812 was just around the corner, and there was a frontier to be pushed back. But E. I. du Pont doesn't seem to have been just another munitions profiteer. For one thing, he was concerned with overall agricultural and silvicultural improvements to his adopted nation—witness all those chestnut trees, and the fact that he introduced Spanish merino sheep to the U.S. to improve the wool supply. He was also interested in the welfare of his workers, and underlined his emphasis on safety by building his own family's home right on the Brandywine, near the powder mills. The family of any employee killed in an explosion was given free tenure in a company-owned house for the rest of their lives, with guaranteed employment for the victim's children.

Ironically, one of E. I. du Pont's own sons was killed in a mishap involving his famously volatile product. And, as if reflecting that early company policy, members of the du Pont family have found two centuries of employment with the mammoth chemical company founded by the "botanist" who fled the French Revolution.

* * * * * * * * * * * * * * *

Back in New England, all of that money from the China and East India trades had to go somewhere. The sharpest minds among the old merchant aristocracy soon came to understand that the 19th century's new technologies would favor not merely those who bought and sold, but those who made things. Two of those burgeoning technologies were the mass production of textiles, and the railroad. Yankee money found its way into both.

One Dr. John Collins Bossidy—the name suggests that other dominant ethnic strain in Boston's history— once tweaked the city's Brahmin establishment with a toast:

(OPPOSITE)

*The grand staircase at Nemours, the 102-room
Wilmington, Delaware, chateau built by Alfred L.
du Pont in 1910.*

PHOTO COURTESY NEMOURS MANSION AND GARDENS,
WILMINGTON, DELAWARE.

(PREVIOUS SPREAD)

*The Chinese parlor at Winterthur was a favorite
place for du Pont gatherings. The original 1837
home was substantially enlarged.*

PHOTO COURTESY THE WINTERTHUR MUSEUM, WINTERTHUR,
DELAWARE.

(ABOVE)

*The library at Nemours, with its finely carved
paneling and warm colors, welcomed company
and encouraged reflection.*

PHOTO COURTESY NEMOURS MANSION AND GARDENS,
WILMINGTON, DELAWARE.

And this is good old Boston,
      The home of the bean and the cod,
   Where the Lowells talk only to the Cabots
      And the Cabots talk only to God.
Francis Cabot Lowell could talk in both directions. This possessor of two of the most formidable names in Yankeedom, and of a good portion of the mercantile fortunes their bearers had amassed, lived at the beginning of the textile revolution.

An Englishman named Samuel Slater had brought the rudiments of mechanized spinning technology to the United States in 1793—you can still visit his mill, on the banks of the Blackstone River in Pawtucket, Rhode Island—and no less a personage than Moses Brown went into business with him. But the American textile industry got its greatest boost when Francis Cabot Lowell came home from a trip to England in 1812 with the working details of that nation's greatest economic treasure tucked into his copious mind. This was the power loom, a device so vital to English industry that its export—or even the export of plans for its construction—was strictly forbidden. Working from memory, Lowell built and patented his own loom. It went into service at Waltham, Massachusetts, in 1814, and, on a larger scale, in the mills established at the entrepreneur's namesake city of Lowell beginning in the 1820s. (Lowell had died, still a relatively young man, in 1817.)

Francis Cabot Lowell must have been a gregarious, clubbable sort during his salad days. He was one of the founders of the most elite of Harvard's undergraduate clubs, the Porcellian, which was originally named the Pig Club because Lowell and fellow founder Robert Treat Paine liked roast pork. As he matured, he seems to have become something of a workaholic. Expecting no less of a commitment from his mill operatives, he nevertheless helped pioneer the idea of factory towns as model communities, in which religious, educational, and social advantages would prevent the vice and misery associated with the English manufacturing cities.

His partner, Nathan Appleton, another Boston Yankee with family shipping money behind him, continued to promote such ideas during the development of the city of Lowell with its model boardinghouses for young, mostly female "operatives." (This was before rapidly expanding business made immigrant labor—and struggles over such niceties as the 13-hour day—inevitable.) Appleton, a scholar and amateur economist, a book collector and keeper of a conversational salon, was also a Brahmin of iron will and purpose. The day before he died, in 1861, he attended the funeral of his daughter. Fanny Appleton Longfellow, wife of the poet, had burned to death in a home accident involving a candle. The same day, Appleton's doctor told him he had two days to live. The old Yankee died on Sunday, only a little ahead of schedule, having told a friend not to bother coming to see him on Monday. "I am not," he had said that weekend, "afraid of anything." He needn't have worried about his elegant, Bulfinch-designed Federal mansion at 39 Beacon Street. The brick bowfronted building has

been kept in fine repair by the Women's City Club of Boston, and is occasionally open for tours.

John Murray Forbes was another heir to an impeccable Boston Brahmin name, and a man distinguished by having personally bridged the China trade and railroad eras. Back when the 19th century was young, Forbes had sailed in Massachusetts vessels bound for Canton and made his fortune before he was 24. As he and the century matured, he took his money and put it on the rails. He led a group of venture capitalists that bought the financially tottering Michigan Central and drove it through to Chicago; with this entry point to the Midwest secured, he

bought a short line railroad and expanded it until it became the Chicago, Burlington, and Quincy. Forbes appears to have packed up his Puritan sense of rectitude and probity and brought it west with him. His friend Ralph Waldo Emerson once remarked, apropos of Forbes's integrity, that he was "not likely, in any company, to meet a man superior to himself." Boston could rise to the occasion of the railroads, but it had trouble coming by the robber baron image.

(ABOVE)

Longwood Gardens, created by Pierre S. du Pont, has more fountains than any other American garden.

PHOTO LARRY ALBEE/LONGWOOD GARDENS, PENNSYLVANIA.

(RIGHT)

The 1,050-acre Longwood complex boasts 11,000 plant varieties in 20 outdoor and 20 indoor gardens.

PHOTO LARRY ALBEE/LONGWOOD GARDENS, PENNSYLVANIA.

The Gilded Age

GROWING UP on the family farm on Staten Island, Cornelius Vanderbilt learned how to handle boats while taking produce across to Manhattan for his father. In 1810 the 16-year-old boy pestered his parents for the loan of $100 to buy a small sailboat of the type called a periauger. Buying his own small craft, "Cornele" figured, would be a ticket off the farm and into a lucrative business ferrying passengers and goods across the Narrows. It was a ticket, indeed . . . a ticket to a fleet of ships that would earn him the nickname "Commodore," to mastery of a system of transportation yet to be invented, and to the greatest fortune amassed by any American of his day.

"I didn't feel as much real satisfaction when I made two million in that Harlem [Railroad] corner," said Cornelius Vanderbilt late in life, "as I did on that bright May morning sixty years before when I stepped into my own periauger, hoisted my own sail, and put my hand on my own tiller."

"Commodore" Cornelius Vanderbilt's hand was always on the tiller. Most of his life, and the bulk of his career, took place before the giddy decades of success and excess that Mark Twain and Charles Dudley Warner dubbed the "Gilded Age." But in many ways, the Commodore set the tone for that era, and he was the first overarching figure in the industry that drove the age.

"Them things that go on land" was Cornelius Vanderbilt's dismissive term for railroads during the first 20 years or so of their existence in America. He had more reason than most people to be wary of them, having suffered two cracked ribs and a punctured lung in the world's first head-on crash, an 1833 mishap in New Jersey. Nor did Vanderbilt have any pressing financial reasons to invest in "them things." Starting with that $100 periauger, he had built an empire out of things that go on water.

"A coarse, tobacco-chewing, profane oaf of a man" was how railroad historian Aaron E. Klein once summed up Cornelius Vanderbilt, but that

The steamship C. Vanderbilt, *weighing over 1,000 tons, traveled at a top speed of 25 miles per hour.*
PHOTO © SHELBURNE MUSEUM, SHELBURNE, VERMONT.

description isn't that uncommon on the resumé of a New York entrepreneur in the first decades of the 19th century. What this particular oaf accomplished, by the age of 20, was the establishment of a regular passenger ferry service between Staten Island and Manhattan, followed by the securing of lucrative contracts to supply military posts around New York harbor during the War of 1812. Investing his profits in bigger vessels, he shouldered his way into the coastal trade linking New York, New England, and the South. By the late 1830s he was running one of America's largest fleets of steamboats, and had been christened "Commodore" by the newspapers.

In 1855 Vanderbilt introduced regular steamship service to Europe, and two years later he launched *Vanderbilt*, then the largest and fastest liner on the Atlantic. By that time he was 63, and rich enough to retire by the standards of any era. But in 1862, he started to buy stock in the New York and Harlem Railroad. He had the bug, and in only two years was out of steamships altogether. Abetted by $20 million in capital and the sheer force of will, he commenced the campaign that brought him control of the New York Central in 1867. At first, the Commodore was uncharacteristically content with command of the rails between New York and Buffalo—"if we take hold of roads running all the way to Chicago, we might as well go to San Francisco and to China," he told his son, William H. Vanderbilt. But the completion of the transcontinental railroad in 1869 convinced him that access to the rough new metropolis on Lake Michigan was a must for any Eastern railroad

that wanted to stay in business. The completion of the New York Central System between New York and Chicago was the Commodore's monument. So was the $100 million he amassed by the time of his death, in 1877, at the age of 82.

As far as more conventional monuments go, we might look to the statue of the Commodore that stands before New York's Grand Central Station, the hand extended as if this frock-coated gentleman is asking for a fare. But such an august apotheosis hardly does the wily boatman justice. He was a far livelier character than that bronze effigy suggests.

Was Cornelius Vanderbilt a coarse oaf? He certainly didn't have much schooling; he was too eager to get out on the water for that. He supposedly read only two books in his life, the Bible and Bunyan's *Pilgrim's Progress*. His grammar was bad and his command of profanity was impressive; he no doubt figured that what was good for the New York waterfront in 1810 was good for the world of high-stakes railroad finance in the 1860s—a conclusion in which he was probably not mistaken.

Still, the Commodore occasionally felt left out of refined society. The more genteel New York business figures, most of whom he could buy and sell by the time he reached middle age, left him out of their social circles, and he felt even more excluded from European society. "I've been to England, and seen them lords, and other fellows, and knew that I had twice as much brains as they had maybe," Vanderbilt once remarked, "and yet I had to keep still, and couldn't say anything for fear of exposing myself." Pangs of that sort turned the Commodore from a bluff disdain to a grudging respect for education, and no doubt helped lead to the million-dollar donation that helped turn struggling Central University, in Nashville, Tennessee, into Vanderbilt University.

What Vanderbilt lacked in erudition, he made up for in his physical presence and strength of will. He stood six foot one, had a leonine head and formidable sideburns, and retained the boatman's strength of his youth well past middle age. At the age of 50, he pummeled a champion boxer into near-insensibility during one of the era's no-holds-barred political

(OPPOSITE)

Fifth Avenue was Vanderbilt territory in the 1880s. Far left, William H. Vanderbilt's home; far right, William K.'s chateau.

MUSEUM OF THE CITY OF NEW YORK.

(ABOVE)

Mrs. Alva Smith Vanderbilt, mistress of Marble House and a Fifth Avenue mansion. She later married Oliver Belmont.

PHOTO COURTESY THE PRESERVATION SOCIETY OF NEWPORT COUNTY.

Fast Trotters on Harlem Lane, N.Y. *John Cameron; colored lithograph; 1870. Cornelius Vanderbilt works his trotters on New York's Harlem Lane, as depicted by Currier and Ives.*

MUSEUM OF THE CITY OF NEW YORK, THE HARRY T. PETERS COLLECTION.

campaigns (Vanderbilt was a Whig; the boxer, who had threatened him, was a Tammany Hall Democrat). He was just as formidable when it came to using his financial muscle. Addressing a cabal of stock manipulators who had temporarily seized control of his Atlantic-to-Pacific transportation enterprise in Nicaragua, he wrote simply, "I won't sue you, for the law is too slow. I'll ruin you." And he did.

The Commodore could be a terrible bully, especially with his wife. When he insisted that the family move from their expansive Staten Island estate to a new house near Washington Square, in Manhattan's fashionable Greenwich Village, Sophia Vanderbilt balked to the point of becoming hysterical. Her husband's response was to commit her to a sanitarium, where she remained for two months. He also threw George Westinghouse bodily out of his office when the young man came to promote his new air brakes. But he could also be reasonable, in his crusty way. He was riding on one of his own trains one day when an employee, who didn't recognize him, told him to put out his cigar. Vanderbilt refused, and the man insisted — even after the Commodore identified himself. That impressed Vanderbilt, who commended the employee for upholding company rules no matter what.

The richest man in America took his pleasures modestly enough, although he wasn't averse to an occasional grand gesture such as building a steam yacht to carry himself, his family, and a few friends on a tour of Europe in 1853. But aside from playing whist with cronies and taking an occasional vacation at Saratoga Springs — his displeasure with some thick-cut fried

(LEFT)

The loggia at The Breakers, built in 1895 and considered the grandest of the Newport "cottages." The efforts of some 2,500 laborers and artisans went into details such as these mosaic-inlaid ceiling vaultings.

(PREVIOUS SPREAD)

The east facade of The Breakers, designed by Richard Morris Hunt for railroad heir Cornelius Vanderbilt II.

Red marble columns topped by bronze capitals flank the main dining room at The Breakers. The entire 70-room structure was built of stone, marble, and alabaster—Cornelius Vanderbilt II wanted no flammable materials used in construction.

Going to the Opera — A Family Portrait, *by Seymour Guy, 1873. The figures in the portrait are William Henry and Louisa Vanderbilt with seven of their eight sons and daughters, spouses or fiancees, and two servants. From left to right, they are: father William H., son Frederick, Mrs. William H., son George, daughter Florence, son William K., daughter Eliza, daughter Margaret, E. F. Shepard (Margaret's husband), servant, daughter Emily, servant, Alice Gwynne (Cornelius II's wife), W. Sloane (Emily's husband), son Cornelius II.*

(BELOW)

William K. Vanderbilt's Marble House, in Newport, incorporates 500,000 cubic feet of its namesake material.

(OPPOSITE)

The Versailles-inspired Gold Room at Marble House.

potatoes at a hotel there is supposed to have led to the invention of potato chips—his favorite pastime was harness racing. Vanderbilt drove his own handsome pair of trotters alone to his lower Manhattan office each day, and in his leisure hours he became such a figure on the suburban roads where fashionable horsemen gathered that he and his equipage were depicted by Currier and Ives. The Commodore stoked himself for the day's activities with his favorite breakfast of three lamb chops and eight egg yolks right up to his eighties. His constitution was so strong that for him, the white of the egg was the part you threw away.

Sophia Vanderbilt died in 1868. The following year, the Commodore married 30-year-old Frank Crawford, a distant relative whom he had met socially at Saratoga. The other eyebrow-raising indulgence of his last decade was an interest in spiritualism. Like most participants in the newly popular seances of that era, Vanderbilt wanted to contact the spirits of departed relatives, particularly his mother and a long-dead son. But being Cornelius Vanderbilt, he also looked to the world beyond for stock market tips.

Vanderbilt himself joined the inside traders of the choir invisible on January 4, 1877. The principal heir to that $100 million fortune was his son, William H. Vanderbilt, and along with the money went control of the New York Central. It was William H. who completed the Central's progression into Chicago, and otherwise put the road on the solid footing that would see it into the 20th century. Unfortunately for William's legacy, he was also the man who uttered the famous words, "The public be damned." There is good reason to believe that the remark, taken out of context, wasn't meant quite that way; but the damage was done. On the eve of the muckraking era it seemed an impolitic sentiment, coming from a big fat man with cartoon-quality muttonchops, a pair of Fifth Avenue townhouses, and a prize racehorse pastured on a piece of midtown Manhattan real estate in sight of the executive offices at the original Grand Central Terminal.

William H. Vanderbilt died in 1885, and after that the Vanderbilts served mostly as directors of the New York Central; within a generation or two, they were

absent from the corporate structure. What they did do, especially in the generation represented by William H.'s sons, was build houses. Fifth Avenue was filled with these now-vanished extravaganzas, especially along the blocks between Fifty-first and Fifty-eighth streets. William K. Vanderbilt put up an immense turreted chateau, and his son built another right next door. Just up the street was Cornelius II's castle, done in the style of a chateau on the Loire and big enough to have served as the Central's main terminal. Cornelius II's greatest extravagance, though, was The Breakers, his "cottage" in Newport, Rhode Island. Designed by Richard Morris Hunt in the style of a Genoese palace of the 17th century, its interior gilt to a fare-thee-well and its grounds landscaped by Frederick Law Olmsted, the 70-room Breakers surpasses even William K. Vanderbilt, Sr.'s nearby Marble House as the most extravagant of Newport's turn-of-the-century mansions. The Breakers would cost an estimated $400 million — four times the Commodore's entire legacy — to build today, assuming one could find the materials and the skilled manpower (2,500 workers, in those days before power tools) to put them together.

But George Washington Vanderbilt III, youngest son of William H., topped even The Breakers. In the early 1890s, he created Biltmore House, a 250-room confection modeled on the French chateaux of Chambord, Chenonceaux, and Blois and set on 125,000 acres outside Asheville, North Carolina. It is the largest private house ever constructed in America, and it still remains in the family. But what began as the fiefdom of a rather shy Vanderbilt interested in experimental forest

(OPPOSITE)

The Gothic Room at Marble House was one of several rooms featuring Alva's favorite styles — this time with French Gothic arches, chimney piece, ribbing, and figurative carving. The room originally held a collection of medieval art objects. William K. Vanderbilt spent $11 million on his Newport home.

PHOTO © RICHARD CHEEK FOR THE PRESERVATION SOCIETY OF NEWPORT COUNTY.

(ABOVE)

Alva Smith Belmont (formerly Vanderbilt) frequently entertained in her Chinese tea house, built in 1914 on the grounds of Marble House. A lavish Chinese costume ball heralded the opening of this delightful tea house. Originally standing directly above the Cliff Walk, overlooking the Atlantic, the sructure was moved back from the edge when the seawall weakened, threatening to send the small, colorful pavilion adrift.

PHOTO © RICHARD CHEEK FOR THE PRESERVATION SOCIETY OF NEWPORT COUNTY.

(ABOVE)

Frederick W. Vanderbilt's Rough Point
(eventually owned by tobacco heiress Doris Duke)
succeeded somewhat better than most Newport
"cottages" at harmonizing with the landscape.
Here we see it on a typical New England overcast
summer day.

(RIGHT)

The solarium at Rough Point: Airiness and
ornament somehow coexist, with a grand Atlantic
vista beyond.

The grand staircase landing at Rough Point, complete with large portraits, is lighted by large windows on the landing featuring stained-glass coats of arms.

PHOTO NEWPORT RESTORATION FOUNDATION, NEWPORT, RHODE ISLAND.

practices is now a major tourist attraction, its surrounding acreage diminished to 7,000 acres.

G. W. Vanderbilt was one of the most earnest and intriguing members of a family that produced a generous share of what society editors used to call "sportsmen." He never went near the railroad business, and seems to have been the first Vanderbilt to realize that inherited wealth (his own legacy amounted to $10 million) might be used to finance a life of study as well as conspicuous consumption. To build a 250-room house is, no doubt, to consume rather conspicuously. But G.W. Vanderbilt took a far more than superficial interest in the development of his estate.

Only 27 when he began to buy his North Carolina acreage, Vanderbilt hired two men who were at the peak of their professions: Richard Morris Hunt as architect, and Frederick Law Olmsted as landscape designer. Unlike many Gilded Age nabobs who were difficult if not impossible patrons, Vanderbilt impressed both Hunt and Olmsted with his sincere interest in their work. "Affectionate solicitude" was the phrase Hunt's wife used to describe his attitude toward Hunt; while Olmsted, in a letter to his landscape architect son, referred to the Vanderbilt commission as a "school" in which a great deal could be learned.

As much as he enjoyed architecture and garden design, G.W. Vanderbilt reserved his greatest enthusiasm for his forests. He hired Gifford Pinchot, father of the U.S. Forest Service, to manage his woodlands. Later, the job fell to

pioneer silviculturist Carl A. Schenck, who founded the Biltmore Forest School. The legacy of modern forestry education, and of the Pisgah National Forest, which comprises much of the original estate, are the most important contributions of a Vanderbilt who, retiring as he was, couldn't have retired to more splendid surroundings.

RAILROAD GIANTS

There were two kinds of railroad men operating in what historian Oliver Jensen has called "the age of bare knuckles." There were the builders and consolidators, men like the Vanderbilts who either created railroad companies and laid track, or at least did a reasonable job of managing roads they had acquired through mergers and takeovers. Then there were the outright scalawags, men whose main interest was the manipulation of railroad stock and the squeezing of value from roads that might well be turned into barren husks by the time the opportunists were finished. "I don't build railroads, I buy them," said Jay Gould, the most notorious exemplar of the latter modus operandi. Both the builders and the manipulators, though, fought with bare knuckles.

One of the great builders was a man remembered to this day in the name of the Amtrak train that runs between Chicago and Seattle. The *Empire Builder* follows the northernmost of the major U.S. rail routes, coursing across the high prairie that reaches from Minnesota's Twin Cities to the foothills of the Rocky Mountains, then traverses both the Rockies and the Cascades before its descent to Puget Sound.

(OPPOSITE)

Biltmore's rich-textured library is home to more than 10,000 volumes selected from George Vanderbilt's personal collection of 23,000 books. A 17th-century tapestry above the black marble fireplace is flanked by walnut figures of Hestia (goddess of the hearth), and Demeter (goddess of the earth) carved by Karl Bitter.

PHOTO USED WITH PERMISSION FROM THE BILTMORE COMPANY, ASHEVILLE, NORTH CAROLINA.

(ABOVE)

Biltmore's banquet hall, the largest and most dramatic room of the house, features a 72-foot ceiling, triple fireplace, and 16th-century Brussels tapestries.

PHOTO USED WITH PERMISSION FROM THE BILTMORE COMPANY, ASHEVILLE, NORTH CAROLINA.

(ABOVE)

A salon in the Stanford White–designed Hyde Park, New York, home of Frederick W. Vanderbilt, completed in 1899.

PHOTO COURTESY NATIONAL PARK SERVICE, ROOSEVELT-VANDERBILT NATIONAL HISTORIC SITES, HYDE PARK, NEW YORK.

(RIGHT)

The largest of the two dining tables in Hyde Park's massive dining room can seat 30 people and was used for formal affairs. The smaller table was used when the Frederick Vanderbilts dined alone.

PHOTO © RICHARD CHEEK FOR THE HYDE PARK HISTORICAL ASSOCIATION.

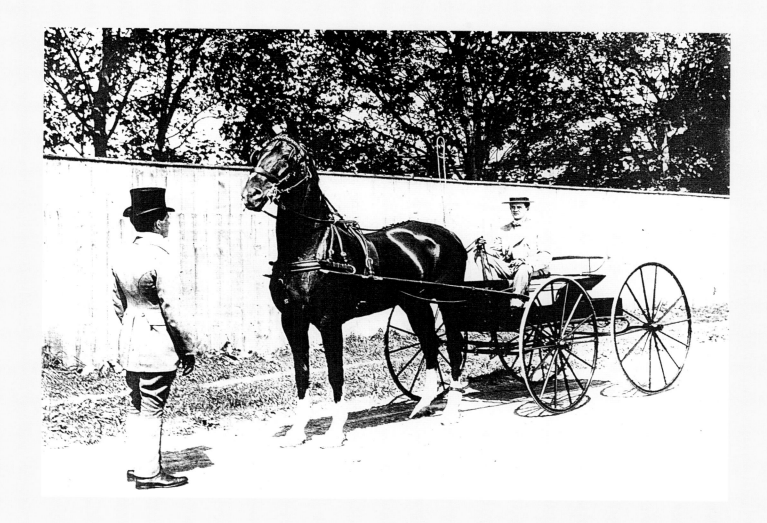

(ABOVE)

The picture of propriety: one of Newport's prominent citizens out for an afteroon ride in a spotless carriage pulled by a proud and impeccably groomed horse.

PHOTO COURTESY THE PRESERVATION SOCIETY OF NEWPORT COUNTY.

(LEFT)

Winters along the New England coast are typically cold and damp, but Newport society always found ways to enjoy the outdoors.

PHOTO COURTESY THE PRESERVATION SOCIETY OF NEWPORT COUNTY.

(OPPOSITE)

From head to toe this Newport family is appropriately attired and prepares to receive guests at an afternoon garden party.

PHOTO COURTESY THE PRESERVATION SOCIETY OF NEWPORT COUNTY.

(OPPOSITE TOP)

With coachmen standing by, spectators enjoy a turn-of-the-century Newport regatta.

PHOTO COURTESY THE NEWPORT HISTORICAL SOCIETY.

(OPPOSITE BOTTOM)

Newport summer sojourners stage a "mattress race" with inflatable rafts on Bailey's Beach, 1921.

PHOTO COURTESY THE NEWPORT HISTORICAL SOCIETY.

(ABOVE)

The Vanderbilts enjoy an afternoon outing on their yacht.

PHOTO BY HENRY O. HAVERMEYER COURTESY THE PRESERVATION SOCIETY OF NEWPORT COUNTY.

(ABOVE)

A Vanderbilt family safari in Africa. Alva, still a
Vanderbilt at the time of the photo, lounges in the
hammock at right.

PHOTO COURTESY THE PRESERVATION SOCIETY OF NEWPORT COUNTY.

(OPPOSITE)

A summer afternoon crowd turns out for a tennis
match at the Casino, Newport.

PHOTO BY HENRY O. HAVERMEYER/COURTESY THE NEWPORT
HISTORICAL SOCIETY.

(ABOVE)

Then as now, Newport's Cliff Walk drew summer strollers, c. 1910. The Breakers stands in the background.

PHOTO COURTESY THE NEWPORT HISTORICAL SOCIETY.

(LEFT)

A summer fete on the lawn at The Breakers, probably during the first decade of the 20th century.

PHOTO COURTESY THE NEWPORT HISTORICAL SOCIETY.

The Empire Builder himself was an émigré from Ontario named James Jerome Hill. His creation was the Great Northern Railway.

Jim Hill had wanted to become a doctor, but he gave up that ambition after losing an eye in a boyhood accident. When he was 18, in 1856, he drifted down to St. Paul, Minnesota, where he hoped to join a fur-trading expedition. But he missed the company's departure, and instead settled down to clerking for a steamboat outfit. By 1865 he was working for himself, forwarding freight and running a warehouse. As a

sideline, he got into the coal business. His assumption was that coal would soon replace wood as locomotive fuel, and that there would be plenty of locomotives to burn it.

Hill's next move was to assume a partnership in the Red River Transportation Company, which ran steamships north to a Canadian settlement called Fort Garry, soon to be renamed Winnipeg. In 1878, he and his partners bought the bankrupt St. Paul and Pacific Railroad, one of Hill's old freight clients. Savvy St. Paul businessmen figured Hill was buying nothing but trouble, because his new acquisition was a poorly built road that served a farming district beset by grasshoppers and depression. But things began to pick up just as Hill was linking up with the lines north of the border, and in 1879 he reorganized the firm as the St. Paul, Minneapolis, and Manitoba.

Hill, by now fully in charge of his road, began planning his next move. It was a scheme that struck the sober citizens of St. Paul as particularly hare-brained, and quickly earned the label "Hill's Folly": James J. Hill was going to run the St. P M&M clear across the Dakotas and Montana, across Idaho and Washington, straight to Puget Sound.

It took until 1893, but Hill pulled it off. His railroad— known after 1883 as the Great Northern Railway—not only spanned the northernmost U.S. route, but the job had been accomplished without any of the federal land grants that had eased the way for other builders of transcontinental lines. Later, Hill also took control of the Northern Pacific and the Chicago, Burlington and Quincy. The Empire Builder had done his job.

Perhaps no other railroad man was as intimately involved in creating the economy and social structure of the territory his lines traversed as was James J. Hill. He advertised for settlers to populate the prairie, distributing seeds and fertilizer, livestock, and the latest information on husbandry and agronomy to the farmers who put their roots down along the Great Northern tracks. (Later, after the region fought its way through drought and hard times, many would say that Hill had overpopulated the high plains.) He was also a wizard at creating complementary shipping patterns, juggling

midwestern wheat, Pacific Northwest lumber, and southern cotton bound for the Orient so that his trains were always making money.

So were Hill's other investments. He once took a flier on a remote chunk of real estate in northern Minnesota, which unbeknownst to buyer or seller contained the Mesabi iron range. He leased the property to U.S. Steel, reaping abundant profits for himself and the Great Northern's stockholders.

With his barrel chest, wiry gray beard, and one good eye that seemed to burn the more fiercely for the absence of the other, Jim Hill was the picture of the crusty capitalist warhorse of the late 19th century. He acted the part, too—if an isolated prairie town eager for a Great Northern connection refused to meet his terms, he would consign it to obscurity by stranding it off the main line. But Hill had a solid respect for men willing to work as hard as he was. On at least one occasion he rode his private car out into the deep prairie snows, then picked up a shovel and put his shoulder to the work while the men he relieved rested and drank coffee in his plush parlor on wheels.

James J. Hill built things big, and he built them solid. Tracks, bridges, rolling stock, locomotives—all were the best he could afford. On Summit Avenue in St. Paul, his massive stone mansion speaks to the same desire to build for the ages. It isn't a cozy house, though we can be sure it was warm enough: its behemoth boilers gobbled enough coal each winter to send a fleet of freight trains across the prairie, and most rooms were equipped with gas fireplaces. The music room with its huge built-in pipe organ seems like a small concert hall, and the dining room like a school refectory; and even giving allowance for its present-day status as a tourist attraction, the halls have a dour institutional feel. But there is one relatively snug room where the spirit of the builder breathes. It isn't difficult to imagine Jim Hill in his office, plotting his next art acquisitions (oddly, he favored modern French painters rather than the safe academicians most rich men went for in his day), planning his quiet bequests to Catholic charities . . . and musing, in the last years before his death in 1916,

on how a one-eyed boy from Ontario might see an iron road to Seattle beginning on the wharves of St. Paul.

The Great Northern was, of course, not the first railroad to traverse the western vastnesses of North America. The Northern Pacific had finished its 14-year task of linking the Great Lakes with the Columbia River valley in 1883, largely due to the organizational genius of a German immigrant named Henry Villard. Villard was, perhaps, the unlikeliest of railroad titans. He first turned up in the United States in 1853, when he was 18. Starting with menial jobs (one was on a railroad crew), the university-trained Villard became a newspaperman and a respected Civil War correspondent. He promoted civil service reform, and married the daughter of the uncompromising New England abolitionist William Lloyd Garrison (their son, Oswald Garrison Villard, would carry on the family's progressive traditions as editor of *The Nation*). But in the early 1870s, Villard returned to Germany to nurse chronic health problems.

Villard's 1874 return to the United States was prompted by a group of German investors, who wanted him to keep an eye on a couple of ailing western railroads in which they held stock. Within a few years, he became president of the Oregon and California and a receiver of the Kansas Pacific. Seeing that the biggest threat to his companies' position in the Northwest market was the still-incomplete Northern Pacific, Villard in 1881 made a bold decision: he would buy the competing line. His

means of financing the acquisition, though, would be even bolder.

Villard approached 50 wealthy Americans, most of whom he knew personally from his years in the U.S., and who knew him as a man of integrity. He asked them to finance an $8 million fund he was amassing for a purpose he could not yet disclose. This was the soon-to-be-legendary "Blind Pool," eventually totaling $12 million, which enabled Villard to purchase the Northern Pacific on behalf of his trusting investors. Installing himself as president, he marshaled the men and material

needed to finish the NP's route to the west coast by 1883.

Ousted as president of the NP and later returned in the role of chairman, Villard in later life pursued interests that ranged far beyond railroads. He bought the *New York Evening Post,* helped organize the Edison General Electric Company, and electrified Milwaukee's street railway system. He represented Deutsche Bank in the U.S., and gave generously to the universities of Washington and Oregon. Although a relatively modest man by railroad baron standards, he also made a

The last word in travel comfort, 1895: Interior of the private railroad car Grand Isle *.*

significant addition to the midtown Manhattan streetscape. The "Villard Houses," as they came to be called, were built between 1882 and 1886 on Madison Avenue between East 50th and East 51st streets. Villard lived in only one of the four Italian Renaissance-style houses, which were designed by McKim, Mead & White (with a later addition by Babb, Cook & Willard) to give the impression of a single palatial edifice embracing a front courtyard. The railroad man sold the other units to friends.

The Villard houses would later be divided between the Roman Catholic Archdiocese of New York and the publishing firm of Random House. Eventually, they faced demolition—but the luxury hotel that was to replace them was instead integrated into the block, so that the houses' façades and a portion of their interior now welcome hotel guests. "Façadomy," some critics call this sort of preservation, but it beats the alternative. Henry Villard himself was a man who appreciated creative approaches to a problem.

The most celebrated of all transcontinental rail routes was the first to have been completed, when the crews of the Union Pacific and Central Pacific met at Promontory Point, Utah, for the driving of the last spike in 1869. The Union Pacific spent much of the next several decades mired in scandal and bankruptcy, eventually becoming the "streak of rust" purchased and rehabilitated by E. H. Harriman, whom we'll meet later on. It was the Central Pacific that produced the legendary team of eyes-on-the-main-chance entrepreneurs known collectively as the Big Four: Leland Stanford, Mark Hopkins, Charles Crocker, and Collis P. Huntington.

They were only a medium-sized four, to begin with. Shopkeepers all, they were easterners who had decamped for California in the wake of the 1849 gold rush. Being men of good sense, they left the actual mining to others and went in for more of a sure thing, staying put in Sacramento and operating on the theory that regardless of whether or not a man found gold, he needed to buy pants, food, and a shovel. Huntington and Hopkins sold hardware; Crocker and his brother owned three dry goods stores; Stanford, who helped found the California Republican Party in 1852, was in the grocery business.

These four merchants were on hand at a meeting in Sacramento one day in 1861 to hear a visionary named Theodore Judah, known as "Crazy" Judah for his fanatical devotion to his cause, lay out his plan for a railroad across the Sierra Nevada—part of an eventual transcontinental route he had been promoting since the early 1850s. Huntington, Hopkins, Crocker, and Stanford didn't think Judah was crazy. They bought enough stock in his scheme to guarantee that it would get off the ground, got the U.S. government to pass the Pacific Railroad Act in 1862, and started construction at Sacramento in January 1863. Along the way they bought out Theodore Judah's share of the Central Pacific, as the new enterprise was called, for $100,000. Judah died shortly afterward, while heading east to find backers to help *him* buy out the Big Four.

But those four erstwhile Sacramento storekeepers held on to the operation, using every trick in the book to get their road built and make the greatest possible amount of money doing it. A firm set up by Crocker

got the construction contract, and the Central Pacific secured the bigger government loans earmarked for mountainous terrain by claiming that the level ground on which tracklaying began was actually in the rugged Sierra foothills. Eventually, the company evolved into the Southern Pacific, a titan of western transportation so formidable that it was the thinly veiled model for the voracious rail colossus in Frank Norris's muckraking classic *The Octopus*.

As partners go, the masterminds of the Central Pacific couldn't have been more different. Stanford,

originally a lawyer, was the most gregarious of the four and a born politician—he served a term as governor of California (1862–1864) and was a U.S. senator from 1885 to 1893, representing his railroad as faithfully as he did his state . . . or more so. Along with the limelight, Stanford loved the good life. He owned a palatial private railroad car, bred prize racehorses at his Palo Alto ranch, and cultivated extensive vineyards. His mansion on San Francisco's Nob Hill was the height of overstuffed Victorian splendor.

Charles Crocker was the man who promoted the

William Van Horne's now-vanished Montreal mansion was a 52-room treasury of paintings, tapestries, and Japanese pottery.

idea of using Chinese labor to build the Central Pacific. His rationale was simple: "They built the Great Wall, didn't they?" Crocker was the field boss of the operation, swaggering up and down the line, all 250 pounds of him, bullying the rails into place and doling out silver and gold coins himself on payday. He had a showy San Francisco mansion, too. One of its notable features was a 40-foot-high spite fence, built around the modest home of the only property owner on his block who refused to sell out.

Mark Hopkins would have been happy with that man's cottage. He was an accountant by training and inclination, and a cheapskate by nature. The only reason "Uncle Mark" ended up in a Nob Hill palace was that his wife insisted on it. His greatest pleasure seemed to have been keeping the railroad's books, and he would no doubt have shaken his head in disapproval at the luxuriousness of the San Francisco hotel that bears his name today.

"Ruthless as a crocodile," "no more soul than a shark." Those were just a few of the phrases used to describe Collis P. Huntington during his heyday as biggest of the Big Four; in retaliation, Huntington called the organized farmers of the Grange movement "Communists." The bald, stocky, white-bearded Huntington honed his pragmatic ruthlessness as he elbowed his way in line for hard-to-come-by construction supplies during the Civil War, and dipped into company slush funds for purposes of legislative persuasion. He never cared for the limelight—he was happy to have Stanford be the Central Pacific president and chief mouthpiece—and despite his Western

notoriety among the Grangers and other anti-monopolists, he alone among the Big Four became primarily a resident of the East. That was where the brains of the Central/Southern Pacific operation could best keep an eye on Wall Street, and on his other interests. When John D. Rockefeller, Sr., moved to New York, his first home was a lavishly furnished brownstone where Huntington had lately installed his mistress.

The San Francisco earthquake of 1906 erased the mansions of the three lifelong Californians among the Big Four, but one monument (aside from their railroad) remains: Stanford University, officially Leland Stanford, Jr., University, created by Stanford in 1885 in memory of his late son.

WILLIAM CORNELIUS VAN HORNE

"Oh, I eat all I can, I drink all I can, I smoke all I can, and I don't give a damn about anything."

The words of an idle sybarite? Not exactly. He may have worked hard at enjoying his creature comforts, but William Cornelius Van Horne worked harder at getting things done. He was an accomplished telegrapher, bookkeeper, art collector, amateur painter, gentleman farmer, and discoverer of nine fossils which bear the designation *van hornei*. And he built the Canadian Pacific Railway.

It's one of the ironies of North American railroad history that while James J. Hill, builder of the Great Northern, was an Ontario boy, William Van Horne was an Illinois native who earned his fame—and a knighthood—in Canada. Alone among the great names

of railroading on this continent, Van Horne acquired his reputation not as a financier, but as a manager. Born in 1843, he had by age 38 worked his way up to the presidency of the Southern Minnesota Railway after starting out as a telegrapher with the Illinois Central. In 1881, when the Canadian Pacific Railway was chartered by an act of Canada's parliament, Van Horne was recommended for the job of general manager by none other than Jim Hill, a member of the CPR syndicate (the two men later became bitter enemies when Van Horne successfully opposed Hill's plan to run

the CPR south of the Great Lakes, where it would be a feeder line for his roads).

Managing the CPR meant building the bulk of the road from scratch, and marshaling the men and materials for this gigantic task revealed Van Horne's genius. During the 10 years preceding his appointment, the Canadian government and its various franchisees had laid only 300 miles of track. In 1882, Van Horne's crews extended the CPR 418 miles through the prairie provinces in 10 *months*. The going was a good deal slower across the stubborn rock and muskeg north of

(ABOVE)

*A windmill at Covenhoven. William Van Horne
was equally fascinated by art and technology, and
was adept at both.*

(LEFT)

*William Van Horne's summer home Covenhoven,
on Minister's Island in New Brunswick: it took
eight men to lift the living room rug.*

Lake Superior, and in the steep passes of the Rocky
Mountains. But Van Horne got the job done, and stood
among the laborers and dignitaries that gathered on
November 7, 1885, at a remote spot called Craigellachie
in British Columbia. At that last spike ceremony, the
general manager was modest and sparing in his
remarks: "All I can say is that the work has been done
well in every way." A tremendous share of that work
had been done by the general manager himself, a man
unafraid to take the throttle of a locomotive and run the
machine over a new high trestle, after the engineer had
looked down and lost his nerve.

Van Horne—Sir William Cornelius Van Horne after
1894—became president of the CPR in 1888, and board
chairman 11 years later. Those were the years when the
stout, bald, elegantly bearded railroader commanded his
empire of trains, steamships, and luxury hotels (several
of which he had helped design) from his office in
Montreal's Windsor Station, and when he might be seen
just about anywhere along the CPR lines in his splendid
private car *Saskatchewan*, crafted of mahogany and
glittering with polished brass. Home for Van Horne
was a baronial 52-room stone mansion in Montreal, its
walls hung with a $3 million collection of Old Masters,
but in summer Sir William would likely be found at his
island farm near St. Andrews, New Brunswick. There
he plunged into landscaping and agricultural tasks,
plotting out vineyards, orchards, greenhouses, and
stables. He expected everyone to work as hard as he
did: when he found a group of his dairymen idly looking
out of a barn window, he sent a team of carpenters to
raise the window above eye level.

Lyndhurst in the Hudson Valley.
Jay Gould's redoubt is now a National
Trust property.

During his last days, in 1915, his doctors had told him not to smoke more than three cigars a day. He followed their orders scrupulously . . . but only after ordering a box of two-foot cigars that would last four hours apiece. Whatever was worth doing, the genius of the CPR figured, was worth doing on a colossal scale.

JAY GOULD

If William Van Horne represented one end of the spectrum of constructive toil during railroading's great era of expansion, there was no shortage of out-and-out rascals at the other end. The most notorious of this crew could be found, toward the latter part of his life, nursing his dyspepsia at his romantic Gothic mansion, Lyndhurst, on the banks of the Hudson in Tarrytown, New York. But there was nothing romantic about Jay Gould. Born in modest circumstances in upstate New York in 1836, he worked as a tanner in Pennsylvania and honed his business skills as a leather merchant in pre–Civil War New York City. Around that time he began speculating in railroad securities, living out his later self-description as a buyer, not a builder, of railroads. His career as a manipulator led to his eventual involvement with the most star-crossed road of his day, the Erie. "The Scarlet Woman of Wall Street," that hapless firm was called, and it certainly had some colorful suitors.

The "Erie Wars" of the 1860s would fill a volume all their own. Suffice it to say that the railroad was the prize in a brazen game played by Gould along with two equally rapacious colleagues named Daniel Drew and James Fisk. At various junctures, the game involved

the issuing of fraudulent stock, the bribing of members of the New York State Legislature, and that extremely rare occurrence, the fleecing of one Commodore Cornelius Vanderbilt. When the dust settled, Vanderbilt had withdrawn in a compromise, Drew was ruined, Fisk was dead, and Gould left the field without the ravished Erie but with $25 million with which to play havoc among the western railroads. (Along the way, he had created the

financial panic called "Black Friday"—September 24, 1869—when he tried to corner the gold market.)

Although they were both pirates at heart, it's hard to imagine two more different operators than Daniel Drew and Jim Fisk. Drew, the Commodore's sometime whist partner, was a rustic Vermonter who had once been a cattle drover. The Wall Street term "watered stock," meaning stock inflated beyond its legitimate value, is said to derive from a practice "Uncle Dan'l" perfected when he was young: letting cattle lick salt and then drink copiously just before delivering them to market, so that he would make more money when he sold them by weight. Like Vanderbilt, he had graduated to railroads via steamboats, although you would never catch him building his own steam yacht. Drew was a lifelong cheapskate, who wore threadbare suits and ate sandwiches at Delmonico's lunch counter while his fellow buccaneers dined on lobster and canvasback duck upstairs. He always carried a Bible, and he said grace over the sandwiches.

"Jubilee Jim" Fisk was another Vermont boy made good—or, more to the point, spectacularly bad. Unlike Drew, he flaunted every dollar he earned or stole, right down to wearing a custom-designed "admiral's" uniform when riding in state on one of the steamboats he wrested from Uncle Dan'l in the Erie Wars. ("If Vanderbilt's a Commodore," he claimed, "I can be an Admiral.") Plump and mustachioed, Fisk was very much the ladies' man, and his favorite mistress was an actress named Josie Mansfield. She was his undoing. On January 6, 1872, Jubilee Jim was shot dead at the Grand Central Hotel in New York by Edward Stokes,

Jay Gould's dining room at Lyndhurst. Chronically dyspeptic, the financier must have enjoyed the decor more than the meals.

The Great Hall of Arden House, last home of Edward H. Harriman.
PHOTO COURTESY ARDEN CONFERENCE CENTER.

another of Josie's admirers. He would have loved his own funeral, a spectacularly gaudy affair organized by his politician friends at Tammany Hall.

And Jay Gould? When he wasn't in seclusion at Lyndhurst, the frail little man with the big black beard might be found at his Fifth Avenue mansion, surrounded by fresh flowers from his Tarrytown greenhouses. That is, if anyone wanted to find him: in the words of a contemporary account, "He has few friends, and is suspicious of all his associates, who return his distrust with equal heartiness." He was once beaten by a Wall Street mob. He owned the New York *World* newspaper, and controlled the Western Union Telegraph Company. His digestion bothered him constantly, and he died, in 1892, at the age of 56.

His daughter, Anna, became the Duchess of Talleyrand-Perigord.

EDWARD HENRY HARRIMAN

Mention the name Harriman today, and anyone versed in 20th-century American politics will recall W. Averill Harriman, the suave, urbane New York State governor and ambassador. People living in the New York metropolitan area might also think of vast Harriman State Park, a component of the Palisades Interstate Park system just north of the New Jersey border. A hundred years ago, though, the name Harriman meant railroads.

The father of both the politician and the park was a small, steely-eyed man with an outsized walrus mustache named Edward Henry Harriman. To him belongs the distinction of controlling more miles of

track than any individual in the history of American railroading. He was neither a builder nor a buccaneer; rather, he combined the boldness and timing of a successful financier with the skills of a master administrator. Having seen the vultures pick the bones of many an unfortunate road, Harriman thought not in terms of overnight profits but of capital improvements that would lead to dependable long-term yields.

E. H. Harriman was born a minister's son in 1848. Leaving school for a job as a Wall Street office boy at 14, he borrowed $3,000 from an uncle and bought a seat on the New York Stock Exchange just seven years later. His introduction to railroad management was a directorship with a small, upstate New York road owned by his father-in-law; by the mid-1880s, he was instrumental in revitalizing the Illinois Central, and doubling that company's earnings.

Harriman hit his stride in 1894, when he led a syndicate that bought a railroad that had been dismissed by J. P. Morgan as "a streak of rust" when it went on the block after going bankrupt the previous year. The Union Pacific, partner with the Central Pacific in spanning the continent in 1869, had since been bled dry by Jay Gould and came in at a bargain price. Harriman, with his genius for management, doubled the UP's earnings within two years, while cutting its freight rates and vastly improving roadbeds and equipment. Next Harriman bought the Central and Southern Pacific railroads, following Collis P. Huntington's death in 1900. He was a director of the Santa Fe and the Erie. With these and a slew of other roads under his ownership or de facto control,

Harriman at his zenith was master of 60,000 to 65,000 miles of track, with another 35,000 miles of steamship lines thrown in. At a 1906 Interstate Commerce Commission hearing, he freely admitted that if there were no antitrust laws to stop him, he would keep buying railroads "as long as I live."

Although Harriman didn't live that much longer—he died in 1909—conservationists might well have wished that he could have kept buying land, as well. Keenly interested in saving forests from exploitation, Harriman acquired 20,000 acres in the Ramapo Mountains of southern New York, and crowned them with his one great extravagance, a 150-room French Renaissance mansion surrounded by formal gardens. Leaving Arden House and the surrounding property to his wife, Mary, along with his $100 million fortune, Harriman stipulated that 10,000 acres be given to the state for use as a park. His other accomplishments outside the realm of pure moneymaking included the adoption of the first pension plan for railroad workers, organization of a relief program for San Francisco following the 1906 earthquake, a flood protection plan for California's

Imperial Valley, and the organization of a scientific expedition to Alaska in 1899. He also left a vastly more efficient American rail system, an achievement which, he might have argued, earned him the right to a dollar or two, or a hundred million, in compensation.

There had been one big disappointment in E. H. Harriman's career. That was his failure to obtain control of the Northern Pacific Railroad, which he had hoped to snatch from under the nose of James J. Hill. The scheme involved the purchase of an outstanding 40,000 shares of Northern Pacific stock, and might have succeeded if a less sensitive nose had been involved. As it was, Hill got hold of those shares before Harriman did, thus cementing what had been his minority control of Henry Villard's old road. Hill's purchase of the NP stock was executed by his New York bankers, partners in a firm whose chairman was in France on one of his frequent art-buying sprees. The partners cabled their boss, who gave his approval to the deal and presumably did not mind being interrupted by the affairs of so important a client as Hill. The banker was John Pierpont Morgan.

J. P. MORGAN

No farmboy, frontier trader, or scion of a small-town preacher, J. P. Morgan was comfortable from birth. The man who rose to become America's master banker never had to worry, as did Astor or Vanderbilt, about fitting in with polite society. As art dealer James Duveen observed, "Morgan was born a gentleman, and did everything he could to fortify that fact and impose it upon an admiring world."

Morgan entered the admiring world in 1837, born into a Hartford, Connecticut, family that had done well in retailing, real estate, and insurance, and was about to do even better in banking. Pierpont's father, Junius Spencer Morgan, became a key figure in the movement of British venture capital to America's growing railroads, and by the time the boy was 20 he was accustomed to transatlantic travel, had studied in Switzerland and Germany, and was beginning to take a hand in his father's enterprises.

For a man whose very name came to signify total control, and absolute mastery of every situation he encountered, it is interesting to note that J. P. Morgan was, for the first 53 years of his life, subsidiary to his father in the older man's banking business. But Junius gave his son an ever-increasing amount of leeway during the boom years following the Civil War, and J. P. Morgan knew what to do with it. He became increasingly involved with the growing railroads, parlaying his role as investment banker into a string of strategic directorships and eventually outright control of a number of major roads. He also backed new technology, becoming an early investor in Thomas Edison's fledgling company as well as one of the first New York customers for Edison's electric lighting apparatus.

By middle age, J. P. Morgan had become one of those individuals who dominates his peers and his surroundings not only by cleverness and will, but by sheer physical presence. Morgan was average in height but weighed a bullish 210 pounds; he had an enormous head, commanding brow, and eyes that reminded the young photographer Edward Steichen of the headlights of a locomotive bearing down on whomever was in their sight. His one physical disfigurement—a nose turned hideous and bulbous by acne rosacea—was at first a cause for shyness and self-consciousness, but came to be a lantern flashed in defiance at the world.

The peak of J. P. Morgan's power and fame coincided with the last quarter-century of his life. From 1890 until his death in 1913, Morgan, for better or worse, represented the power of centralized finance in

their resources to halt a cascade of bank failures that threatened the nation's economy. This was the last time, in those days before the creation of the Federal reserve system, that a private citizen would (or could) assume such a leadership position.

Morgan may have been a private citizen, but he lived like a Renaissance doge. His image was perhaps enhanced by the fact that unlike financial titans who view conspicuous consumption as a badge of celebrity (or even as the vehicle for their celebrity), Morgan gave the appearance of a man whose appetites existed in and of themselves, and would be every bit as grand even if no publicity were to accrue to them. "As long as he was in active life, and in whatever field he entered, he bought the highest-priced corner lot," wrote his son-in-law and biographer Herbert Satterlee. "He added championship horses to his stable, built the best steam yacht, and purchased the most notable pictures."

That summed up Morgan's magnificence, as much as anything. Like most of his fabulously wealthy contemporaries, J. P. Morgan lived on a lavish personal scale: He employed a succession of four splendid yachts, all named *Corsair*, to ferry friends and business associates up the Hudson from New York to his riverside country house, Cragston. He was commodore of the New York Yacht Club. He bred prize collies and cattle, had his gargantuan cigars custom-made in Cuba from select-harvest tobacco, and ate eight-course breakfasts. "Always resist everything except temptation," he once told an associate, and his Lucullan appetites extended to some of the most beautiful women of the age, whom he entertained in those off hours when

the United States. His passion was for organization, and reorganization. With the railroads hauled out of the chaos of the wide-open heyday of the Goulds and Drews, Morgan turned to the steel industry, consolidating the Carnegie, Frick, and other competing firms into U.S. Steel, the nation's first billion-dollar company. (In 1901, a billion dollars represented 4 percent of the national wealth of the United States.) The other accomplishment for which Morgan is most widely remembered is his role in the Panic of 1907, putting together a coalition of banks willing to commit

he wasn't singing hymns with Episcopalian bishops. But "the most notable pictures," and a collection of equally notable manuscripts and books, were Morgan's greatest extravagance.

Starting humbly enough at age 14 with President Millard Fillmore's autograph, Morgan went on to collect shards of medieval stained glass in towns he visited as a student in Europe; later, he graduated to ancient Egyptian pieces. But his ambitions as a grand acquisitor really burst forth after the death of his father, when he became known among transatlantic art dealers as a man who would swallow entire collections, and outbid anyone for anything.

Morgan bought Chinese ceramics, medieval tapestries, Etruscan and Babylonian antiquities, Old Master drawings, and works by such artists as Memling, Bellini, and Fragonard. Turning to manuscripts and printed works, he acquired a Gutenberg Bible (the Morgan Library now possesses three, more than any other institution in the world), illuminated medieval books of hours, and handwritten letters of Jefferson, Washington, Napoleon, and

The Andrew Carnegie Mansion, featuring the Arthur Ross Terrace. The mansion is now the Smithsonian's Cooper-Hewitt National Design Museum.

Elizabeth I. Beginning with Thackeray, Morgan collected manuscripts of works by Dickens, Keats, Milton, and other authors of the first rank. The financier's trove of paintings, sculptures, and works on paper eventually required a home of their own, and so Morgan commissioned McKim, Mead & White to create the neoclassical library building adjacent to his brownstone home at Madison Avenue and East 36th Street in Manhattan. This building, at the heart of which is Morgan's ornate private study, is today's Morgan Library, one of New York's great museums and reference institutions. The institution's first director remarked that it "apparently contains everything but the original tablets of the Ten Commandments." She was using only mild exaggeration. Opened at the bequest of Morgan's son in 1924, 11 years after the great banker's death, it is as much a monument to its creator as that billion-dollar edifice called U.S. Steel.

ANDREW CARNEGIE

The cornerstone of Morgan's great steel trust was the colossal iron and steel business of Andrew Carnegie, the one great figure of the age of American winner-take-all capitalism who is remembered as much for his philanthropies as for the way in which he amassed his riches. To the ages, Carnegie means—Carnegie *is*— libraries, more than 2,500 of them throughout the English-speaking world, 1,689 in the United States alone. The libraries, donated to communities that agreed to provide them with land and an annual budget, were only part of his bequests, which by the time of his death in 1919 exceeded $350 million.

"Little Andy" Carnegie—he would grow to an adult height of only five feet two inches—was born in 1835 in Dumferline, Scotland, the son of a reasonably prosperous handweaver. Both his father and mother were political radicals, their beliefs a foundation for the progressive—if necessarily compromised—attitudes of the future industrialist.

With handloom weaving doomed to mechanization, the Carnegie family emigrated to western Pennsylvania in 1848. Andrew's first job was as a bobbin boy in a cotton mill, earning $1.20 a week. After that came a stint as a messenger for a telegraph company, during which he began to cultivate the contacts in the Pittsburgh business community that would serve him well in later years. Carnegie used his telegraphy skills in his next job, with the Pennsylvania Railroad, where he rose to the position of superintendent of the Pittsburgh division. He remained with the Pennsylvania until 1865, by which time his investments had become numerous and lucrative enough to enable him to strike out on his own. By far the most important of those new ventures was his controlling partnership in an iron forging company, at the threshold of an era in which iron and steel would become the physical foundation of American economic expansion.

The succession of enterprises that would by 1892 become the Carnegie Steel Company owed its phenomenal success to Andrew Carnegie's embrace of the Bessemer process after 1873, and his subsequent focus upon steel manufacture. But just as important was Carnegie's organizational genius, and his ability to delegate responsibility to talented researchers and

managers. He once suggested that his epitaph should be, "Here lies a man who was able to surround himself with men far cleverer than himself."

They were clever men indeed, but there is more than a little undue self-deprecation in Carnegie's remark. He was, after all, a man who could spot an opportunity or a business trend with remarkable acuity, and he was so dedicated to his work (and, it should be said, to his widowed mother) that he didn't even marry until he was 51 years old. But it wasn't modesty, uncharacteristic as it was for a Gilded Age industrialist, that startled so many of the steel man's peers. It was his unsettling opinions on the rights of labor, extending even to his endorsement of the idea of unions.

The man who put the phrase "Death to Privilege" on his family's coat of arms was veering alarmingly toward the radical politics of his ancestors—or so it seemed to those who didn't appreciate the ambiguity of Carnegie's professed beliefs, or the gap between what he said and what he did. Typical was Carnegie's dithering on such issues as the eight-hour day—first he adopted this radical innovation, then went back to 12-hour shifts when economy so dictated. But the worst blight on his record was the bloody suppression of the steel strike at a Carnegie mill in Homestead, Pennsylvania, in 1892. Engineered not by Carnegie himself (he was abroad at the time) but by Henry Clay Frick, cleverest of those clever Carnegie lieutenants, the Homestead debacle nevertheless permanently darkened Carnegie's reputation as a friend of labor. Ultimately, he was the responsible party.

The other great peculiarity which set Andrew Carnegie apart from so many of his contemporaries was his view of philanthropy. Other rich men gave away money, but Carnegie, in his essay "The Gospel of Wealth," was the first to articulate the idea that the possessors of great fortunes were merely stewards, obliged to return their riches to society.

Carnegie lived up to his own high ideals. He began building his famous libraries in 1882, starting with a bequest to his home town of Dumferline, Scotland.

The main staircase at Skibo Castle, the Carnegie family's retreat in Scotland. The stained glass windows show scenes from Scottish history, the farthest to the right the history of the Carnegie family.

PHOTO SKIBO CASTLE, SCOTLAND.

His greatest outpouring of philanthropy, however, occurred over the nearly two decades of his life which remained after he sold his steel company to the giant U.S. Steel combine assembled by J. P. Morgan in 1901. Carnegie received nearly a half billion dollars in the sale, roughly half of which was his following payments to his associates. Carnegie was merely a conduit for this vast sum, which was soon directed not only to libraries but to the endowment of foundations that continue to underwrite research, education, and charitable projects to this day. Among them are the Carnegie Corporation of New York, endowed in 1911 with $125 million; the Carnegie Institute of Washington; the Carnegie United Kingdom Trust; and the Carnegie Trust for the Universities of Scotland. He also gave liberally to institutions promoting peace, and built the Hague Peace Palace in the Netherlands as a center for international arbitration. All in all, Carnegie managed to give away some $350 million in his lifetime, and—after reasonable provisions for his wife, daughter, and other relatives—his coffers were virtually empty when his will was probated.

By no means did Andrew Carnegie live as a pauper in order to finance his philanthropies. He was happy to spend substantial amounts on such sentimental frivolities as an 1881 coach trip throughout the length of Great Britain, crowned by his triumphal entry into Dumferline to make his library donation in person. In 1897, he bought the ruined castle of Skibo in the Scottish Highlands, and spent lavishly to transform it into a romantic ideal of a laird's estate complete with salmon streams, bagpipers to welcome visitors, and a vast pipe organ for entertainment at meals.

Carnegie and his family spent five months a year at Skibo; the rest of the time, they lived at the "most modest, plain, and roomiest" house he built in 1902 at Fifth Avenue and East 91st Street in Manhattan. Now the Smithsonian Institution's Cooper-Hewitt National Design Museum, the 64-room Georgian mansion *was* plain in its way, compared to the midtown palaces of other moguls, and stood in what was then a very unfashionable neighborhood—before Carnegie came along, it had been left to squatters and their shanties. Ever the practical man, Carnegie built the first private home in New York to have a steel frame, an Otis passenger elevator, and central heating. There was even a system for drawing air over tanks of cool water, in an early attempt at air conditioning.

That sense of practicality, of the virtue of a plainness that was so hard for a fabulously rich man to achieve, was a thread that ran through Andrew Carnegie's life. His library at Skibo was a telling bit of evidence: having had his friend Lord Acton recommend some eight thousand titles, he assigned the acquisition of the works to Hew Morrison, head librarian at the Carnegie Library in Edinburgh. When the books were delivered, Carnegie was deeply displeased. Without his permission, Morrison had them handsomely rebound. "I never said one word to you about changing the bindings of these gems," Carnegie wrote Morrison. The rebindings were, he went on, "an insult to the great Teachers from whom I draw my intellectual & emotional life."

HENRY CLAY FRICK

If Andrew Carnegie is remembered—to some, perhaps too charitably—as a rosy-cheeked and benign presence who scattered libraries across the land the way Johnny Appleseed did Pippins and Macs, his one-time colleague and eventual enemy Henry Clay Frick left behind a quite different set of impressions.

Unlike Carnegie, Frick was born into money; his grandfather was a wealthy distiller. Frick made his own fortune by providing coke (coal baked to eliminate impurities and leave pure carbon) to the burgeoning western Pennsylvania iron and steel industries, eventually integrating his business with that of Carnegie and becoming chairman of the Scotsman's vast enterprise.

Frick, as we saw earlier, was under no illusions as to the rights of labor. "Of all slave drivers, for spite and kick,/ No one so cruel as Tyrant Frick," went the chorus of a poem that appeared in a union publication during the steel man's heyday. If it can be argued that the American business landscape was heavily populated with slave drivers at the time, there is no denying that Frick's devotion to opposing organized labor and employing scab workers was particularly ardent. He was one of the few Gilded Age captains of industry to actually have been the target of an assassination attempt: in the aftermath of the Homestead debacle, Frick was shot and seriously wounded by a young anarchist named Alexander Berkman, who had presented himself at the executive's office. This incident, and the fact that Carnegie eventually muscled

The Living Hall of the Frick mansion. Carrère and Hastings, New York's master Beaux-Arts architects, designed the $4-million treasure-house.

PHOTO THE FRICK ART REFERENCE LIBRARY, NEW YORK.

Frick out of his company ("I'll see him in hell, where we both are going," was Frick's reply to a proposed reconciliation shortly before his death in 1919), would rank among the salient events of Frick's life—if it weren't for the man's outstanding achievements as an art collector and museum benefactor.

Frick began collecting paintings seriously around 1895, his tastes at first running to the French Barbizon School but eventually deepening to include Flemish, Dutch, Italian, and Spanish masters. In 1906, he bought an entire Manhattan block, on Fifth Avenue between 70th and 71st streets, and commissioned Carrère & Hastings, architects of the New York Public Library, to build a $4 million neoclassical mansion on the site. Finished in 1914, it was meant to serve both as a home for the Frick family and, eventually, as an art museum. (Ironically, one of the reasons Frick left his turreted Pittsburgh mansion was that he felt the steel city's air was bad for his paintings.)

After the death of Frick's widow in 1931, the white stone pile on Fifth Avenue was subtly transformed from a cool, formal home into an intimate and engaging gallery. Splendid works by Tiepolo and Fragonard, Van Eyck and Vermeer, Holbein and Watteau are among the treasures of the Frick Collection, things of great beauty enshrined in the personal palace of a man who was all coke and iron.

JOHN DAVISON ROCKEFELLER

When J. P. Morgan died, and his taxable estate was tallied at $77.5 million, one of his contemporaries archly remarked, "And to think that he wasn't even a rich

man." There was only a handful of individuals on earth who could have spoken those words with anything like a straight face; and in fact they were spoken by the man with the straightest face of all. The son of a rascally traveling salesman whom Morgan's family would have cut dead socially, he had successfully come to grips with America's newfound appetite for petroleum. His name was John Davison Rockefeller.

Although at least one modern mogul's paper fortune is 50 times as large as Rockefeller's in 2002 dollars, no American was ever richer in terms of the percentage of the gross domestic product his holdings represented. At his peak, Rockefeller was worth just shy of one billion dollars. In 1902, he earned the equivalent of a modern billion—$58 million—in dividends from his Standard Oil Corporation and other investments. His sister said it best: "When it was raining porridge, John's dish was always right side up."

John's dish, and the porridge that filled it, have long been the stuff of American legend. There used to be a line in a 1950s commercial jingle, "Better coffee Rockefeller's money can't buy," and although the Rockefeller family asked the coffee company to change the wording to "a millionaire's money," it's a telling fact that years after the departure of John D. Senior, his name and that of his descendants remained a synonym for fathomless wealth.

To the extent that we still retain an image of Rockefeller the man, 65 years after his death, it is an image of a frail, parchment-skinned character with birdlike features and a prim, almost otherworldy expression: a hairless alien from the planet Money. If

that is the lasting impression, it is because Rockefeller lasted so long. He died in 1937, just short of his 98th birthday, and for the last 40 years of his life he was the victim of alopecia, a disease which causes the loss of body hair. By 1901, his body was as smooth as an egg. He couldn't do much about eyebrows, but he kept a collection of wigs in varying lengths, and wore them in succession to look as if he were going from one haircut to another.

The entrance gate to Kykuit.

The Rockefeller of the 19th century was a different creature altogether, a trim, straight-backed man with a dark moustache who allowed himself neither the paunch nor the extravagant whiskers of other magnificoes of his age. He was a product of the nondescript villages of upstate New York—was there ever a more fertile breeding ground for future tycoons?—and he came of age in the new midwest metropolis of Cleveland, Ohio, where his father had brought the family in the early 1850s. It was there that Rockefeller got his first job, as an assistant bookkeeper in a produce and commodities shipping firm. Cleveland was also the young man's playing field when, at the age of 18, he launched a partnership as a commission merchant.

Because of Cleveland's proximity to the newly discovered oilfields of western Pennsylvania, petroleum soon became one of the commodities in which Rockefeller traded. When the opportunity arose, he moved into refining. Those were the years when kerosene was taking over from whale oil as America's principal source of illumination, and Rockefeller's fortune was secured by the thirst of millions of lamps long before Henry Ford created a demand for another petroleum distillate, gasoline, which of course Rockefeller's Standard Oil Company was ready and eager to supply.

Rockefeller's meteoric rise from Cleveland refiner of kerosene to master of the greatest of all preregulation American monopolies was the result not only of spiraling demand, but of the industrialist's now-legendary demolishing of competition by, among other means, forcing railroads to give his high-volume business preferential shipping rates. The black side of the Rockefeller legend grew accordingly, so that by the time of the court-ordered breakup of Standard Oil into several regional companies (a process that only made Rockefeller richer, since he owned stock in all of them), he was excoriated by the muckraking press as a gouging manipulator, the man who had finally taken capitalism too far. But there was always another side to John D. Rockefeller, and the decades of his long retirement gave him ample occasion to show it. He was, quite simply, the greatest of all American philanthropists.

Even as a young bookkeeper making only several hundred dollars a year, Rockefeller earmarked a portion of his wages for charitable contributions. If his strict Baptist faith gave him the assurance that a man ought to work hard and earn all he could, it also imbued him with the notion that the money was to be reinvested in the community through philanthropy. During his lifetime he gave away $530 million, primarily to educational and research institutions—"Instead of giving alms to beggars," he once remarked, "[it is more worthwhile] to remove the causes which lead to the existence of beggars." He also handed out his famous dimes, thousands of them, not as alms but as tokens representing thrift. The dimes also provided an outlet for the puckish side of John D.'s nature. Despite the common impression of him as a grim old moneybags, he had a considerable dry wit.

Rockefeller the devout, Sunday-School teacher Baptist also avoided the extravagance and show of his plutocrat peers. He smoked no cigars, rented no

The Japanese Tea House Garden at Kykuit,
Pocantico Hills.

private rooms at Delmonico's for champagne-soaked soirees, captained no yachts, and kept no bejeweled mistresses. Certainly he was no miser of the Hetty Green stamp—that Wall Street operator was worth tens of millions, yet she lived in a walkup flat in Hoboken. Rockefeller dressed soberly but well, and kept a huge, rambling summer home outside Cleveland even after he moved to a New York brownstone. Perhaps his greatest extravagance was his estate at Pocantico Hills, in New York's Westchester County, but the building of Kykuit, his mansion on the property, originated with his son, John D. Rockefeller, Jr.

The younger Rockefeller hired architects Chester Aldrich and William Delano to create a 1906 house with a wraparound porch and steep-sloped roof and dormers, barely more than upper-middle class in its outward appearance. But between 1911 and 1913, Junior had the facade transformed into the classically pilastered and pedimented version that exists today, with a full third floor replacing those bourgeois dormers. And yet the house remained a modest mansion rather than a billionaire's palace, in keeping with Rockefeller Senior's simple tastes. Its most majestic aspect is its view of the Hudson River valley, and its greatest extravagance was the old man's private golf course. His religion forbade him cards and dancing, but golf was good exercise in God's fresh air.

RETAIL MAGNATES

Toward the close of the 19th century, great new fortunes again owed their existence to the business of selling things. But these were different times than those

"I am more drawn to the plastic, three-dimensional, than to pure line and color," said Nelson Rockefeller; Henry Moore was a favorite sculptor.

in which the Derbys and Crowninshields of Salem made their money by importing luxury goods and leaving them for others to merchandise. The mercantile Midases of the late Victorian age were shopkeepers on a grand scale, men who built multistory temples of commerce. Or, in the case of individuals like Aaron Montgomery Ward and Richard Warren Sears (the man who hired Alvah C. Roebuck to repair his mail-order watches), they created their empires out of catalogues rather than bricks and mortar.

Back in the days when Commodore Vanderbilt was piling up his steamship dollars, an Irish immigrant and one-time schoolteacher named Alexander Turney Stewart was building America's first retail fortune. Beginning in 1823, and eventually operating out of a six-story "marble palace" (it was actually painted cast iron) on lower Broadway, A. T. Stewart ran a dry goods business that catered to the New York carriage trade, carrying the finest in silks, lace, cashmere, and ready-made Paris gowns. Stewart employed some two hundred clerks, whom he personally instructed in package wrapping techniques that would save paper and string, and took in $3 million a year during the mid-1800s.

Moody and unpleasant in disposition, allegedly quite stingy with his employees, Stewart was largely ostracized from Knickerbocker society. But if he sulked over his exclusion from the company of the people who wore the finery he imported, at least he was able to do so in what was in its time the largest mansion in New York—a pillared palazzo on Fifth Avenue at 34th Street built, unlike his store, out of real marble. By the end of

Stewart's life, he was one of the three richest men in New York. The others were Cornelius Vanderbilt and William Backhouse Astor, John Jacob Astor's son.

Stewart's establishment was, strictly speaking, an enormous dry goods store, and not a department store in the modern sense. But his innovation of assigning plainly displayed, no-haggle prices on his merchandise was adopted by later retailers whose fame and fortunes rested on huge, multi-department operations that quickly became the model for emporiums throughout the United States. Rowland Hussey Macy, a

Nantucketer who served for four years on a whaling ship while still in his teens and later tried his hand at selling provisions to miners during the California gold rush, took up the fixed-price policy when he and his brother opened a dry goods store in Haverhill, Massachusetts, in 1851. The Haverhill venture failed, but Macy at age 36 was ready to give retailing one more try. He opened his new business as R. H. Macy and Company, on 14th Street in Manhattan, on October 28, 1858.

The stocky, full-bearded R. H. Macy drove himself

*The marble-pillared palazzo of Alexander Turney
Stewart, 1894, in its time the largest mansion
in New York.*

hard, determined to find in middle age the success that had eluded him for years. He had a sharp temper and a sailor's command of profanity, and some of his attempts at keeping overhead down were almost comical. He wouldn't hear of having shades on his gas lamps, saying that since he had paid for the gas, he wanted the light unimpeded. But several of his innovations have a decidedly modern ring: Macy's, in its founder's day, pioneered the idea of using prices such as "$4.99" to make an item look cheaper than one marked at $5.00, and by 1875 — two years before R. H. Macy's death — the store's advertisements declared, "We will not be undersold." As for other Macy's traditions, history has not told us what R. H. thought of Thanksgiving Day parades.

Marshall Field, born in Massachusetts' Berkshire Hills in 1834, struck out for Chicago at the age of 22. He was so intent on setting aside capital that when he was hired as a clerk in a wholesale dry goods firm, he lived in the store in order to save half of his $400 annual salary. Eight years later, having become a partner and general manager, his interest in the business was worth $260,000. By 1881, the firm whose back room he had once slept in was known as Marshall Field & Company. Quiet and unassuming, Field kept a low profile in Chicago social circles but was everywhere at once in his store. He pioneered the use of advertising to create a demand for goods he had already purchased, rather than wait for demand — and wholesale prices — to rise on their own.

Marshall Field donated the land for the new University of Chicago, and his bequests made possible the city's Field Museum of Natural History. The retailer surely had a sentimental streak, because the gift he was proudest of was that of a library to his hometown of Conway, Massachusetts. Another, less tangible part of his legacy lives on wherever retailers remember who they are working for: coming upon one of his clerks arguing with a customer one day, Field spoke the words that became his store's motto: "Give the lady what she wants."

With the population of the United States expanding rapidly during the last decades of the 19th century, the carriage trade wasn't the only path to retail riches. One man who realized this was Frank Winfield Woolworth, who managed to pay cash to build the tallest building in the world — cash, his contemporaries enjoyed remarking, that had come to him in the form of five- and ten-cent pieces.

Unlike R. H. Macy, who drifted into retailing, F. W. Woolworth seems to have had his heart set on selling things right from the start. Born on a northern New York State farm in 1854, he took a job at age 19 as a general store clerk just for the experience, drawing no wages for the first three months. In 1878, he talked his employer into trying a new gimmick he had heard about, a table stocked with goods priced at a uniform five cents.

Staked by his former boss, F. W. Woolworth opened his first store in Utica, New York, in 1879. Every item sold for a nickel — but those nickels added up to only $150 in profits after three months, so Woolworth closed the doors of his shabby rented premises and went off to try again in Lancaster, Pennsylvania. This time, things sold so well that the young man expanded to a couple of other Pennsylvania cities, hired his brother to help him, and took a chance on a table of ten-cent items at his new Scranton location. It was there that the famous sign first went up: "5 & 10 cent store."

By the early 1890s, there were some thirty Woolworth stores, and sales had surpassed $1 million a year. The 20-year path from that landmark to another—the Woolworth Building, the 720-foot Gothic-inspired "Cathedral of Commerce" completed in 1913—was a steady story of Woolworth store openings on both sides of the Atlantic, and of the founder's transformation from a lean, hungry young man to a 250-pound, white-mustached tycoon whose doctors were perpetually warning him that he was digging his grave with a fork. F. W. Woolworth, who largely ignored the physicians (he died just shy of his 65th birthday in 1919), was a man whose tastes in his maturity extended not only to gargantuan meals and posh suites on ocean liners, and to the usual architectural excesses of his peers, but to music— specifically, organ music.

Woolworth loved to show off the great pipe organ he had installed in the drawing room of his Fifth Avenue mansion. He had a hand in designing it himself, creating an instrument that operated like an enormous player piano with controls that would not only synchronize the music with displays of colored lights, but with illuminated paintings of the composers whose works were being played. As his father put it during a visit to the house, "Well, Frank, you always did like to lay it on thick." And as the old man

bemusedly admired his son's musical extravagance, no doubt the piano tinkled in yet another new Woolworth's store, as a clerk sat at the keyboard to promote the latest sheet-music tune. That emporium, in the eyes of its distant owner, was an undoubted boon to its community. "The more stores we create," F. W. Woolworth once said, "the more good we do for humanity."

JOSEPH PULITZER

If selling was a path to riches as the 20th century approached, so was telling. The idea of a press empire was something new in the world, a phenomenon made possible by the twin advances of wider literacy and mechanized printing. As Joseph Pulitzer cruised in his yacht between Jeykll Island, Georgia, and Bar Harbor, Maine, or surveyed Manhattan from his office perch in the dome of the *World* Building on Park Row, he may not have mused on how much he owed to the success of public education, or to the development of the rotary press earlier in the 1800s; but those developments had nonetheless put him where he was. And that was at the pinnacle of the American newspaper industry.

Joseph Pulitzer was a man of paradoxes. Brought up comfortably in Hungary, where he was born in 1847, he had to struggle as a young man in the United States after his family lost its money. He launched his career writing for German-language newspapers, but began his meteoric rise after purchasing the English-language St. Louis *Evening Dispatch* and creating that city's *Post-Dispatch* in 1878. His greatest achievement was the transformation of the New York *World*, nearly

moribund when he bought it from Jay Gould in 1883, into a great liberal organ—and yet in his personal life, Pulitzer surrounded himself with much the same luxury as the captains of industry whose power and excesses he excoriated.

Pulitzer was a great shaper of public opinion, yet he chose to remain aloof from the back-room politics that attract many powerful publishers. "He believed in Liberty, Equality, and Opportunity," his biographer Don Seitz wrote. "Fraternity was not in his code." The aloof press czar put a tangible stamp on his hatred of intrusion, creating soundproof rooms at his homes in New York and Bar Harbor. He worked himself into infirmity and blindness, but was so fond of music as a means of relaxation that he always included a competent pianist among his secretaries.

Perhaps most paradoxical of all is the fact that the immensely cultured Pulitzer, whose great legacy is the series of prizes honoring literary, journalistic, and musical excellence, was the man most responsible for nurturing the strain of sensationalism in the American press. Or perhaps not: receiving guests at his home, his favorite greeting was, "Tell me a good story." Whether Pulitzer Prize material or red meat from the police blotter, "a good story" was at the heart of this master pressman's business.

In 1883, the year Joseph Pulitzer bought the New York *World*, a rich young man from California was managing a successful circulation drive for the Harvard University humor magazine, the *Lampoon*. Within three years he had dropped out of Harvard—he always had a problem with authority, and was an indifferent student at best—and gone to New York to take a reporter's job on the *World*. All the while, he was pestering his father to give him a money-losing paper, the San Francisco *Examiner*, which the older man owned. Father finally capitulated, and William Randolph Hearst never looked back.

Titans of the Early Twentieth Century

WILLIAM Randolph Hearst is the only great American tycoon known as much through a fictional portrayal as through his actual persona. Ever since Orson Welles gave us the figure of Charles Foster Kane in his 1941 film *Citizen Kane*, art has blurred reality in our understanding of the Hearst saga. But the real William Randolph Hearst was a character who lived, worked, and played on an even larger scale than Welles's creation.

Hearst began his rise in the newspaper industry on the strength of his father's success in an entirely different pursuit. George Hearst was one of the men made into millionaires by Nevada's Comstock Lode of silver ore; in later life, he became a California land baron and a member of the state's U.S. Senate delegation. His foray into newspaper ownership with the *Examiner* was merely a political maneuver. For William Randolph Hearst, who talked his father into letting him take over the paper in 1887, the transformation of the *Examiner* was an object in itself.

Hearst turned the *Examiner* around, employing a mix of banner headlines, sensationalized writing, and campaigns for civic reform. Moving into his old training ground—and the domain of Joseph Pulitzer—he bought the New York *Morning Journal* in 1895 and applied the same methods, hiring top editorial talent away from Pulitzer and pioneering the use of Sunday comics and "sob sister" columns. The *Journal* was the primary vehicle for Hearst's first, and still most notorious, nationwide campaign: the stirring of war fever over Spanish colonial occupation of Cuba. The publisher backed Cuban insurgency against Spain, and instructed his correspondents to exaggerate (and in some instances manufacture) instances of Spanish atrocity in putting down the rebellion. "You furnish the pictures and I'll furnish the war," was his legendary reply to artist Frederic Remington, issued after Remington reported that there was "no

(ABOVE)
An aerial view of La Cuesta Encantada, "the Enchanted Hill."

PHOTO VICTORIA GARAGLIANO.
© HEARST CASTLE ®/CA STATE PARKS.

(OPPOSITE)
Working with architect Julia Morgan, William Randolph Hearst began work on La Casa Grande, crown jewel of his San Simeon estate, in 1919.

PHOTO VICTORIA GARAGLIANO.
© HEARST CASTLE ®/CA STATE PARKS.

Hearst told Julia Morgan that he wanted to build "a little something": La Cuesta Encantada rises above the coastal mist.

Hearst's main house at San Simeon is in Spanish Mediterranean style, but the structures surrounding the outdoor Neptune pool are purely classical. Fragments of ancient Roman columns, bases, and capitals make up the Roman temple.

trouble" in Cuba. Of course Hearst got his war, following the sinking of the USS *Maine* in Havana harbor. Hearst's papers trumpeted Spain's responsibility for the tragedy, even though it still remains a mystery nearly a century later.

Flush with the success his sensationalized Spanish-American War reportage had brought to his papers, Hearst rapidly expanded his press holdings during the early decades of the 20th century. He added Chicago papers in 1900 and 1902, and entered the Boston and Los Angeles markets in 1904. By 1927 Hearst was publishing 25 dailies and 17 Sunday papers in 17 cities. Twenty-four magazines were eventually added to the Hearst fold, as were radio stations, newsreels, and motion-picture production. It has been estimated that by the late 1940s, one-third of the U.S. population — some 40 million people — were readers of Hearst publications. And they heard directly from the man at the center of this empire: Hearst was constantly on the phone with his underlings, directing editorial policy, and was himself the author of columns and editorials published throughout his newspaper chain.

Sensationalism was Hearst's constant modus operandi, but the causes it served shifted over the course of his long career. Originally enough of a reformer to have supported the 1896 and 1900 presidential candidacies of populist William Jennings Bryan and fumed against the Standard Oil monopoly, Hearst grew increasingly conservative; his early support of Franklin Roosevelt evaporated during FDR's first term, and a Hearst visit with Adolf Hitler in 1934 left the publisher open to charges that he was a

The indoor Roman Pool at La Casa Grande was inspired by an ancient Roman bath.

fascist sympathizer. Throughout the first three decades of his career Hearst pursued his own political ambitions, succeeding in getting elected to the U.S. House of Representatives but failing in bids for the Senate, New York City mayoralty, and New York State governorship. Like Charles Foster Kane in *Citizen Kane*, his great goal was the presidency. But he came no closer than a vigorous battle for the Democratic nomination in 1904.

William Randolph Hearst's thwarted political longings pale before his success as creator of the grandest personal surroundings ever enjoyed by an American plutocrat. He was an inveterate and omnivorous collector, spending an estimated million dollars a year on art and antiques. Hearst enjoyed the luxury of distributing his acquisitions among a string of lavish estates, including his home in New York, his Welsh castle, and his Bavarian-style retreat near Mt. Shasta. But the greatest architectural obsession of the publisher's life—and, at perhaps $30 million, the most expensive residence ever constructed by an American— was the California estate today known as "Hearst Castle," which its builder called "La Cuesta Encantada"—the Enchanted Hill.

The palette on which Hearst worked was the Piedra Blanca Ranch, a 48,000-acre property near San Simeon that his father had bought in 1865. Hiring Julia Morgan, America's first notable woman architect, he began to piece together his dream castle in 1919, when he was already 56 years old. Hearst would build at San Simeon for most of the rest of his life, all the while using the place to entertain luminaries ranging from Buster

(ABOVE)

Whimsical characters adorn the wrought-iron doors made by Edward Trinkkeller, a California craftsman, at la Casa Grande.

(RIGHT)

The Refectory at la Casa Grande: Hearst made sure there was a bottle of ketchup within reach of each of his dinner guests.

Keaton to Winston Churchill. It was also the ultimate stage setting for his mistress, Marion Davies, a Hollywood actress whose career he relentlessly promoted and whose relationship with him he made no effort to conceal—even as Hearst papers stood as champions of what a later generation would call "family values."

The twin Mediterranean towers of the main house, La Casa Grande, stand 137 feet high, and the scale of everything else on the Enchanted Hill is cued to their grand proportions . . . and to the grand proportions of Hearst himself, all six feet three inches and 220 pounds of him. There are 56 bedrooms, 61 bathrooms, 41 fireplaces, and terraces designers were told to treat as "rooms without walls." At the center of it all was a refectory with a dining table that could seat 22 guests, none of whom had to reach far for the bottles of ketchup that Hearst insisted accompany every dinner. It was a nice proletarian touch, for a man who had bought the contents of European palaces and monasteries—entire rooms, stained glass windows, elaborately carved staircases and paneling, tapestries— and installed them in his castle as patents of the New World nobility he craved for himself.

Hearst's landscaping at San Simeon—now a California state historic site—rivals La Casa Grande and its surrounding pools, terraces, and guest houses. He thought nothing of having mature oak and cypress trees moved and replanted, or of planting a barren hilltop with pines even though a road had to be built for the purpose. He kept a private zoo, and played night tennis on a court lit by 28 1000-watt bulbs.

One guest, George Bernard Shaw, is said to have remarked of San Simeon, "It's the way God would have done it, if He had Hearst's money." Ultimately, even Hearst didn't have the money. The place was still unfinished when he died, at age 88, in 1951.

Men such as Joseph Pulitzer, William Randolph Hearst, and, later, the Time-Life titan Henry Luce took journalism out of an era in which it had been a local product meant primarily for local consumption, and made it into a vehicle for mass culture in what Luce would herald as the "American Century." During the decade of Hearst's first great triumphs, the 1890s, a power-station engineer from Dearborn, Michigan, would create an actual rather than a figurative vehicle, one easily recognizable in the advertising pages of Hearst and Luce publications for years to come. Mass-produced popular culture was one of two great hallmarks of the American Century, and the mass-produced automobile was the other. It was created by Henry Ford.

HENRY FORD

With the exception of John D. Rockefeller, Sr., no American capitalist has so captured the world's imagination as Henry Ford. In Aldous Huxley's novel *Brave New World*, the phrase "the year of Our Ford" is substituted for "A.D." to indicate the debt owed the industrialist by an advanced technological society. The facts of Ford's life are legend: He built his first car, the "Quadricycle," in 1896, and was able to drive it on the streets of Dearborn only after taking a sledge-hammer to the doorway of the shed he used as a

(ABOVE)

Henry Ford enjoys his son Edsel's performance at
the player piano during a camping trip in
Maryland, 1921.

(RIGHT)

Henry and Clara Ford at Fair Lane, with
grandchildren Henry II and — in Henry's lap —
Benson Ford, 1923.

(ABOVE)

Henry Ford demonstrates a prototype at his Detroit plant, 1907. A year later, he sold the first of 15 million Model Ts.

PHOTO FROM THE COLLECTIONS OF HENRY FORD MUSEUM & GREENFIELD VILLAGE.

(RIGHT)

Henry Ford (far right) on a 1920s fishing trip with Thomas Edison (next to Ford) and Harvey Firestone (second from left). At far left is Christian Edison, the inventor's son.

PHOTO LIBRARY OF CONGRESS.

Henry and Clara Ford, on a 1906 trip to the Grand Canyon. The automaker had a lifelong love of the outdoors.

The Fords visit England during the late 1920s: at right are Lady Nancy Astor and her son, William Waldorf Astor.

workshop. After several false starts manufacturing more expensive cars, he introduced the inexpensive, mass-produced Model T in 1908 and captured nearly one-half of the world automobile market within 10 years. Along the Rouge River near Detroit, he built the first completely vertically integrated automobile plant, capable of taking iron ore and coke and turning them into cars—and then, in a move that the *Wall Street Journal* called "the most foolish thing ever attempted in the industrial world," he saw to it that his workers could afford the machines they were building by paying

them an unheard-of five dollars a day.

Henry Ford, a lean, plainspoken Midwesterner raised on a farm and a stranger to wealth and fame until he was in his forties, had one of the most complex and contradictory natures of all the great American captains of industry. The man who could bestow five dollars a day on his employees was also capable of creating a "sociological department" that would visit workers' homes to make sure they and their families were living in a seemly manner and not squandering the Ford largesse—and, much

*The Field Room, with its massive stone fireplace
from a nearby tavern, was a favorite evening
gathering place for Ford family and friends.*

PHOTO FAIR LANE (THE HENRY AND CLARA BRYANT FORD HOUSE).

worse, allow his henchman Harry Bennett to use his company security apparatus to viciously put down attempts at unionization during the 1930s. (In 1932, four pro-union marchers were shot dead by Dearborn police working closely with Ford security.)

The very model of the practical engineer, as comfortable in the machine shop as behind his desk, Henry Ford could nevertheless extol the transcendental philosophy of Ralph Waldo Emerson, and became a believer in reincarnation. Responsible for accelerating the pace of American urbanization and transforming rural landscapes across the continent, he remained all his life a lover of nature, particularly birds, and struck up a friendship with the great naturalist John Burroughs, with whom he went on several camping trips. (Thomas Edison joined these excursions, as did tire manufacturer Harvey Firestone.) And at Dearborn, Ford created Greenfield Village, a vast assemblage of museum-piece historic structures honoring small-town pre-industrial America, even as his automobiles helped the nation put an incalculable distance between its past and its future.

Ford was an idealist and pacifist who sought to end World War I by traveling to Europe in 1915 on a "Peace Ship," remarking that he wanted "to make the world a little better for having lived in it." He was an early champion of fair wages and employment practices for blacks, who made up 10 percent of his workforce by 1926 and could even be promoted to supervisory positions over whites. Yet in his newspaper venture of the early 1920s, the *Dearborn Independent*, he published a continuous stream of anti-Semitic invective apparently

born of his identification of Jews with an international banking conspiracy.

By 1918, virtually half of all the automobiles on earth were Model Ts, and the success of his plain, reliable little car ("any color you like, as long as it's black") had brought Ford's wealth near the billion-dollar mark. He was not the man to spend it lavishly; sometimes, as in the case of the uncashed $75,000 check his wife once found in one of his suit pockets, he didn't spend it at all—but he did build an estate. With a characteristic nod to nostalgia, he named it Fair Lane, after the district in the Irish city of Cork where his grandfather had once lived. Also characteristic was Ford's siting of his mansion not in the fashionable Detroit suburb of Grosse Point, but in his boyhood home of Dearborn, where one day he would also construct Greenfield Village.

Ford spent a million 1914 dollars to build Fair Lane, and it is pleasant to imagine what that sum could have bought if it had been placed in the hands of Frank Lloyd Wright, the carmaker's original choice as architect. Wright was unavailable, though, and the task devolved to a pair of lesser talents who came up with a dull limestone fortress that hardly did more for its Rouge River setting than the Ford factory downstream.

Its stodgy appearance aside, Fair Lane did have its comforts. Bathroom faucets offered either well or rainwater, hot and cold, as well as hot-air jets for hair drying. There was an indoor swimming pool, a bowling alley, and a golf course. Ford could relax in a rustic den whose fireplace mantel bore Thoreau's admonition, "Chop your own wood, and it will warm you twice."

The bulk of the mansion's energy supply, however, was dependent on a powerhouse that Ford had designed himself. Its generators ran on water power from a dam in the Rouge River, and polished brass instruments shone against its green walls with marble trimming. Best of all, for the man who counted John Burroughs among his friends, was the maze of heating pipes that extended outdoors to keep five hundred birdbaths from freezing in winter.

Born during the Civil War, in an America vastly different from the one he and his machines helped create, Henry Ford died at 83 in 1947. That would be the Year of Our Ford 39, if we mark the beginning of the era with the introduction of the Model T.

Henry Ford's heyday coincided with the years in which dozens of entrepreneurs put their names on hubcaps and radiators. Many of those names have long survived the shakeout of independent auto companies that reached its peak in the 1920s and '30s and still continues today; many others did not. Buick, Dodge, Olds, Nash, Willys, Packard: these were all men, not merely cars. One such name survives not only on an automobile, but in the most beautiful Art Deco building in the world.

Walter P. Chrysler

Walter P. Chrysler was the Kansas-born son of a Union Pacific engineer. He trained as a machinist in railroad maintenance shops, eventually becoming superintendent of a locomotive plant. But his life truly began on a day in 1908 when he fell in love with a gleaming new Locomobile at an auto show in Chicago. Chrysler borrowed most of the $5,000 needed to buy the Locomobile, which he took apart and put back together repeatedly until he understood its every working. His first professional involvement with cars came in 1911, when he went to work for the Buick Motor Company; 14 years later, having risen to a vice-presidency at the new General Motors and retired a millionaire, he created the Chrysler Corporation at the age of 50. The remaining 15 years of his life secured his reputation as an automotive visionary, a master machinist-manager. They also gave him the opportunity to place his name on

(ABOVE)
His company's name has been diluted by merger, but Walter Chrysler will always be associated with New York's most sublime skyscraper.
Photo Library of Congress.

(Opposite top)
Mr. and Mrs. Walter Chrysler, with another Chrysler in the background, Palm Beach, 1937.
Photo Morgan Collection/Getty Images.

(Opposite bottom)
Art collector Walter Chrysler, Jr., son of the automaker, at a 1950 sale of his Impressionist paintings.
Photo Getty Images.

The George Eastman House and west garden.
The mansion now houses the International
Museum of Photography.

PHOTO: BARBARA DUORRO GALASSO/
COURTESY GEORGE EASTMAN HOUSE.

a sublime inanimate object that shouted out its connection with the motor age.

The Chrysler Corporation didn't build the Chrysler Building; Walter Chrysler did. Designed by William Van Alen and completed at a cost of $14 million in 1930, the sleek structure was topped with a crested, elongated dome and spire of chromium nickel steel and ornamented with enormous replicas of Chrysler hubcaps and radiator caps. It reigned as the tallest structure in the world until the Empire State Building was completed in 1931. When we look at the untarnished majesty of that Art Deco dome today, it's hard to imagine it as anything other than a public monument. When the Chrysler Building was new, though, it reportedly had one very special private aspect. Two flights up from Walter Chrysler's baronial 56th-floor office, contemporary sources reported, was a duplex apartment designed for Chrysler himself. No photographs of this aerie exist—but breakfast at Tiffany's aside, it is hard to imagine a more spectacular New York experience than living in the Chrysler Building. And it was a midwestern machinist who did.

One of the most respected American entrepreneurs of the 20th century was a notable failure as an automaker. Only those who are well into their fifties, or who are dedicated auto buffs, remember cars called the Kaiser, the Frazer, or the Henry J. Manufactured during the late 1940s and early '50s, they were the creations of Henry J. Kaiser and his partner, Joseph Frazer; the Henry J. was a stripped-down economy car (one early suggestion for its name, ironically enough, had been "Mustang") that appeared at the beginning of

a decade that would be known for chrome ostentation. But Henry J. Kaiser was too much of a success at virtually everything else he attempted to be remembered for a failed carmaking enterprise.

Born in 1882 in upstate New York—again, was there something in the water?—Kaiser first tasted success as a paving contractor on both sides of the U.S.–Canadian border in the Pacific Northwest. (His future father-in-law had told Kaiser he would deny him his daughter's hand in marriage unless he sold his interest in a Lake Placid photography shop and started earning real money.) The contractor's big break came in 1931, when a consortium his company had joined won the bid to build Hoover Dam, on the Colorado River in Nevada. Attacking the job with an energy remarkable in a fat, placid-looking man, Kaiser finished the job on time and later went on to build the Grand Coulee Dam on Washington's Columbia River.

Kaiser's greatest achievement, though, came when he entered the shipbuilding industry at the outset of World War II. With Navy contracts in hand, this supremely capable marshaler of men and materials turned out 1,490 vessels between 1941 and 1945, including 821 of the 10,000-ton "Liberty Ships" that lumbered through the world's oceans carrying supplies for the Allied effort. Using the subassembly method, in which major portions of each ship were prefabricated then brought together only as needed, Kaiser's workers trimmed months from traditional production schedules. One crew actually managed to assemble a Liberty Ship in four days, 15 hours, and 26 minutes from the time the keel was laid.

Kaiser's name echoed down through the postwar years in the steel and aluminum industries, in television broadcasting, and of course in the money-losing Kaiser-Frazer enterprise. It survives to this day in the Kaiser-Permanente health maintenance organization, an outgrowth of a medical plan he created for his workers. But Kaiser's reputation as a paragon of the can-do spirit was secured during those frantic days of World War II, when Liberty Ships came down the ways like rolls from an oven.

GEORGE EASTMAN

On broad, handsome East Avenue in Rochester, New York, stands a stately Georgian Revival mansion that houses one of the world's greatest museums of photography. Its spacious rooms contain not only the museum collections, but also many reminders that the man who built the place was very up-to-date: how many houses had central vacuum systems in 1905? If kitchen aromas lingered over the decades, though, they would convey something a good deal more quirky. George Eastman, who brought photography to the masses,

liked to relax not in a darkroom but by baking
lemon pies.

If lemon pies seem a modest amusement for a man
once estimated to be the sixth richest in the nation,
remember that George Eastman was himself so
unassuming that a newly hired watchman at his factory
once turned him away at the gate when he stated his
name, replying, "Glad to meet you, I'm John D.
Rockefeller." Perhaps the watchman had never seen
Eastman's photograph—an irony in itself—or perhaps,
he had, and simply couldn't associate that kindly,
serious, high-school-principal face with the name on
his paycheck. That name was ubiquitous in Rochester,
but the face was seldom in the society pages.

Thanks to George Eastman, photography itself was
ubiquitous by the beginning of the 20th century. As a
23-year-old bank employee in 1877, Eastman had
spent nearly 50 dollars on a camera. In the Rochester
of that day, there were only two other amateur
photographers—the wet plate process was that
complicated. Eastman mastered it, and indeed became
so enamored of photography that he did little else with
his spare time. But he felt the whole procedure could
be simplified. With his 1878 invention of a machine
that would coat photographic plates with an emulsion of
gelatin and silver bromide, followed by his development
of paper-backed roll film several years later, Eastman
had done just that. In 1888, he put his roll film into a
hand-held camera he called the "Kodak," having coined
the name because he liked the "firm and unyielding"
sound of the letter "k."

The George Eastman who moved into his newly

finished mansion in 1905 had made a resounding
success of his Eastman Kodak Company, but he never
stopped improving his products. His was the genius
behind the development of motion-picture film for the
Edison-invented cameras that made possible a great
new medium for entertainment and information; in the
1920s, he would even accompany the explorers Osa and
Martin Johnson as they took Eastman films on safari to
record a rapidly vanishing Africa. He ran a huge
business, far and away the leader in the industry it had
pioneered, from his office at Rochester's Kodak Park.

(ABOVE)

George Eastman in his study at Rochester.

PHOTO COURTESY GEORGE EASTMAN HOUSE.

(OPPOSITE)

George Eastman liked to breakfast in his
conservatory, while his house organist played.
This table awaits the inventor on an October
morning in 1919.

PHOTO COURTESY GEORGE EASTMAN HOUSE.

Along with endless rolls of film, he developed a joint reputation as a kind, courtly man with a seemly but sumptuous lifestyle, and as a philanthropist whose gifts to education and health care institutions stagger the imagination.

Eastman never married. Other than a housekeeper, eight maids, and a maid for the maids (all well paid, with a then all-but-unheard of two to three weeks vacation each year), the only woman who ever lived in the big house at 900 East Avenue was his elderly mother, who died in 1907. There were also two butlers,

Film producer Samuel Goldwyn and his wife, Frances, enjoy a game of cards at their Hollywood home in the 1930s.
PHOTO GETTY IMAGES.

as well as whatever auxiliary help was needed on occasions such as New Year's 1914, when nine hundred guests were present at the Eastman mansion.

"A platinum mounted farm," was how one guest described Eastman's estate, for in its early days the mansion and its formal gardens were adjoined by vegetable gardens, greenhouses, and barns for chickens and cows. The "platinum" part of the description refers of course to the house itself, where Eastman rose every morning to the sound of his enormous Aeolian organ, played by his house organist, breakfasted amid potted plants and cut flowers in his airy conservatory, and delighted in showing visitors his billiard room, darkroom, home theater, and trophies from African safaris. And, of course, there was the little upstairs kitchen where Eastman baked his lemon pies.

None of these extravagances precluded Eastman's commitment to philanthropy. He gave away nearly $100 million, including bequests to dental clinics for poor children, Tuskeegee Institute, and the University of Rochester. He built his city's Eastman School of Music, and Eastman Theatre. He gave ambulances to France during World War I. And he was the "Mr. Smith"—a mystery for nearly two decades—who financed the core campus buildings of the Massachusetts Institute of Technology. In 1924, he gave $9 million in stock to Kodak employees. "Men who leave their money to be distributed by others are pie-faced mutts," he once remarked. "I want to see the action in my lifetime."

Eastman knew when that lifetime had run its course. At age 77, he was in pain and growing weaker,

the victim of a degenerative spinal disease. He had once asked his doctor to show him exactly where his heart was, and on the afternoon of March 14, 1932, he put a bullet through it. Alongside his bed was a note that read, "To my friends, My work is done— Why wait?"

As all those miles of Eastman motion-picture film spooled through cameras and projectors, they made the fortunes of a group of individuals as tough and determined—and easily as colorful—as any American entrepreneurs before or since. In the 19th century, a showman was a man like P. T. Barnum, who could pack a circus tent or museum of curiosities, or sell out a string of performances by Jenny Lind. Edison and Eastman changed all that, and created a new breed of showman who could reach audiences in hundreds of places at once.

HOLLYWOOD MOGULS

"Poor, poor, poor," was how the man born Shmuel Gelbfisz described his boyhood in the Jewish ghetto of Warsaw. If that description fit the early years of Sam Goldwyn, it could just have easily been applied to Louis B. Mayer, born amid the anti-Jewish pogroms of Czarist Russia, or Jack Warner, born in London, Ontario, after the immigration of his parents from Russia. All of these men came to maturity in the first years of the 20th century, and all of them tried their hands at something else before they got into—or, rather, behind—the movies.

Gelbfisz (he took the name Goldwyn in 1918, after several years as Goldfish) walked 500 miles from

Warsaw to Hamburg, where he took a ship for England before sailing to Canada. Making his way to the United States—again, on foot—he became a successful glove salesman for a firm in Gloversville, New York. One day in Manhattan, he happened to take in a nickelodeon show. He was so fascinated with the new medium of motion pictures that he talked his brother-in-law, Jesse Lasky, into starting a film production business. The founding of Metro-Goldwyn-Mayer (with which he was associated only in 1924, the year it was organized), and a later career as an independent producer all date

to that day when the glove salesman decided to pass an August afternoon watching the "flickers" at the Herald Square Theater on 34th Street.

Louis Mayer (he added the "B." himself, saying it stood for Burt), spent his school days in Saint John, New Brunswick, where his teacher once asked each member of the class what they would do with a thousand dollars. No houses or boats or shopping sprees for Louis—"I'd put it into a business," he answered—or, at least, he later said he did, which may as well be the same thing. The business he soon found

(ABOVE)

Louis B. Mayer, the real roar behind the MGM lion, arrives in the U.S. on the SS Paris, *October 1934.*

PHOTO MGM STUDIOS/COURTESY GETTY IMAGES.

(RIGHT)

Louis B. Mayer's Santa Monica beach house in the 1930s: Mayer's route to this idyll took him from the Ukraine by way of Saint John, New Brunswick, and Haverhill, Massachusetts.

PHOTO GETTY IMAGES.

himself in was scrap metal, his father's trade. On his own in Boston, he followed the same line of work . . . until one day he, too, went to a nickelodeon show. Mayer soon leased a theater in Haverhill, Massachusetts, and started screening the latest films. A chain of picture show venues followed, as did a film distribution business. Then came production, and Mayer's long career with Metro-Goldwyn-Mayer.

Jack Warner and his brothers borrowed against the family horse to buy their first projector, and launched their careers by showing *The Great Train Robbery* on a

bedsheet in Youngstown, Ohio. They opened their first theater in New Castle, Pennsylvania, in 1903. Jack Warner was only 11 years old then, but he would become the driving force of Warner Bros., the production company the brothers founded in 1923. That same year, the Warners signed their first superstar: a war-orphaned German Shepherd named Rin-Tin-Tin. Five years later, they made the movies talk with *The Jazz Singer*.

Collectively, these movie men who had started with nothing came to create a particular image of how

American millionaires were expected to act in the 20th century. It was the southern California version of the plutocrat's lifestyle, a far cry from J. P. Morgan steaming along on the *Corsair* or ensconced in his dark library like a Borgia pope. Jack Warner tooling through Beverly Hills in his Bentley, presiding over cocktails alongside his two swimming pools, or losing a quarter of a million dollars playing Baccarat with King Farouk at Monte Carlo; Louis B. Mayer not only raising but riding prize horses at his ranch, or bragging about slamming through nine holes of golf in an hour, as

(ABOVE)
Jack Warner in 1962, with the two stars of Warner Bros.' Whatever Happened to Baby Jane? — Bette Davis, left, and Joan Crawford, right.
PHOTO GETTY IMAGES.

(OPPOSITE)
A film industry luncheon, c. 1925. Louis B. Mayer sits at the head of the table; fifth from left is William Randolph Hearst, seated next to his mistress, actress Marion Davies.
PHOTO GETTY IMAGES.

if the game was a race—none of this was in the old Newport style. Sam Goldwyn, in his Savile Row suits, might have come the closest to projecting the old upper-class image. It was something he worked hard at: from the time he was a boy, he once said, he had "wanted to be somebody."

WALT DISNEY

Walt Disney's background couldn't have been more different from those of the film pioneers who hailed from the Jewish ghettos of eastern Europe. He was a Protestant Midwestern boy, and like Henry Ford he always placed great stock in the characteristics of that moral and physical terrain of his youth—a world embraced just as fervently by the immigrant movie moguls, as any Andy Hardy film will attest. As Ford did with Greenfield Village, Disney eulogized small-town America in his "Main Street U.S.A." environments at Disneyland in California and Disney World in Florida. But, like Ford, his great contribution to American culture was homogenization. Ford made the shopping mall and the fast-food restaurant possible. Disney filled these places with characters recognizable to everyone. In addition, he made the theme park, rather than raffish old carnivals like the one he depicted in *Dumbo*, the paradigm of American amusement.

Whether or not Walt Disney set out to do these things, or whether they would have emerged anyway as an inevitable consequence of mass tastemaking and mass communications in a democratic society, is almost beside the point of what the man wanted to do with his life and his business. Born in Chicago in 1901, Walter

Rail buff Walt Disney put train rides in his theme parks. At his home he often took guests on his own scale railway.

PHOTO GENE LESTER/GETTY IMAGES.

(ABOVE)

The family behind family entertainment: Walt Disney, c. 1955, with his wife Lillian, daughter Diane, and grandchildren.

PHOTO GETTY IMAGES.

(OPPOSITE)

Howard Hughes with Ginger Rogers.

PHOTO LIBRARY OF CONGRESS.

Elias Disney grew up on a farm in Missouri. In the years just after World War I, he worked as a commercial artist in Kansas City, where he met and briefly went into business with Ub Iwerks, the animation artist who was to be so important to the development of Disney's signature screen products. Disney arrived in Hollywood in 1923, at first hoping to become a film director, but soon landed a contract to create a series of combination live action-animated shorts called *Alice in Cartoonland*. Next came *Oswald the Rabbit*, followed by an idea Disney had for a mouse

named Mortimer. He liked mice; he had once kept several of them as pets in his Kansas City office. Renamed Mickey, and graced with the most famous pair of ears in the history of capitalism, the plucky rodent was launched in a silent short called *Plane Crazy* .

Sound and color, the *Silly Symphonies*, *Snow White*, and all the other full-length features, live action films, nature documentaries, the television programs, and the theme parks—it has become trite to point out that it all began with Mickey Mouse. Just as overworked is the revelation, hardly a surprise to anyone any more, that

Walt Disney didn't, and couldn't, draw Mickey. His genius was not for cartooning, it was for organization.

By the time he reached late middle age, Walt Disney was as rich as, or richer than, many of his moviemaking counterparts, but we must search in vain for any evidence of the flamboyance or conspicuous consumption that often characterized the breed. Disney bought his suits off the rack, not from Savile Row; he was fond of steaks and chili, not the oeuvre of any private French chef, and he bought mid-priced American cars almost until the end of his life. He

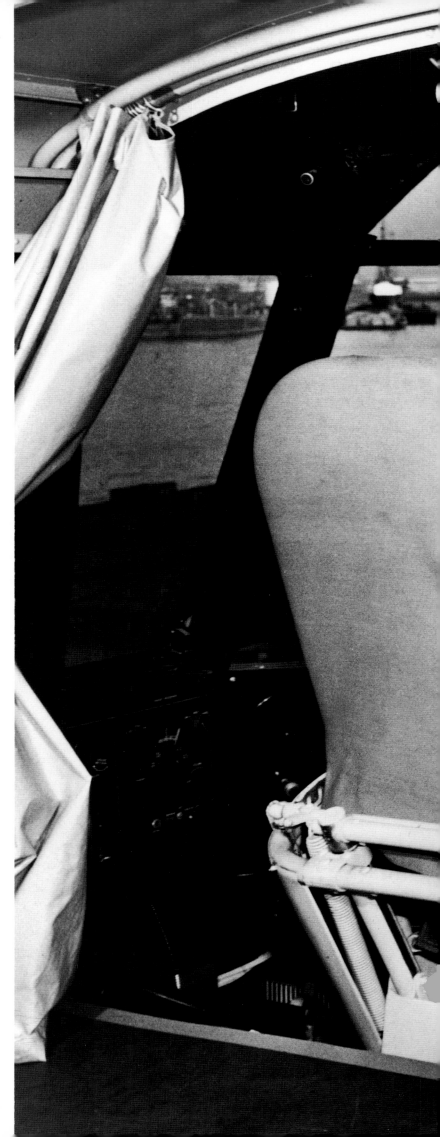

eventually took to driving a Jaguar that had been used
in his film *That Darned Cat*, although that departure
from custom might be written off as the economy of
getting more use out of a paid-for prop. His one
expensive indulgence was a half-mile-long model
railroad, with rolling stock big enough to ride on, that
he constructed on the grounds of his Los Angeles home.
Disney puttered endlessly with his train, even after his
young daughters grew tired of it; visit the Disney home,
and you were likely to get a ride.

Not much fodder there for the modernist sensibility,
which would prefer to find, beneath the aggressively
wholesome exterior, a rakehell Disney. But all of the
man's energies seemed to have been channeled into his
work. That work culminated, not surprisingly, in the
creation of two model environments — in California
and, posthumously, in Florida — as scrupulously
engineered as his little home railway.

HOWARD HUGHES

To any American middle-aged or younger, mention of
the name Howard Hughes will likely bring to mind the
grotesque caricature of a mysterious hermit billionaire,
an addled, secrecy-obsessed invalid who spent his days
bedridden in darkened rooms, watching the film *Ice
Station Zebra* over and over again. This was the portrait
of Hughes that emerged during his last days in the early
and mid-1970s, when he was at the center of a
controversy involving a spurious "as told to" Hughes
biography and a shadowy figure in the Byzantine twists
of the Watergate affair. Anyone older, though, might
recall Hughes as the glamorous titan of the midcentury

*The heavy cornice of the Music Room at
Whitehall is dominated by almost life-size figures
holding musical instruments.*
PHOTO © FLAGLER MUSEUM.

film and aircraft industries, a tall, handsome character as closely involved with his leading ladies as he was with test-flying his planes. Such recollections made the image of the scrawny, bearded eccentric with uncut fingernails even more bizarre.

Howard Robard Hughes grew up rich. When he was three, his father invented the rotary bit that would eventually be used to drill three-quarters of the world's oil wells. Young Howard was heir to the Hughes Tool Company, which he used as the springboard to one of America's most spectacular, and most unconventional, business careers. It was also one of the most lucrative: at his peak, Howard Hughes was a billionaire, second in worth only to oilman J. Paul Getty.

Hughes parlayed his father's drill-bit fortune into the creation of the Hughes Aircraft Company, as well as a career as a movie producer and director. He also controlled Trans-World Airlines. Obtaining his pilot's license in 1928, Hughes spent the next two decades enthralling the public with his exploits as a flyer. He set short-distance and transcontinental speed records during the 1930s, and in 1938 circled the world in three days, 19 hours, and 17 minutes, a record that earned him a tickertape parade. A movie fan magazine put him on the cover alongside one of the more serious of his Hollywood romantic interests, posing the question, "Will America's hero, Howard Hughes, marry Katharine Hepburn?" The wedding never took place. And in November 1947, Hughes piloted his wooden-fuselage, eight-engine, 190-ton HK-1, nicknamed the "Spruce Goose," on a 1,000-foot flight that lasted less than a minute. The $40,000 prototype, designed as a troop carrier but never adopted by the U.S. military, has a 320-foot wingspan and was the largest aircraft ever.

What caused Hughes's descent into an eccentricity that finally crossed the line into madness? For one thing, he was the victim of obsessive-compulsive disorder, a form of mental illness that had not yet been described when he began to fuss inordinately over germs, paper tissues, and even the precise half-inch square dimensions he required for the diced vegetables in his beef stew. He also wrestled with drug addiction, which began when he was administered morphine following a near-fatal 1946 plane crash and continued with massive doses of codeine and Valium during his final years. Finally, there was syphilis. Hughes was warned by doctors that he had contracted the primary stage of the disease as early as the 1930s. After his death in 1976, an autopsy showed evidence of tertiary-stage syphilis, which is invariably accompanied by profound mental deterioration.

Howard Hughes slid toward death in fanatically and expensively guarded privacy, over the course of several years in which he holed up in a Las Vegas hotel he owned and, finally, in Acapulco. And yet his protracted demise was paradoxically a public one, followed by a media that picked up on every Gothic tidbit. The fascination was fed by the Watergate angle, having to do with secret Hughes contributions to Richard Nixon's campaigns, and by the bogus biography. But in the end, there was one central story line that held the public rapt: here was a man so rich, and yet so miserable.

Along with Hughes's pioneer aeronautical designs,

one additional engineering contribution was remembered when he died. He had designed a brassiere for Jane Russell to wear in his 1943 film *The Outlaw*.

Although the film tycoons used southern California as the setting for the mammoth extravaganzas of their own life stories, a lesser known but hardly less successful group of men chose a different place in the sun. Henry Flagler, James Deering, and John Ringling couldn't have come about their fortunes through more widely divergent paths. But they all found in subtropical Florida the ideal setting for extravagant and highly individualistic architectural expression.

HENRY FLAGLER

Although he was instrumental in helping John D. Rockefeller launch the Standard Oil Company, Henry M. Flagler is best known today for what he did with his millions during the latter part of his life. Flagler was the man who first realized the enormous potential of the Florida coast, where he developed destination resorts such as the Royal Poinciana Hotel in Palm Beach and

St. Augustine's Ponce de Leon. He built the Florida East Coast Railway, which eventually leaped across miles of salt water to reach Key West. And when Flagler decided to create his own Florida retreat, he did it in just as grand a style.

Whitehall, Flagler's 55-room, 60,000-square-foot Beaux-Arts extravaganza on Lake Worth in Palm Beach, was completed in 1902 as a gift for the 72-year-old tycoon's third wife, Mary. Built around an open central courtyard, the mansion was designed by Carrère and Hastings—architects of New York's Public Library—and decorated in a variety of Italian Renaissance and French *ancien regime* styles. A red tile roof gives a warm, Mediterranean feeling to the structure that belies its interior formality, which is reinforced by marble floors, damask-covered walls, and a 4,400-square-foot reception hall topped by a painted ceiling depicting "The Crowning of Wisdom."

Visitors to Whitehall, today fully restored as a museum, might nevertheless wonder if the peripatetic Flagler, restlessly at work almost until his death in 1913, might have felt more at home in the smaller quarters preserved adjacent to the great house . . . his private railroad car.

JOHN RINGLING

Ca' d'Zan, in Sarasota, is the house we might expect a great showman to build. John Ringling was one of the five Ringling Brothers, who founded one of the world's most popular circuses in 1884 and eventually bought out their competitor, Barnum and Bailey.

In 1924, at the age of 58, John Ringling started

building his Sarasota winter home. Intending that his
showplace also serve to house his Venetian art
collection, Ringling and his wife Mable turned to
Venice for architectural inspiration, incorporating many
of the Gothic elements that characterize the palazzi
lining the Grand Canal: one series of columns
surrounding a second-floor gallery even suggests a
principal motif of the Doges' Palace. The name Ca'
d'Zan is likewise Venetian. In the distinctive dialect of
the *Serenissima*, it means "house of John"—although
today's curators are quick to point out that Mable
Ringling had as much to do as her husband with its
striking colors and textures. Ca' d'Zan, which cost the
Ringlings $1.5 million despite the fact that it is not an
immensely large house, is distinctive for its stucco
exterior walls in a subtle rose color, its bright marble
terraces, and for a wealth of intricate terra cotta
detailing on interior as well as exterior surfaces.

Even though he was nearly ruined by the 1929 stock
market crash, John Ringling retained a magnificent
collection of Baroque paintings, including the world's
largest private holding of the work of Peter Paul
Rubens. Ca' d'Zan's galleries were opened to the
public in 1930, during Ringling's lifetime, and the circus
king's quirky, cheerful structure remains a popular
museum today.

JAMES DEERING

Fly in low over Biscayne Bay on the approach to
Miami International Airport, and one of the most
arresting sights below is a particularly ponderous-
looking boat moored just offshore from a splendid

(ABOVE)

The ballroom at Ca' d'Zan, 1924–1927.

COLLECTION OF THE JOHN AND MABLE RINGLING MUSEUM OF ART,
THE STATE ART MUSEUM OF FLORIDA. PHOTO GIOVANNI LUNARDI, 2002.

(OPPOSITE)

The west facade tower at Ca' d'Zan, 1924–1927.

COLLECTION OF THE JOHN AND MABLE RINGLING MUSEUM OF ART,
THE STATE ART MUSEUM OF FLORIDA. PHOTO TERRY SHANK, 2002.

Italian Renaissance villa.

But look again—that boat is filled with marble statuary, and the reason it looks so ponderous is that it, too, is made of stone. The "Great Stone Barge," as it is called, is simply one of many highly individualistic extravagances at Vizcaya, James Deering's bayside estate.

Deering, a vice-president of the International Harvester Company, began building Vizcaya (the Basque name is that of a Spanish province on the Bay of Biscay) in 1916 as the centerpiece of a 180-acre property that included a dairy farm, stables, greenhouses, and 10 acres of formal Italian gardens. Not content with merely replicating the furnishings and architectural elements he admired, Deering and a consultant, artist Paul Chaflin, scoured Europe for the statuary, paneling, mantelpieces, tapestries, and paintings that today make Vizcaya an important museum chronicling some 400 years of art and design.

Vizcaya's Italian Rococo Music Room incorporates walls and ceilings from Milan's Palazzo Borromeo; the tinted plaster ceiling in the Reception Room once adorned the Rossi Palace in Venice. These and other authentic elements are complemented by specially commissioned touches such as an embroidered linen ceiling (in Deering's bathroom); silk wall coverings by Scalamandre; and, in the Tea Room, painted canvas walls depicting classical ruins.

And there is the Great Stone Barge, laden with its allegorical maritime statues by Stirling Calder. It isn't going anywhere, but no matter: James Deering already brought much of the world to Vizcaya.

(Left)

The Tea Room at Vizcaya. The bronze and wrought-iron gate once graced a Venetian palazzo.

Photo courtesy Vizcaya Estate.

(RIGHT)

Vizcaya is surrounded by 10 acres of Italian gardens, with typical Renaissance emphasis on symmetrically placed statuary and fountains.

PHOTO COURTESY VIZCAYA ESTATE.

Modern Moguls

JUST as Joseph Pulitzer and William Randolph Hearst used advances in printing to create their newspaper and magazine empires, a new breed of media barons built their fortunes on the revolution in wireless communications pioneered by Guglielmo Marconi at the beginning of the 20th century. Although the careers of these czars of mass communications began in the radio days of the 1920s and '30s, they came into the full measure of their power and influence with the postwar arrival of television.

On the night of April 14, 1912, a 21-year-old wireless operator sat at his station in New York's Wanamaker department store. Operated by the Marconi Wireless Telegraph Company, the station was thought of by many people as little more than a gimmick, a clever publicity device for the store. But there was nothing frivolous about the dots and dashes of Morse Code that came across David Sarnoff's earphones that night. They relayed the desperate situation of the White Star liner *Titanic*, foundering in the north Atlantic after a glancing but fatal collision with an iceberg. Sarnoff, manager of the Marconi station, was one of the few people on the east coast of North America with what would later be called a "real time" connection with the disaster.

Impressed as they were with young Sarnoff's coolness and competence as the *Titanic* tragedy played itself out, the young man's superiors were less enthusiastic when he submitted a memorandum, four years later, suggesting that Marconi's wireless technology might outgrow its utilitarian role and make possible a "radio music box," enabling listeners to enjoy "concerts, lectures, music, recitals, etc. which may be going on in the nearest city within their radius." "Harebrained," was one Marconi official's opinion of the idea.

David Sarnoff was too serious a man to harbor harebrained ideas. Born in a Russian Jewish shtetl in 1891, he had sailed in steerage with his family to America, and learned English from newspapers he picked out of the trash on the Lower East Side of Manhattan. He had started

(ABOVE)
NBC founder David Sarnoff (left) with the man who made his industry possible, radio inventor Guglielmo Marconi.
PHOTO GETTY IMAGES.

(OPPOSITE)
Ted Turner at the helm in 1979, off the New England coast. Two years earlier, he had won the America's Cup.
PHOTO CHRISTOPHER CUNNINGHAM/LIAISON.

David Sarnoff at the New York World's Fair, 1939. NBC began regular television broadcasts that same year.

with Marconi in 1906, learning Morse Code and wireless operation well enough to advance from office boy to station manager by the time of the *Titanic* sinking. Then, in 1919, he had another opportunity to present his "music box" idea. The Marconi Company had been bought out by a bigger firm, whose initials were to become as much a part of Sarnoff's identity as his own: the Radio Corporation of America.

Sarnoff sold RCA management on the idea of radio broadcasting, and on the business of selling radios. By 1927 he was the man in charge of RCA's fledgling 25-station network, the National Broadcasting Company.

David Sarnoff was not only a radio pioneer, shepherding NBC through the medium's formative years and golden age of popularity in the 1930s and '40s. He was also the visionary and technical wizard who saw the potential of television, and made sure his company had the talent and technology to plunge into the new medium when the time was right. Amazingly, he told his RCA superiors as early as 1923 that television would become "the ultimate and greatest step in mass communications"—a belief that led him, in 1928, to secure a government permit for New York's first experimental television network. Regular programming began in 1939. "Sarnoff was the visionary," CBS executive Frank Stanton later recalled. "He had the guts." In the postwar years, when TV really took off, it was Sarnoff's guts—and gut instincts—that led him to develop an extensive network based on black-and-white broadcasting when rival CBS was still hoping that color would be the entry-level technology.

For all his pioneer involvement with the electronic media that would transform American tastes and lifestyles, David Sarnoff seemed like a tycoon from an earlier era. Formal and formidable, almost stuffy, he easily wore the title "General" earned during his reserve service in World War II, when he built an Allied radio network after the D-Day invasion. He lived in a 30-room Manhattan town house, and ruled his empire from an oak-paneled office with a private barbershop in Rockefeller Center's RCA Building. Perhaps most surprising of all were Sarnoff's cultural tastes. His favorite activity at Rockefeller Center, when he could get away from his desk, was to listen to Arturo Toscanini and the NBC Symphony rehearse. He hated NBC's own "Amos 'n' Andy" radio show, not because it was racist but because it was frivolous. "If comedy is the center of NBC's activities, then maybe I had better quit," he once said. But Sarnoff didn't quit, and more than a few comedies went out across the radio and TV airwaves in his time. He was too good a businessman to have decreed otherwise.

WILLIAM S. PALEY

In the 1950s and '60s, many of the most momentous decisions in the television world—from the airing of landmark documentaries to the development of the frothiest situation comedies—were made around an antique chemin-de-fer gaming table that belonged to a one-time cigar manufacturer named William S. Paley.

Unlike David Sarnoff, who came into radio and television by way of his technical capabilities, Bill Paley got involved in mass communications because of . . .

well, because of cigars. His father manufactured the La Palina brand, and Paley—born in Chicago in 1901—began in 1928 to supervise a show called "The La Palina Smoker" that the family firm sponsored on the shaky young Columbia radio network. Paley had heard the new medium for the first time in 1925, and it fascinated him. Using his share of the proceeds from the family's sale of stock in its cigar company, Paley bought a controlling interest in Columbia in 1928. At 27, he was president of a radio network.

Bill Paley didn't build CBS while grumbling about comedy offerings taking the place of high culture—"I am not a highbrow," he once asserted. "I do not look down on popular taste." Right from the beginning, he went after broad popular appeal, and he went after advertising. Soon after heading for New York to take charge at Columbia headquarters, he signed Paul Whiteman, the era's most successful mass-appeal jazz bandleader. "True Story" soon went on the air as a CBS radio version of the popular pulp magazine. Paley's network brought America George Burns and Gracie Allen, Jack Benny (who would defect to NBC, and then later rejoin the CBS fold) and Fred Allen, and introduced stage superstar Will Rogers to radio. Later, in the mid-1930s, Paley lured Al Jolson, amateur hour host Major Bowes, and Nelson Eddy from NBC.

Babe Paley strikes a characteristically stylish pose as her husband, CBS chief William Paley, frames a photo at the Paleys' Jamaica retreat.
PHOTO GETTY IMAGES.

Meanwhile, he relentlessly courted advertisers such as Chrysler Corporation and American Tobacco.

Paley's talent-scouting expeditions to Manhattan theaters and nightclubs came naturally to a man who was a lifelong bon vivant and big spender. In 1928, flush with his cigar money, he had paid $16,000 for a Hispano-Suiza, one of the most elegant automobiles of that or any age. In 1930, he moved into his first big New York apartment, a triplex that he had redecorated at a cost of $10,000 per room. His bachelor pad had eight radios, a dressing room with a built-in massage table and room for three hundred suits, and a silver-painted barroom with a circular aluminum staircase leading to a roof garden. It was all an Art Deco test run for the house he built after marrying his first wife, Dorothy Hart Hearst (Paley had swept her away from her first husband, Jack Hearst, son of the master of San Simeon). That six-story extravaganza had a black maple floor inlaid with brass, and a staircase carpeted in zebra skins. But the Paleys moved out after only three years. Bill's tastes were growing more refined. He had also begun to collect art. Beginning with Matisse, he eventually acquired works by Lautrec, Cezanne, Gaugin, and Picasso.

Paley would eventually own estates on the north shore of Long Island, at Squam Lake in New Hampshire, and on Lyford Cay in the Bahamas, as well as a spectacular Fifth Avenue apartment. With Dorothy—and, later, with his second wife, best-dressed-list perennial Barbara Cushing "Babe" Paley—he would entertain on a lavish scale. The Long Island place in particular was the scene of weekend parties that prompted one visitor to claim he was "overcome by the brilliance and charm and beauty and style of life at the Paleys'."

But Bill Paley's truest domain was the office from which he ran the Columbia Broadcasting System. After 1964, that antique chemin-de-fer table stood in his private quarters at Black Rock, the sleek, severe CBS headquarters building. By then, Paley's legend was well ensconced in the public imagination: there was the Paley who had built a superb news organization around Edward R. Murrow and his colleagues, the Paley who had earned CBS television its reputation as the "Tiffany Network." It hardly mattered that Paley had not at all been unaided in his accomplishments, that he had held onto his faith in radio long after TV seemed the wave of the future, and that the "Tiffany Network" broadcast series such as "The Beverly Hillbillies" and "Petticoat Junction." The effervescence and drive of the cigar man turned radio whiz was what mattered, so much so that Paley survived, albeit in a diminished role, as a part of CBS management until his death in 1990. A fellow entertainment magnate sized up the old man as well as anyone, remarking after a first meeting that "I have seen pure willpower."

TED TURNER

One summer day in the early 1980s, a traveler dining at a restaurant in the tiny native community of Eskimo Point in Canada's Northwest Territories (now Arviat, Nunavut Territory) looked up from his lunch of caribou stew and whale meat at the television mounted above the bar. The news was on, and an incongruous stream

*"Captain Outrageous" Ted Turner—no stranger
to rough waters or bold tacking maneuvers—
sailing off the Florida coast.*

of images from the world's capitals and trouble spots
pressed its way in upon this subarctic outpost on the
shores of Hudson Bay. That was marvel enough, made
possible by the big satellite dish planted on the edge of
the tundra. But just as remarkable was the phrase in
the newscaster's signoff: "from Atlanta." Not Toronto,
not Winnipeg, but Atlanta. Why was Atlanta sending
the news to Eskimo Point?

The answer was simple: because Ted Turner wanted
to send it there, and just about everywhere else. The
man called "Captain Outrageous" had been struck by
the idea that people shouldn't have to wait until the
news came on, but that it should always be on. His
answer was the Cable News Network.

The path Turner took to CNN—and to the sale of
his media and sports empire to Time-Warner, later AOL
Time-Warner—began with his father's outdoor
advertising company, which the younger man parlayed
into a string of radio stations and, eventually, his entry
into the Atlanta television market. When cable and
later satellite broadcasting came on the scene, Turner
took his Atlanta operation national, creating the first
"superstations."

When his countrymen first took notice of Ted
Turner, it wasn't because of CNN but because of his
fame as a yachtsman. A sailor since boyhood, he took
his first national championship in 1963. Captaining
Courageous, he won the America's Cup in 1977. Around
the same time, he was busy establishing credentials in
what were, for him, non-participatory sports. He had
bought the Atlanta Braves baseball team in 1976, and
begun the arduous task of building that organization

Ted Turner's legacy may ultimately rest as much on his vast Western landholdings as on his broadcasting triumphs.
PHOTO JOHN C. AMOS/CORBIS.

into the perennial National League contenders they would become a decade later. In 1977, he bought pro basketball's Atlanta Hawks. With his sports teams and the meteoric growth of Turner Broadcasting, Turner was rapidly becoming the face of the new Atlanta.

He was also, in those days, becoming the "Mouth of the South," known for his freewheeling bluster, shoot-from-the-hip remarks, and good-old-boy insouciance. Having picked up the habit of chewing tobacco from his Braves players, he would work away on a wad, spitting into a glass, while meeting buttoned-down executives from the New York offices of CBS—which, at one point in the early '80s, he attempted to buy. His cigar origins notwithstanding, it isn't easy to imagine Bill Paley chewing tobacco.

Ironically, Ted Turner toned down his flamboyant style during the same decade in which he made headlines through his high-profile marriage (his third) to actress-activist-fitness entrepreneur Jane Fonda. At one World Series after another the two sat in front row seats, doing the Braves' signature "tomahawk chop" (not Fonda's most politically correct moment); and they seemed, as the years passed, like a celebrity institution. But the Turner-Fonda union ended, after 10 years, in 2000. Jane announced that she had become a Christian; Ted had never professed anything stronger than agnosticism. If any of her beliefs had rubbed off on him, they likely had more to do with his growing social activism than with religious dogma.

Ted Turner's ultimate legacy may rest not with his revolutionizing of the television news business, nor with his personal exploits as what the society columns used

Malcolm Forbes welcomes Elizabeth Taylor to his seventieth birthday party at his palace in Tangiers, Morocco.

to call a "millionaire sportsman." Over the past two decades, what had been a muddled Turner political philosophy has jelled into a commitment to environmentalism and world peace. He gives $50 million each year to his Turner Foundation, and in 1997 announced that he was donating one billion dollars—at the time, roughly a third of his resources—to the United Nations. Parceled out at the rate of $100 million annually for 10 years, the money is to be earmarked for addressing population and women's rights issues, children's welfare, the environment, and global security.

Turner's best gift to America may turn out to be a good part of itself: over the years, he has acquired nearly two million acres of real estate, most of it in the West, making him the nation's largest private landowner. Turner has bought one enormous ranch after another, and has worked hard to restore these properties to pristine condition—removing fences, replanting native vegetation, restocking indigenous animals such as bison. What will be the eventual disposition of landholdings equal in size to Rhode Island and Delaware put together? Turner, in his early sixties, has yet to make public a plan. But given his record of charity and environmental concern, it's difficult to imagine all that land being sold to pay estate taxes, or turned back over to agribusiness and development. It will be interesting to see just what Ted Turner has in mind.

MALCOLM FORBES

It was the evening of May 20, 1986, and a bagpiper was welcoming guests to a Hudson River pier in Manhattan.

Malcolm Forbes cradles one of his collection of Fabergé eggs, crafted for the Russian imperial court.

Alongside the pier lay the magnificent *Highlander V,* a yacht that looked more like a small ocean liner than a large pleasure boat. Like the vessel's name, the bagpiper was a nod to the Scottish antecedents of the man who was celebrating the maiden cruise of his fine new toy. Malcolm Forbes was having a party.

This latest in a line of Forbes yachts named *Highlander* was a toy decked out with toys. Secured to its decks were two speedboats, a Cigarette and a Donzi, alongside launching davits; a Bell Jet Ranger helicopter; and a pair of Forbes's favorite Harley-Davidson motorcycles—he owned more than 60 motorcycles. Inside were sumptuous salons and staterooms, and a restaurant-worthy galley capable of turning out, as it did during that star-studded launch party, a feast of lobster, prime tenderloin, and choice wines. Near the entrance to the main salon stood the man himself, shaking hands and offering cigars. Malcolm Forbes was doing what he did best, having fun.

Highlander was not only the Forbes yacht but the *Forbes* yacht, flagship of an institution which, in the hands of a less flamboyant man, might have been associated more with bottom lines than mooring lines. *Forbes* was—and is—a business magazine, the sort of publication that had traditionally been concerned with making and keeping money rather than with spending it with cheerful abandon. "Capitalist tool," was the puckish sobriquet he gave his publication, standing Marxist cant on its head. But *Forbes* was also its owner's tool for pure enjoyment, his device for turning advertising and circulation into yachts,

hot-air balloons, a castle in Morocco, and even a collection of Fabergé eggs.

Forbes was founded in 1917 by Malcolm Forbes's father, Bertie Charles Forbes, a Scottish immigrant. Malcolm, 35 when his father died in 1954, took over what was a staid and respected publication. Distancing his magazine from the first of those attributes without sacrificing the second, the new publisher ventured increasingly into profiling the

(ABOVE)

In addition to this inflatable, Forbes owned some 60 real Harleys.

(LEFT)

Malcolm Forbes loved balloons, and he loved his stately homes: this temptation was obviously too great.

Capitalist Tool: The Forbes yacht Highlander V,
equipped with helicopter, twin speedboats, and
Harley-Davidson motorcycles.

personalities of American business leaders. He also
introduced the annual "*Forbes* 400" feature, ranking
America's richest individuals in much the same way
that *Fortune* magazine listed leading corporations.

But Malcolm Forbes was destined to be
remembered more for the way he spent his money
than the way he made it. Aside from that succession
of *Highlanders* and his Fabergé eggs, he owned a Fiji
Island, Lauthala; a 40-acre New Jersey estate; a
home along England's River Thames; and a castle in
Tangiers, Morocco. The Tangiers palace was the
location of one of the most talked-about parties of the
1980s, Forbes's 70th—and last—birthday party, in
1989. The publisher flew 1,000 guests to the
celebration, at a cost of $2 million. He appeared in
formal Scottish attire, kilt and all, amid a crowd of
wellwishers that included celebrities as diverse as
Donald Trump, Julio Iglesias, Walter Cronkite, and
Trump's sometime motorcycling companion,
Elizabeth Taylor.

Balloons—not the party kind—were Malcolm
Forbes's abiding passion. He went aloft in a balloon
for the first time in 1972, but by the end of the
following year he had not only qualified as a pilot but
set six world records in hot-air ballooning. In 1974,
he became the first man to fly one of the craft coast-
to-coast across the United States.

The surface of a hot-air balloon, of course,
offers a lot of advertising space. On the record-
setter, the words "*Forbes* " and "Capitalist Tool"
filled it out nicely.

SAM WALTON

If the 1980s had anything to offer in the way of a populist tycoon to counterbalance the image of Malcolm Forbes in his final opulent decade, that individual was a pickup-driving Arkansan named Sam Walton.

By the time Walton died in 1992, he had lead the *Forbes* list as the richest American for seven years. He got there by practicing, and preaching to his employees, the gospel of volume. Walton bought as cheap as he could, sold as cheap as he could, and counted on a vast multiplication of those narrow margins in all of his Wal-Mart stores.

The story of Wal-Mart's origins would have been a familiar one to Frank Woolworth or Rowland Macy, although Sam Walton started on a slightly stouter shoestring than they did. Having worked as a management trainee at a J. C. Penney store before World War II, Walton bought his first store, a Ben Franklin five-and-ten franchise, in Newport, Arkansas. It was 1945, and he was 27 years old.

Having lost his lease on the Newport property, Walton bought a second Ben Franklin franchise in Bentonville, Arkansas, in 1950. Then, two years later, he did what he would keep on doing for the rest of his life: he opened another store. By the early 1960s he had 16 of them, and he had no desire to stop there or anywhere else within sight. And alongside of his commitment to steady growth and high-volume, low-margin retailing, Walton stuck to another principal that many of his colleagues had overlooked. He always located in or near small towns, figuring that such places had been bypassed by other chains and individual operators but nevertheless offered tremendous opportunities.

In 1962, Walton opened the first store bearing the Wal-Mart name. By the end of the decade, there were 18 of them, along with 14 variety stores Walton still ran under different names (some were still Ben Franklins). All the stores were in the South—in fact, even as late as 1976, all 125 Wal-Marts were within a day's drive of company headquarters in Bentonville.

Wal-Mart, which had gone public in 1970, reached the $1 billion sales plateau 10 years later. The 1980s would be the decade in which Americans outside the South would begin to become aware of Wal-Mart, as the company's expansion reached a pace that put more and more stores well beyond a day's drive of Bentonville (by the century's close, there would be more than three thousand Wal-Mart stores, employing some 825,000 workers).

And it was during the 1980s that Sam Walton became something of a folk legend. The image was one he had shrewdly cultivated within his empire, with his flying visits (often literally, in his small plane) to store after store for pep talks with employees who would be awed by their contact with down-home "Mr. Sam." But Sam Walton really *was* down-home. He bought his shoes—where else?—at Wal-Mart. He never bothered to have his phone number unlisted. His idea of recreation wasn't a trip to the tables at Monte Carlo or racing a 12-meter yacht, but a quail hunt on property he leased in south Texas, where his camp was made up of old trailers. In his aging pickup truck, the rangy, silver-

The Oracle of Omaha: master investor Warren Buffett announces the Disney-Capital Cities merger, 1995.

PHOTO PORTER GIFFORD/LIAISON.

haired Walton looked like a man who had taken a break from his Saturday morning chores to pick up a few necessities in town.

But that's not putting it quite right. In the world he had created, he wouldn't be heading to town, but to the Wal-Mart out on the highway.

WARREN BUFFETT

For one man who has consistently occupied the highest echelons of the *Forbes* list of richest Americans—he often holds second place, behind Bill Gates—the business of making money is not something that follows from providing a particular product or service. It is a function of a finely honed investment strategy that involves many businesses, many products, and many services. Warren Buffett is the consummate investor, and his skill has made him a billionaire many times over.

The son of an Omaha broker, Buffett bought his first stock at age 11. By the time he was in high school his investments, and his skillful management of a chain of paper routes, were paying so well he almost didn't bother with college. But studies at Wharton and at Columbia sharpened Buffett's analytical abilities even more acutely, and by the time he was in his twenties he was busy at his lifetime occupation of beating the Dow. His company, Berkshire Hathaway—named for a textile mill he once controlled—has spawned scores of millionaires, acolytes of the Buffett philosophy of buying sound stocks and holding onto them. At Berkshire's famous annual meetings, rapt investors gather to receive the wisdom of the "Oracle of Omaha."

Equally famous is the Buffett lifestyle, or what most billionaires would consider the lack of one. There are no yachts, no stables of Ferraris, no villas on the Riviera: Warren Buffett still lives in a house he bought for $31,500 over 40 years ago, still wears inexpensive off-the-rack suits, and still favors cherry Coke . . . which tastes even better when you're on the board of directors.

STEVEN SPIELBERG

Viewers tuning into ABC on the evening of November 13, 1971, might have thought they were in for the usual Saturday night TV movie fare, and at first they saw little to suggest anything different. The week's offering was a made-for-television film called *Duel*, about a motorist pursued across a lonely desert landscape by a homicidal trucker driving an evil-looking 18-wheel gas tanker. More perspicacious viewers, however, might have realized that they weren't merely watching a

(ABOVE)

Along for the ride: Non-golfer Steven Spielberg accompanies Bill Clinton during a presidential round in 1998.

PHOTO MARK WILSON/NEWSMAKERS/LIAISON.

(OPPOSITE)

Source of the Force: George Lucas, creator of the Star Wars *and* Indiana Jones *film franchises, in a reflective moment at his Skywalker Ranch.*

PHOTO JIM WILSON/NEW YORK TIMES CO./GETTY IMAGES.

standard-grade chase movie slapped together to fill a time slot, but an unusually adept bit of directing — the beginning, perhaps, of a promising career.

The director of *Duel* was a 24-year-old named Steven Spielberg. Ohio-born and raised in New Jersey, Arizona, and California, Spielberg had been fascinated by his father's 8mm wind-up movie camera, and by '50s TV fare such as "The Twilight Zone and "Davy Crockett." It is doubtful that he ever wanted to be anything but a film director. He signed his first contract with Universal at 22, having spent much of the preceding year hanging around the studio, using an informally expropriated office and soaking up whatever knowledge and advice he

could by watching other directors at work. That contract led to *Duel*, and *Duel* led to the world beyond television.

A list of the Spielberg films of the subsequent 30 years reads like a history of American popular entertainment in the late 20th century — *Jaws, Close Encounters of the Third Kind, E.T.*, the *Indiana Jones* and *Jurassic Park* series, *Schindler's List*, and *Saving Private Ryan*. Along the way, Spielberg became wealthy beyond the most exaggerated standards of the old Hollywood. By the time the waters had calmed after *Jaws*, his net worth was reported at $200 million, and by the early 1990s he was earning some $70 million per year. "Spielberg is a tycoon, like Rockefeller," Federico Fellini once remarked — but there has never

been any locus with which to associate Spielberg's great wealth, no Kykuit or San Simeon or even anything like the faux-baronial surroundings of earlier Hollywood moguls. Steven Spielberg's personal world, like that of so many of his earlier films, seems rooted in suburban America; his baseball caps and denim jackets come across as less of a pose than something simply comfortable to work in.

GEORGE LUCAS

George Lucas is Steven Spielberg's only serious rival as the master modern mythmaker of American film. Lucas was born in Modesto,

California, in 1944, and as anyone who has seen his *American Graffiti* might suspect, Lucas had a midcentury California kid's passion for drag racing. But not long after high school, he was nearly killed in an auto accident. His dream of racing faded during his months of recuperation—a time during which, legend has it, he began thinking about something called "the Force."

Lucas was part of a new generation who entered the motion picture industry by way of film school. At the University of Southern California, he directed a short called *THX-1138:4EB*, which won a national award and was expanded into a feature in 1970. But it was *American Graffiti*, a paean to hot rods and rock 'n' roll, that launched Lucas's career. The film's success gave him time to work on an idea he had, for a space movie in the old Flash Gordon spirit. After his script was rejected by several studios, Twentieth Century-Fox gave *Star Wars* the go-ahead . . . provided Lucas would trade the usual director's fee for a 40 percent share of the profits, and all merchandising rights.

Any director or producer would be more than satisfied to have devised a franchise as phenomenally successful as *Star Wars*. But one day on a beach in Hawaii, Lucas asked Spielberg if he had ever heard of the Ark of the Covenant. What followed was the *Indiana Jones* series, like *Star Wars* still a work in progress.

The master of Lucasfilm, and of the special-effects company Industrial Light and Magic, is for all his reported net worth of $3 billion no more of a high-profile spender than his frequent collaborator Steven

Spielberg. But Lucas does own a sizeable corner of the world on which he has put his unmistakable stamp. He manages all his wizardry from a 3,000-acre northern California property called, most appropriately, Skywalker Ranch.

HIGH-TECH GIANTS

Henry Ford and John D. Rockefeller were the supreme exponents of the products that defined 20th-century America—the automobile, and the fuel it ran on. Bill Gates and Steve Jobs, two tycoons who rose to phenomenal wealth and power during the century's closing decades, just as succinctly represent our era and its iconic machine.

To carry the analogy further, Gates takes on the role of a latter-day Rockefeller because he makes the software on which most of the world's computers run. And, like Rockefeller, his crucial position as master of one of the most vital components of the world's economy has made him unimaginably wealthy: at the peak stock value of his Microsoft Corporation, William H. Gates III flirted with a net worth of nearly $100 billion, roughly the amount of the U.S. federal budget at the time John Kennedy became president.

Steve Jobs doesn't have that much money (although he is safely a billionaire), nor does he control nearly as large a market share in his part of the industry as Gates does in his. Apple Computer, which Jobs co-founded with Steve Wozniak in 1976, enjoys only a single-digit portion of the personal computer pie. Michael Dell's eponymous machines, which run on Gates's software, are far more common on America's desktops. (Apple

always ran on its own operating system, which it never chose to license—the source, most analysts say, of its stunted growth.)

But Jobs looms large not because he represents some odd Stanley Steamer in a world of Fords. He is part of contemporary business folklore because his first Apple machines did as much as anyone's to create the personal computer market, while his Macintosh and iMac products both reinvigorated it; because he came back from a humiliating forced departure to revive the company he created; and because he has used his visionary genius to transform the animated motion-picture industry through his studio Pixar, producers of *Toy Story* and *A Bug's Life*.

Gates and Jobs display marked differences in style, and in their public projection of themselves. Gates, as the years go by, comes across more and more as the suit-and-tie captain of industry, his image magnified Big Brother style on giant screens above the podiums at which he speaks. Jobs, meanwhile, still cultivates his persona as the intense, offbeat character in jeans and black turtleneck, the Zen-inspired vegetarian who mesmerizes devotees at MacWorld expositions as if he were about to pull a rabbit out of a hat—a feat that, repeatedly throughout his career, he has figuratively accomplished.

But the two men, both born in 1955, have a great deal in common. They started young, and succeeded young. They both inspire fierce loyalty, and intense dislike. Neither suffers fools cheerfully, and each of them determinedly sets the bar for non-foolhood exceptionally high.

LARRY ELLISON

"You can't win without being completely different. When everyone else says we are crazy. I say 'Gee, we must really be onto something.'" The man who made that remark might be different, but few would call him crazy. Larry Ellison launched Oracle Corporation in

1977, aiming to revolutionize computer databasing. Oracle grew to dominate the database software market, helping companies like Boeing, Yahoo, Coors, and BMW smoothly manage oceans of vital information. Along the way, CEO Ellison—a college dropout—has become one of the world's richest men. For a while his wealth even surpassed that of his archrival, Bill Gates.

Always impeccable in his $7,000 suits by Armani and Zegna, Ellison cuts a distinctive figure in an industry where it is always "casual Friday." He also fits the mold of the billionaire sportsman soaring over the Pacific in his own Italian fighter jet or racing his 78-foot yacht *Sayonara*. An Asian theme extends to several other passions: he collects Samurai helmets and Chinese ceramics, and lives in a $40-million replica of a Japanese palace complex among the redwoods in California's Silicon Valley nirvana.

JIM CLARK

"All I've ever done," Jim Clark explains, "is build businesses." Clark is the founder of such profoundly influential companies as Silicon Graphics—a pioneer in the field of three-dimensional computer modeling—and Netscape, which helped to transform the World Wide Web from an obscure academic tool to a part of daily life in homes and offices around the world. The personal rewards for these earth-shaking achievements have included a fortune in excess of $500 million, and the most advanced private sailboat ever created—the sailboat *Hyperion*.

To the naked eye, the 155-foot-long vessel is both grandiose and classically elegant, but, by Clark's own admission, "There is nothing that is terribly unique about this boat." The round-bottomed hull shape with its bulb fin keel, and the giant sail that furls into the boom, can be seen on other boats. The mahogany-trimmed staterooms are certainly luxurious, but they hardly represent a revolution in interior design. The ship's captain, Allan Prior, concurs: "There's nothing that's really different from other boats that are built. It's just bigger." Such comments, though, downplay the real wonder of this boat, which begs to be loved not only for its body but for its mind. Behind the scenes of this marvel runs more than 40 miles of copper wire, a central nervous system that collects information on every aspect of *Hyperion*'s operations, and routes it to touch-screen control centers located at 22 separate locations around the ship. A network of Silicon Graphics computers monitors the vessel's engines and generators, its navigation systems, and even its climate controls and video library. It can alert the crew to potential danger, such as changes in hull stresses and weather conditions.

Media coverage of *Hyperion*—which Clark has called "sensational"—has claimed that he will be able to sail the boat by remote control from his desk, halfway around the world. While acknowledging that it's possible, and the boat is prepared for it, Clark and his engineers maintain that this has never been their intention, and they have not even written the necessary software. "You have to ask yourself . . . what is sailing all about?" says systems manager Jim Bokxem. "It would mean that suddenly there is no crew, you step on the boat, push the button, and the boat starts to sail." Where, for a person who loves sailing, would be the fun in that?

BILL GATES

When all is said and done, though, it is the more conventional-seeming Gates who holds the popular imagination, who has become a household word. The reason is simple: he is the richest man in the world.

Bill Gates, a lawyer's son from Seattle, learned the FORTRAN and BASIC computer languages in high school. While he was a student at Harvard in the 1970s, he teamed with his friend Paul Allen to create a form of BASIC for a primitive personal computer called the Altair. Entering into an agreement with Altair's manufacturer to provide the software, the pair in 1975 formed a company they called Microsoft.

Settled into the Seattle suburbs, Microsoft grew throughout the late 1970s as a company that supplied variations of BASIC, FORTRAN, and COBOL for the microprocessors that powered minicomputers—the term then used for machines smaller than mainframes, but still larger than desktop personal computers. In 1981, IBM introduced an initial entry into that field, the PC. At its heart was an operating system supplied by Microsoft, called MS/DOS.

The IBM PC became the paradigm for the personal computer industry as it exploded in size throughout the 1980s and '90s, and MS/DOS followed as the operating system for all of the IBM "clones" that soon came to

dominate home and office computing throughout the world. The success of Microsoft—and of Bill Gates—followed in lockstep with the PC revolution. By 1987, the 32-year-old Microsoft CEO had become the youngest self-made billionaire in history. The ubiquitous Windows platform has since cemented both Microsoft's dominance of the industry, and Gates's place at the top of the Forbes 400 heap (for a short period around the turn of the century, he was displaced by Larry Ellison of Oracle). "Ubiquitous" is in fact an innocuous synonym for the definition of Microsoft which the U.S. Justice Department had on its mind when—shades of Rockefeller's Standard Oil, 1911—it instituted the antitrust proceedings which, as of this writing, are still grinding through the courts.

The media custodians of captain-of-industry folklore like to keep things simple, and "computer nerd" has certainly been a convenient pigeonhole in which to place Bill Gates. The slight frame, the big glasses, the floppy, '70s-style haircut—all of these superficial aspects tend to keep Gates in line with the stereotype.

Tales of Gates's cheeseburger-and-milkshake eating habits have also contributed, as have reports that he drives a Lexus—a coveted car among the upper middle classes, but hardly the chariot of a plutocrat. But there is more here than meets the eye: yes, Gates has included Lexuses among his stable of cars—but they have shared garage space with Ferraris and Porsches, including a Porsche 959 costing nearly $400,000. At this point, of course, price tags are virtually meaningless to Gates.

If, in its superficial way, a Porsche 959 helps mitigate Bill Gates's old computer-nerd image, his charities of recent years have done a great deal to alter the common impression that Gates has been particularly inattentive to the needs of the society that made him so rich. He once remarked that he was saving the task of philanthropy for a later period in his life, but that has changed. Perhaps in response to the chiding of fellow billionaire Ted Turner, whose remark "What good is wealth sitting in the bank?" was aimed in Gates's direction, the Microsoft chairman now doles out vast sums through his Bill and Melissa Gates Foundation. In 2000, the Gates bequests totaled $5 billion dollars.

Where would the richest man in the world live? As for the rest of us, the requirements might be simply stated: a nice private setting, not too far from work. For Gates, this means a four-and-a-half-acre site on Lake Washington, in the Seattle suburbs. He bought the land in the late 1980s and opened the design for his new house to competition. The winning entry was a subtle, contemporary Pacific Northwest–style residence made up of connected pavilions, linked by underground passageways and served by a 20-car garage, a reception hall capable of accommodating more than 100 guests, and a caretaker's house that would easily please a garden-variety millionaire. The home's most striking component, though, is its computerized bank of images—artworks and scenery—that can materialize on wall-sized screens, allowing residents and guests to alter their surroundings at will.

For now, at least, that house on the shores of Lake Washington marks the end of the line in a journey that began on the wharves of Salem, back when the Yankee ships were everywhere.

The Gates' home commands spectacular views of Seattle's Lake Washington. Its exterior features natural materials in traditional Pacific Northwest style, but the technological wonders concealed within include a 22-foot-wide video display composed of 24 rear-projection television monitors, each with a 40-inch screen.

PHOTO MIKE SIEGEL/*SEATTLE TIMES.*

Index

WILD
SOUTH AFRICA

WILD
SOUTH AFRICA

Photographs by LEX HES
Text by ALAN MOUNTAIN

The MIT Press
Cambridge, Massachusetts

First MIT Press edition, 1998

Library of Congress Cataloging-in-Publication Data
Mountain, Alan.
    Wild South Africa / photographs by Lex Hes; text by Alan Mountain.
        p.   cm.
    Originally published: London : New Holland Publishers , 1998.
    Includes bibliographical references and index.
    ISBN 0-262-13347-4 (hc. : alk. paper)
    1. South Africa.   2. South Africa – Geography.
    3. Natural history – South Africa.
    4. Conservation of natural resources – South Africa.   I. Hes, Lex.   II. Title.
D1721.M68 1998
916.8'02–dc21   98-17954
                                                                                 CIP

Senior Designer: Lyndall du Toit
Editors: Jane Maliepaard and Ann Baggaley
Project Manager: Mariëlle Renssen
DTP Cartographer: John Loubser
Picture Researcher: Carmen Swanepoel

Reproduction by Hirt and Carter Cape (Pty) Ltd
Printed and bound by Tien Wah Press (Pte) Ltd in Singapore

CONTENTS

INTRODUCTION

FOCUS ON THE EASTERN COASTAL PLAIN   *page 58*

FOCUS ON THE COAST   *page 92*

FOCUS ON THE BUSHVELD   *page 122*

FOCUS ON THE DESERTS *page 150*

FOCUS ON THE MOUNTAINS *page 176*

PHOTOGRAPHIC ACKNOWLEDGEMENTS

The publishers and photographer extend their thanks to the following people who kindly loaned their photographs for inclusion in this book. All the photographs in the book, with the exception of those listed below, were taken by **Lex Hes**.

PA = Photo Access
SIL = Struik Image Library

A Bannister (ABPL Image Library): pp. 51, 75 (bottom right), **Roger de la Harpe (ABPL Image Library):** 76 (top); **Keith Begg (ABPL Image Library):** p. 35 (top left); **Peter Chadwick (ABPL Image Library):** p. 38 (bottom right); **Peter Craig-Cooper:** front cover; **Duncan Butchart:** pp. 106, 107 (top), 145 (top and bottom); **Pat de la Harpe (PA):** p. 77 (top right); **Nigel Dennis:** pp. 84 (bottom), 128 (top right and bottom); **Gerhard Dreyer (SIL):** pp. 100 (top), 107 (bottom right), 109 (top), 110, 111 (top right), 113 (bottom right); **Gerhard Dreyer:** 196 (bottom); **HPH Photography (PA):** p. 79 (top); **J & B Photographers (PA):** p. 88 (top); **Wayne Matthews:** p. 78; **Steve McKean:** p. 81; **Alan Mountain:** pp. 19, 23 (right), 25 (top and centre), 49, 52, 53, 66 (bottom), 68, 80 (bottom left), 82, 85 (top), 93, 94 (right), 95 (left), 121 (bottom), 126; **Colin Paterson Jones:** p. 199; **Peter Pickford (SIL):** p. 74; **D Rogers (PA):** pp. 146 (bottom), 147, 148 (top); **Lorna Stanton:** front cover (middle inset), pp. 144; 203; **Hein von Hörsten (SIL):** p. 167; **Lanz von Hörsten (SIL):** pp. 50, 129 (bottom), 181, 198; **Alan Weaving (PA):** pp. 77 (bottom), 84 (top).
Source unknown: p48

Illustrations appearing in the preliminary pages are as follows:

HALF TITLE	*A rare photograph of Leopard* (Panthera pardus) *drinking.*
FRONTISPIECE	*The Matlabas River in the Marakele National Park with Sprobolus* sp. *grass in the foreground.*
PAGE 4	*The flower of the beautiful King Protea* (Protea cynaroides).
PAGE 5	*The Black-backed Jackal* (Canis mesomelas) *is a common resident in many parts of South Africa.*
PAGE 6	*Fish Eagles* (Halieetus vocifer) *usually perch high up in trees where they have a good vantage point.*
PAGE 7	*A camel-like rock form created by erosion in the Cedarberg.*
PAGE 10	*A view of the beach looking south from Black Rock in Maputaland.*
PAGE 12	*Aloe pillansi with the Vandersterrberge in the background near Helskloof in the Richtersveld.*

ACKNOWLEDGEMENTS

I would like to thank John Hanks and Pippa Parker for getting me involved in this project. To my brother, Mick, goes my gratitude for his assistance and guidance on various aspects of the geology section in the Introduction. My thanks also go to Lex, who was always ready to help when my information was a little thin. Finally, I would like to thank Lyndall du Toit, both for her enthusiasm – particularly when the road became very rocky – and the flair she brought to the design of the book.

Alan Mountain

During the making of this book I met many people who were incredibly helpful in pointing me in the right direction to get the photography required. I would like to extend my thanks and appreciation to the following:

Mike Doran of Trimark Agencies
Sasol Limited for providing me with fuel
Raymond Bezuidenhout and his staff at Fotofirst Nelspruit for top quality film processing

Staff at game and nature reserves and conservation departments around the country who went out of their way to help:
Joggie Ackerman at Mkambati Game Reserve in the Transkei
John Adendorf at Zuurberg National Park
Keith Cooper of the Wildlife and Environment Society
John Hanks of the Peace Parks Foundation
Mark Johns at Kogelberg Nature Reserve
Kobus Jooste of Cape Nature Conservation
Amber Millard of the Kwazulu Bureau of Natural Resources
Vic Moller of Berglust in the Waterberg
Dirk Ockhuis and Louis van Dyk of Cape Nature Conservation in the Cedarberg
Peter Openshaw at Giant's Castle Game Reserve
At Lapalala Wilderness, Peter Morrison, Haneke van der Merwe and especially Clive Walker who was truly an inspiration to be with in the field
K.C. Voges of the Department of Water Affairs and Forestry in the Outeniqua Mountains
At the West Coast National Park, Otto van Kaschke, Johan Taljaard and especially Matthew Norval who so willingly gave his time

The following individuals helped me out in so many different ways:
Patrick Bodham-Whetham of Wilderness Safaris
Braam van Wyk and Duncan Butchart who answered my queries on plant identification
Andy Coetzee at Rocktail Bay Lodge who is an inspiration
Dave and Janet Cruse are always there and willing to help
Brian Jones, who does wonderful animal rehabilitation work at Moholoholo
Wayne Mathews is a good friend who showed me wonderful plants in Tembe Elephants Park and guided me around the Richtersveld
Alan Mountain wrote an illuminating text
Roger and Anne Miller of Kokstad
Peter and Diane Norton
Zeph Nyati and Clive Poultney of the Mboza Village Project who introduced me to the peaceful life on the Pongola flood plain
Donald Strydom of the new Crocodile River Reptile Park in Nelspruit and his staff at Swadini Reptile Park allowed me access to some of their truly beautiful reptiles
Staff and management at Sodwana Bay Lodge
The staff at New Holland Publishers especially Jane Maliepaard, Carmen Swanepoel and Lyndall du Toit

The final word of thanks and appreciation must go to my wife and children for coping, with great strength, with my many months of absence. To Lynn and Tammy and Dale, I say thank you.

Lex Hes

FOREWORD

John Hanks
Peace Parks Foundation

Africa is a continent in transition. With the highest human population growth rate of any major region in the world, extensive areas of land are being transformed by the activities of man. Industrial and urban development, arable lands, timber plantations, road and rail links, and power lines have changed the face of Africa. In the vast communal areas, which cover much of the continent, overcrowding and absolute poverty have left the local residents with little alternative but to destroy the resource base on which their survival depends. Deforestation, overgrazing, accelerating soil erosion and desertification have become the dramatic and selective images of those who portray Africa as a continent in crisis.

Wild South Africa has encapsulated the antithesis of this anthropocentric pernicious transformation, and has succeeded admirably in prose and pictures in describing South Africa's truly wild places. These are the crown jewels of wilderness, which have survived intact through a combination of good fortune (by virtue of their remoteness), and through exemplary management by responsible conservation authorities. In many cases, these wild areas have embraced some of the most important and extraordinary extravagances of life's diversity, a variation in form, function and colour that has no equal anywhere in the world. South Africa's remarkable biological diversity is an international treasure, but like every treasure it must be protected from those who want to steal it (or through ignorance destroy it), for the benefit of those who want to use it or simply to view and enjoy it.

With legitimate and rapidly increasing human demands for more land for human settlement and for food production, and with poverty being one of the greatest destroyers of the environment, will these wild places survive if they do not pay their way? This is a real dilemma for conservationists. On the one hand, there is no doubt that the wild places of South Africa are rapidly gaining recognition as one of the world's premier nature-based tourism destinations. Yet many of these areas are ecologically fragile, and without careful management the impact of tourism can lead to inappropriate development, environmental destruction, and pollution. If complete preservation is the goal, then there should be no tourism development at all, a luxury that very few countries can afford. There is no doubt that tourism has the potential to become one of the most significant routes to the economic development which South Africa so desperately needs if it is to overcome widespread poverty. The economic rationale is compelling. In 1996, tourism generated 480,000 jobs, and contributed 4 per cent to the country's GDP. If present growth of tourism continues, by 2005 tourism could contribute 10 per cent to the GDP, generating some 40 billion South African rands annually and creating two million jobs. No other industry in South Africa has the potential to make such a significant and sustainable contribution to local economic growth and employment creation.

What is the future of the wild places so beautifully described in this book? Strict preservationists will be horrified by the thought of a 'tourist invasion', and all the detrimental consequences. Yet without this tourist income, either directly to the area concerned or through cross-subsidization from those centres that can carry a high visitor density, it will be difficult – if not impossible – to stop the insidious wave of human encroachment and settlement. The challenge for the guardians of these sanctuaries is to insist that the principles of *responsible tourism* be strictly adhered to. These include responsibility to the environment, responsibility to local communities (in terms of job creation and a genuine sharing of the benefits of economic development), a respect for local cultures and customs, and a commitment to guaranteeing the safety, security and health of the visitors to these remote areas.

Successful tourism is fostered and promoted by good publicity. There can hardly be a better way to do this for the wild places of South Africa than through a book such as this, a wonderful stimulus to visit and enjoy some of the less-known parts of the country, and a superb reminder of precious moments spent away from intrusive human developments. It also brings a message of hope to those who dwell on the selective images of despair. Africa still has much to be proud of, a precious heritage worth fighting for.

INTRODUCTION

A LAND OF BEAUTY AND DIVERSITY

Situated at the southern tip of the great African continent, South Africa is a land of hauntingly beautiful landscapes. Underlying the fundamental structure of the country's topography are three broad features – a high interior plateau, low-lying coastal margins that fringe the entire subcontinent and, separating the two, a virtually continuous escarpment made up of an irregular chain of rugged mountains. The plateau, which averages between 1300 and 1800 metres (4265 and 5906 feet) above sea level, is characterized by spacious plains that stretch out to flat horizons beneath piercing blue skies. Here the topographic pattern is one of large-scale features that gradually merge into one another. The same is true for climate, soil and vegetation types where boundaries are poorly defined and their occurrence widespread. The eastern regions of the plateau, which are relatively well watered by the rains brought over the escarpment from the Indian Ocean, are characterized by rolling grasslands that are green and grow fast in summer, but which turn brown and become stunted and then die back in winter. In the western half, the rolling grasslands give way to thornveld and then to semidesert dwarf scrub and finally, in the extreme west, to desert as the rain clouds from the east become increasingly less fecund.

Where the inland plateau descends to the coastal margins it is usually in abrupt steplike escarpment edges that are mountainous – often soft and rolling, occasionally dramatic and grand or, where the flow of the earth's unstable crust was opposed in palaeontological times, contorted and folded. Valleys have cut deep into these mountains and where they do so in the wetter eastern parts of the country, their wounds are soothed by evergreen riverine forests which hide their scars and contain the erosive force of the rivers that steadfastly flow at their feet. In the drier western regions of South Africa intermittent rivers, which often flood their banks when the sudden desert storms come, have left searing gashes in the landscape.

The coastal marginal lands are also stepped between the sea and the Great Escarpment which skirts the interior plateau. Smaller than the abrupt edges of the latter, these steps are made up of a series of steep-sided river basins that become interlinked as rivers from the escarpment meander through them on their way to the sea. The rugged beauty of these dramatic landscapes embraces some of the fairest valleys in Africa which are framed by great hill after great hill, producing a serried range of low mountains which seem to pile up upon each other while busily reaching up to the heights of the escarpment in the far distance.

Along the coastal margins, where the interplay between the action of the sea and the prevailing weather produces vistas of great beauty, variables such as the climate, soils and vegetation change abruptly from place to place and, as a result, environmental diversity is high. In the subtropical northeast of South Africa, for example, the warm offshore Mozambique Current, together with the continuity of a tropical climate along the low-lying Mozambique Plain, combine to create a diverse tropical flora which embellishes a necklace of estuaries, lakes and wetlands. A great variety of birds, mammals, trees and plants congregate in profusion around these aquatic jewels, adding interest to this wilderness paradise. The coast is characterized by long narrow beaches of silica sand sandwiched between an almost continuous barrier of forested sand dunes and the Indian Ocean.

Further south along the aptly named Wild Coast there is no coastal lowland separating the ocean from the low hills that build up to the escarpment; instead, the ocean and the hills meet head-on in mortal combat. Crashing waves constantly pound the shores until slowly, inexorably, the land gives way to the sea in places. In this unending battle, dramatic and varied beauty is born: rocks are eroded into natural sculptures that defy description; cliffs with sheer faces worn smooth by incessant wave action rise rigidly out of the sea; huge jagged holes are drilled through solid rock to create great archways which gradually become bigger until they, too, eventually collapse; and huge caverns are carved out of rock by the repetitive action of swirling water forcing its way into the smallest weak spots. This is a truly wild coast, washed by even wilder waters, that shows neither mercy to mariners who come too close nor remorse when a ship is dashed to pieces in the crossfire between land and sea.

Once large tracts of indigenous forest thrived along the narrow coastal margins of the southern and eastern coasts of South Africa. Today the remaining forests are restricted to specific areas along a 200-kilometre (124-mile) stretch of coast between George and Humansdorp in the southern Cape. The tall evergreen hardwood trees that comprise these forests fight for survival against the inroads made by humankind, whether it be through increased development and urbanization or the establishment of large-scale exotic plantations.

Beyond Humansdorp and stretching south to Cape Point and then extending northwards along the Cape's west coast to Vanrhynsdorp is South Africa's only winter rainfall region. Covering the often stark and jagged mountains that feature so prominently in this region, and the valleys that nestle in between, are tracts of Cape *fynbos* – one of the wonders of the floral kingdom. In an area of less than 90,000 square kilometres (34,740 square miles), no less than 8600 plant species occur, of which some 5800 are endemic. Cape *fynbos* has an exuberance in diversity that is delicate and subtle and therein lies its greatest danger. As a result of its lack of flamboyance, the importance of *fynbos* to the ecology of the Western Cape and its value, in particular, in protecting precious water sources and the natural environment is not fully understood by many people. As a result, it stands threatened by encroachment through afforestation, farming, indiscriminate clearing, repeated untimely burning and invasion by alien vegetation.

Along the west coast of South Africa an amazing miracle is performed by nature each year. In late winter and early spring, the broad coastal margin of Namaqualand is transformed from a

barren semidesert to a brightly carpeted wonderland as wild flowers of almost every hue make their short debut – a magical display of nature's genius. Namaqualand's unique flora includes not only carpets of flowers, which grow from seeds carefully stored in the ground from the previous season, but also geophytes – plants with bulbs, corms and tubers – and dwarf shrubs and succulents that vary in shape, size and form. In total, there are over 4000 plant species which contribute to the transformation of the barren summer landscape into a late winter wonderland.

ABOVE *The distinction between High Berg and Low Berg in the KwaZulu-Natal Drakensberg is clearly evident in this view of the Tseketseke River valley area, with Cathedral Peak in the background. The High Berg is characterized by two distinct features: domes and buttresses, which form part of the main escarpment, and freestanding columns, pinnacles and spires, which were once part of the main escarpment but have since been separated from it through erosion. The Little Berg comprises grass-covered plateaus, or terraces, with rivers and streams running between them, that extend eastward in almost fingerlike projections before terminating in prominent sandstone cliffs.*

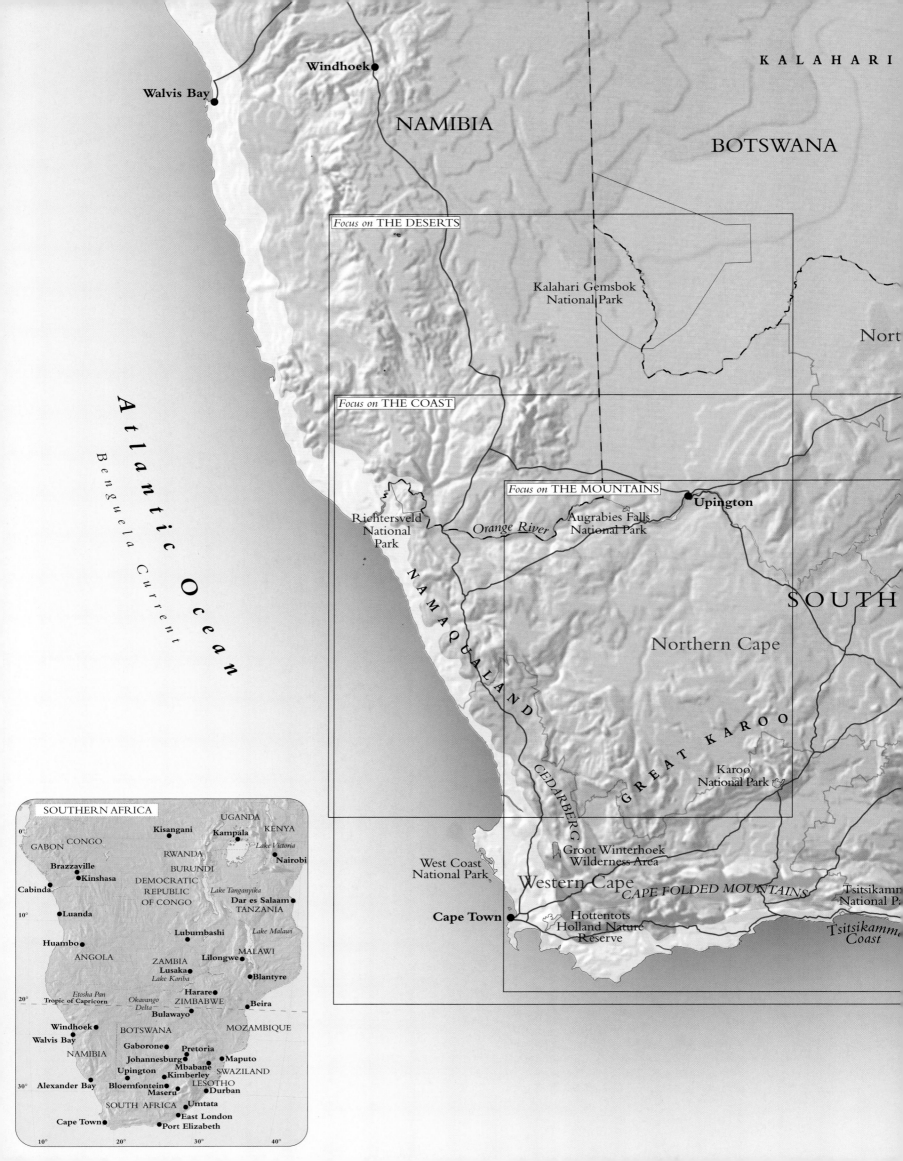

Windhoek

Walvis Bay

KALAHARI

NAMIBIA

BOTSWANA

Focus on THE DESERTS

Kalahari Gemsbok
National Park

Nort

Focus on THE COAST

Focus on THE MOUNTAINS

Upington

Richtersveld
National
Park

Orange River

Augrabies Falls
National Park

SOUTH

A t l a n t i c   O c e a n

B e n g u e l a   C u r r e n t

N
A
M
A
Q
U
A
L
A
N
D

Northern Cape

G
R
E
A
T
K
A
R
O
O

Karoo
National Park

C
E
D
A
R
B
E
R
G

West Coast
National Park

Groot Winterhoek
Wilderness Area

Western Cape *CAPE FOLDED MOUNTAINS*

Tsitsikamm
National P

Cape Town

Hottentots
Holland Nature
Reserve

*Tsitsikamm
Coast*

SOUTHERN AFRICA

UGANDA

Kisangani

Kampala   KENYA

GABON   CONGO

RWANDA

Lake Victoria

Nairobi

Brazzaville

Kinshasa

BURUNDI

DEMOCRATIC

Cabinda

REPUBLIC

Lake Tanganyika

Dar es Salaam

OF CONGO

TANZANIA

Luanda

Lubumbashi

Lake Malawi

Huambo

ANGOLA

MALAWI

ZAMBIA   **Lilongwe**

Lusaka

Lake Kariba

Blantyre

Etosha Pan

Harare

*Okavango
Delta*

ZIMBABWE

Beira

Tropic of Capricorn

Bulawayo

MOZAMBIQUE

Windhoek

BOTSWANA

Walvis Bay

Gaborone

Pretoria

Maputo

NAMIBIA

Johannesburg

Mbabane

SWAZILAND

Upington

Kimberley

Alexander Bay

Bloemfontein

LESOTHO

Durban

Maseru

SOUTH AFRICA

Umtata

Cape Town

East London

Port Elizabeth

ZIMBABWE

DESERT

Focus on THE BUSHVELD

MOZAMBIQUE

N

Limpopo River

Kruger
National
Park

Northern Province

Marakele
National Park

Olifants River

Pietersburg

Limpopo River

WATERBERG

Madikwe
Game Reserve

Gaborone

Pilanesberg
National Park

Focus on THE EASTERN COASTAL PLAIN

Nelspruit

Maputo

Pretoria

Johannesburg

Mbabane

Mpumalanga

Gauteng

SWAZILAND

Tembe Elephant Park

Vaal River

Ndumo Game
Reserve

← *Kosi Estuary & Lake System*

Lake Sibaya

Mkuzi
Game Reserve

Mgobezeleni Lake System

← Maputaland's Marine Reserves

Free State

Royal Natal
National Park

Hluhluwe–Umfolozi
Game Reserve

St Lucia Estuary & Lake System
(Greater St. Lucia Wetland Park)

imberley

Mont-aux-Sources

KwaZulu-Natal

Bloemfontein

Giant's Castle
Game Reserve

Maseru

AFRICA

LESOTHO

Natal
Drakensberg
Park

Durban

Orange River

Indian Ocean

Agulhas Current

Dwesa & Cwebe
Nature Reserves

The Wild Coast

astern Cape

East London

Port Elizabeth

LEGEND

| 0 | 50 | 100 | 150 |

| 0 | 25 | 50 | 75 | 100 |

International Boundaries — — —

National Roads ———

National Parks & Conservation Areas ———

| Metres | 0 | 100 | 200 | 500 | 1000 | 2000 |
| Feet | 0 | 328 | 656 | 1625 | 3250 | 6500 |

Height above sea level

GEOLOGY

It is currently estimated that the geological history of the earth extends back about 4.6 billion years. At some indeterminate time after this, development of the earth's crust began to take place despite the fact that a large proportion of the surface of the globe was still covered by water. Over aeons of time, the earth's crust continued to expand and develop – often violently and convulsively – as the processes of weathering and sedimentation steadily moulded, reshaped and added to the natural landscape. Outpourings of volcanic rock built the nucleus of a single continental land mass that was subsequently intruded by vast amounts of molten granite generated in the crust. These ancient rocks were deformed and metamorphosed by movements of the earth's crust, and were subjected to atmospheric weathering and erosion. The action of wind and water transported the weathered products into low-lying basins, internal seas and the surrounding ocean where they consolidated to become layered sedimentary rocks. Sediments which accumulated in deep basins on the margins of the continental land mass were slowly metamorphosed and ultimately accreted to a megacontinent, thereby increasing its area. At this time, there were no recognizable continents as we know them – only the megacontinent, Pangaea, meaning 'all lands'. This primitive land mass began to break up about 200 million years ago when the southern land mass, Gondwana, separated from the northern part, Laurasia.

The disintegration of Gondwana, in turn, was initiated at about the end of the Jurassic Period, about 130 million years ago, with the opening of a rift that slowly widened and eventually became the South Atlantic Ocean. Thereafter the great islands and continents of the world began to resemble their present form.

Reconstruction of the process of continental drift, which continues to the present day, has been greatly facilitated by the fossil record left behind. Particularly good correlations occur between Africa, South America and Antarctica. The Cretaceous Period (130 to 65 million years ago) saw the beginnings of modern flora and fauna, as we know them, but in their development many species have come and gone. From these times, South Africa began to take on the appearance it has today. The effects of weathering and erosion on the great variety of rock formations have sculpted a landscape of amazing diversity and produced a country of breathtaking beauty.

During the first several billion years of land-building, ancient geological formations of rock underwent great upheaval and geological revolution, the magnitude of which is difficult to imagine. Within the continental land mass, movement caused by convection within the earth resulted in the fragmentation of the crust into stable blocks surrounded by zones in which the rocks were subjected to greater degrees of movement and uplift. The oldest rocks known in southern Africa occur in one such zone. They are gneissic metamorphic rocks exposed in the Sand River south of Messina in South Africa and are reliably dated, by radiometric means, at 3.8 billion years old. These rocks are thought to be of sedimentary origin and therefore derived from even older rocks of which no visible records remain. The next oldest rocks are located within the adjacent stable block to the south and can be found in isolated parts of Mpumalanga

BELOW *Exposed bands of sedimentary rocks show evidence of erosion due, partially, to chemical decay and mechanical weathering resulting from the combined forces of thermal shattering (caused by huge diurnal variances in temperature) and wind action.*

Province and Swaziland. They are remnants of volcanic rocks that were formed 3.5 billion years ago.

About 2.5 billion years ago the crystalline basement of southern Africa was fully developed and was buried beneath a cover consisting of mainly sedimentary rocks, including the gold-bearing Witwatersrand strata, but incorporating volcanic episodes and major intrusions of igneous rocks, such as the Bushveld Igneous Complex which is situated north of Pretoria. This period was followed by a phase of mountain building that involved folding and crumpling of the rock strata, and was accompanied by the intrusion of granites.

One consequence of this period of deformation was the formation of a large sedimentary basin along the southern and western margins of the southern part of the supercontinent, Gondwana. The sediments in this basin were deposited about 500 million years ago and are represented today by the Cape Supergroup. They are significant for their content of well-preserved marine fossils which have made it possible to correlate these strata with sediments deposited in the same geological period in other parts of the world. The rocks of the Cape Supergroup were extensively folded and twisted through a south-westward movement of the continental land mass that is interpreted by geologists as a failed initial stage in the breaking up of the supercontinent into smaller blocks of individual continents.

Subsequent to the building of the Cape mountain chain, a vast internal sedimentary basin formed within the southern part of Gondwana in the region known today as the Karoo. Into this basin poured enormous quantities of sediment derived from the erosion of the surrounding highlands. The thick sedimentary

ABOVE The folding of rock strata is due to compressive forces in the earth's crust. The character of any fold structure depends upon the intensity of the compressive forces creating it, together with the nature of the rock. Here is an example of an asymmetrical, or inclined, upfold which has been pushed over to form an overfold. In cases like this, where the fold is overturned to the extent that the axial plane lies virtually horizontal, it is said to be recumbent.

rocks thus formed are collectively known as the Karoo Supergroup. Karoo rocks cover most of South Africa but at their greatest extent, they occurred as far north as the equator and both eastwards and westwards beyond the present shores of South Africa. In these sediments is a record of the vast changes that took place in Gondwana over a period of about 200 million years. Continental ice sheets spread into the subcontinent from the north, and major climatic changes brought first temperate, then tropical forests. In a later phase, which was characterized by arid conditions, wind-borne desert sands were deposited. Ultimately, the vast weight of the sedimentary deposits in the Karoo basin ruptured the earth's crust and continental flood basalts poured out to form a layer of over 1000 metres (3281 feet) thick. The present-day Drakensberg mountains are paltry remnants of vast lava sheets that once extended over much of southern Africa.

A fascinating and valuable aspect of the Karoo period is the fossil record of the age of the dinosaurs that is contained in its rocks. These rocks exhibit a continuous thread of evidence of evolutionary progression from fish through amphibians to reptiles and the origins of mammals. This comprehensive fossil record has made possible our understanding of the development of the continents as they exist today.

GEOGRAPHY AND CLIMATE

South Africa is 1.2 million square kilometres (463,200 square miles) in extent. From its northern boundary, the Limpopo River, the country spreads out to fill the southern extremes of the great African continent, ending at Africa's southernmost point, Cape Agulhas – an inauspicious and windswept headland surrounded by low sand dunes and shallow reefs. The country is washed by the waters of two major oceans – the warm Indian Ocean along its east and southern coasts and the cold Atlantic Ocean along its west coast.

There are no great climatic extremes in South Africa since the factors which affect the climate of the subcontinent, namely latitude, distance from the sea, ocean currents and altitude above sea level, tend to counterbalance each other. For example, except along the coastal lowlands, a decline in latitude (which normally results in an increase in temperature because of closer proximity to the equator) is countered by an increase in altitude in which there is a temperature drop of 10°C (50°F) for every 150-metre (492-foot) increase in altitude. Thus, although Cape Agulhas is the most southern point in Africa, its mean annual temperature of 16.8°C (62°F) compares with Johannesburg's mean annual temperature of 16.2°C (61°F), because the city is situated at an altitude of 1970 metres (6464 feet). The diurnal temperature range is also influenced by distance from the sea. This is due to the fact that a land surface absorbs more heat from the sun during the day than a water surface, but loses it more quickly through radiation at night. There is consequently a greater range in temperature between day and night in the high-lying interior than at sea level. Ocean currents do influence South Africa's weather, with the cold Benguela Current along the west coast resulting in an appreciable lowering of temperature and a build-up of fog banks along the coastline. The warm Agulhas Current increases temperatures along the east coast, causing warmer, more humid weather conditions along the eastern coastal margins than on the interior plateau. The western coastal margins are arid and cooler than equivalent latitudes on the east coast.

On the whole, South Africa is a dry country with an annual average rainfall of only 464 millimetres (18 inches) – compared to the world average of 857 millimetres (34 inches). Some 21 per cent of the country receives less than 200 millimetres (8 inches) annually, another 48 per cent between 200 and 600 millimetres (8 to 24 inches) and only 31 per cent enjoys a total above 600 millimetres (24 inches). The amount of rainfall reduces from east to west. West of an axis drawn between Kimberley and East London, the average annual rainfall that occurs on the interior plateau is less than 500 millimetres (20 inches), resulting in barren, desertlike conditions. East of the line the average rainfall is above 500 millimetres (20 inches) so vegetation is more prolific. The highest annual totals (more than 1000 millimetres, or 40 inches), occur along the KwaZulu-Natal coastal lowlands, at isolated places in the mountains of the Western Cape and along stretches of the eastern escarpment. The lowest precipitation occurs along the west coast of southern Namibia where less than 100 millimetres (4 inches) is recorded annually. Characteristic of South Africa's rainfall is a high degree of variation about the mean and the tendency for this to increase as rainfall decreases. Thus the western half of the country not only experiences low rainfall but also a very unreliable supply, while the eastern half experiences higher and more reliable rainfall.

In the Western Cape, between the mouths of the Olifants and Bree rivers, rain falls in winter. Within the borders of this region the mean annual rainfall varies considerably but in general the mountainous regions have the best precipitation. Further east along the coastal margins and southern slopes of the escarpment ridge between Swellendam in the west and Port St Johns in the east, the rain falls throughout the year with the heaviest preponderance shifting from the winter months in the south of the zone to the summer months in the north. In the remainder of the country rain falls predominantly in summer.

BELOW *De Hoop Nature Reserve's 50-kilometre (32-mile) coastline is lined by pristine dunes, fynbos and wetlands. Seven distinct ecosystems support some 40 mammal, 11 reptile, and 1400 plant species, as well as a rich birdlife.*

ABOVE *These Thonga girls are sorting fish caught in hand nets at Tete Pan on the Pongolo floodplain in Maputaland. Fish have traditionally provided an important source of protein for the people of this region because, until the tsetse fly was eradicated in the middle of this century, cattle breeding was not possible due to the fatal cattle disease, nagana, which was conveyed by the parasite.*

BELOW *People living on the borders of South Africa's wild places are caught between two worlds – those of rural simplicity and urban modernity. Here a Zulu herdboy reflects on this dichotomy while strumming on an amazingly tuneful homemade guitar.*

SOUTH AFRICA'S INDIGENOUS PEOPLE

It is not known who were the first people to tread the soil of southern Africa. The San, previously known as Bushmen (a name that today carries pejorative connotations), are certainly the oldest of the people of South Africa of whom there is any definite historical record. Simple evidence of this lies in the traditions of the other native peoples of South Africa which indicate that when they entered the country the San were already scattered over large parts of its surface. Archaeological research has shown that there existed in the southern subcontinent a number of different stone implement industries, clearly separated in time as well as in character. These industries are grouped chronologically into the Earlier, Middle and Later Stone Age cultures. The stone implements and rock art associated with the San all belong to the Later Stone Age, and furthermore it is only in deposits of this age that skeletal remains of the San have been found. The Early and Middle Stone Age cultures must consequently be regarded as previous to the San. There is a lack of continuity in type between the Middle and the Later Stone Age cultures which thus precludes the possibility that the latter, with the San stone industries forming part of it, developed in South Africa out of the former. At the same time, scattered all over East Africa, especially in Tanzania, Kenya and Uganda, are stone implement industries and, in places, rock paintings so closely resembling those of the San that they are regarded as having a common origin. These facts indicate that the stone industries associated in South Africa with the San were not indigenous to the country, but instead illustrate that the San migrated into the region from the northeast and were preceded by two pre-existing stone cultures. An interesting fact, however, is that no skeletal remains have yet been discovered north of the Zambezi River which are similar to those of the San, nor are there any peoples living outside South Africa who may be regarded as definitely San in race. Attempts have been made to establish a connection between the San and the Pygmy peoples who inhabited the equatorial forests of Africa, more especially in the Zaire and Congo regions, but anthropologically the two groups differ so substantially that it is not possible to establish a single racial identity. Anthropologists believe that as increasing numbers of Hamitic and Negroid peoples, who were more extensive in number and more powerful, invaded the East African region from the north, those San who were not exterminated or absorbed gradually migrated southwards, keeping along the more open grasslands of the eastern mountainous zone, where they could still conduct their hunting and gathering way of life. They, in turn, presumably exterminated or absorbed their predecessors in the region, the Strandlopers, whose remains date back to about 150,000 years ago, and who it is believed were largely confined to the coastal margins, living mainly off shellfish and the fruits of the sea which were easy to harvest. The time of arrival of the San on the soils of southern Africa is indeterminate, but researchers have found arrowheads and ostrich eggshell beads in Border Cave in northern KwaZulu-Natal, which provide us with concrete evidence that their early ancestors roamed the veld of southern Africa at least 30,000 years ago.

The Khoi are believed to constitute the next wave of people to inhabit South Africa. Anthropologists believe that the Khoi were probably originally San, but had acquired a large Hamitic admixture. There are strong points of similarity and divergence between the two groups. Their racial characteristics are similar and their languages have much in common, such as the occurrence of several 'click' consonants, similarities in word meanings

ABOVE *Young Xhosa boys explore the veld along the top of the cliffs created by the Magwa River as it slowly, but inexorably, cuts back through sandstone rock strata laid down many millions of years ago.*

and in various aspects of grammar. Factors which justify their distinction (but not separation) from the San include certain grammatical usages and the fact that while the San were hunters and gatherers only, the Khoi were pastoral people with herds of long-horned, straight-backed cattle and flocks of fat-tailed sheep. The Khoi were also Iron Age people who were able to smelt metal ores for the manufacture of their implements, weapons and ornaments, whereas the San were strictly of the Stone Age. However, scientists believe that the common elements between the Khoi and San people are sufficiently significant enough to warrant the conclusion that they are of the same racial stock and their languages belong to the same language family; indeed that the Khoi were once San people. For convenience the two groups have been brought together and are referred to as the Khoisan peoples of South Africa.

Normally described today as black Africans, Negroid Bantu-speaking peoples (classified on the basis of linguistic, rather than racial or anthropological, criteria – these being the use of an agglutinative language in which the root *ntu*, or its derivatives, means 'person') followed, many believe, in various swirling migrations, some of which came down the lowland coastal plain that stretches along Africa's great eastern seaboard. Others moved

down the centre of the continent or migrated down the sub-continent's drier western regions. These people were agricultural-ists and pastoralists and as their populations grew, so pressures on the environment increased; indeed the main motivation that constantly drove the Bantu-speaking people southwards in search of new areas for settlement was the depletion of the natural resources and land fertility within an accessible radius of where they had first settled. It was probably about 2000 years ago when the earliest ancestors of South Africa's indigenous Bantu-speaking peoples crossed the Limpopo River and started planting the first agricultural crops to be grown in South Africa.

In more recent years people came from Europe to settle on the shores of South Africa. At first it was only a handful of people who belonged to the Dutch East India Company and their task was to grow vegetables and hunt for meat to supply passing company-owned ships as they ploughed their way across the seas to and from their trading stations in the East. But this handful soon grew and the small settlement and garrison established at the foot of Table Mountain eventually became a town. At the same time, successive waves of white settlers radiated out from Cape Town, crossing the rivers and mountains that lie to the east, and equipped with ploughs, guns and tools to build homes and farms.

At first the impact on the environment of black migration from the north and white migration from the south was contained by the limited numbers of people involved. But as population numbers increased and trade multiplied, so the impact of humankind's destructive hand escalated and nature's integrity began to be increasingly violated. This has now intensified to such an extent that today, even with active conservation agencies and formal conservation programmes in place, the only real wild places left in South Africa are those that were protected from man's predation as a result of their remoteness and inaccessibility. The hope for the future is that people are beginning to understand that nature cannot be taken for granted and that caring for the environment is essential for the survival of humankind. But in South Africa the ravages of poverty, which have been worsened by the unequal distribution of land among the nation's people, make this understanding difficult. Therefore it is only when conservation, allied to the sustainable utilization of natural resources, can be shown to have tangible and lasting benefits for local communities that there will be any real hope for the long-term future of South Africa's wild places.

RIGHT *For the San people, who once roamed freely across the vast plains of the Kalahari Desert, the donkey has become an important means of transport. A father and daughter move home with all their worldly wealth.*

BELOW *San rock paintings are the ancient reminders of a people who were the first to record their presence in southern Africa. A characteristic feature of San art is the depiction of animals and their relationship with humankind.*

BOTTOM *Digging sticks were used by South Africa's early inhabitants to wrest roots and tubers (used for food and medicines) from the hardened soil. Hollowed out stones were placed at the tip of these digging sticks in order to give them additional weight and strength.*

PLANT LIFE

In South Africa natural vegetation depends more on climate than on soil and the most important climatic factor is rainfall. Due to the generally low levels of rainfall much of the country is semi-arid and consequently the predominant vegetation types relate to these conditions. As a result of this low and variable rainfall, South Africa is poorly endowed with indigenous forests.

Indigenous forests

True timber forests, with creepers and tree vines entwined around magnificent hardwood trees, such as Yellowwood (*Podocarpus* spp.), Stinkwood (*Ocotoea bullata*), and Assegai-wood (*Curtisia dentata*), as well as an abundance of epiphytic mosses, lichens and ferns, are largely confined to a well-watered strip which begins at George in the south and extends intermittently in an easterly and northeasterly direction as far north as the Drakensberg mountains in Mpumalanga. The most extensive, and best known, of these indigenous forests occur in the George–Knysna–Tsitsikamma district where they cover about 45,000 hectares (111,195 acres) along a narrow coastal belt situated between the sea and the Outeniqua–Tsitsikamma mountains. At Clarkson the forests peter out and do not reappear until the Amatola Mountains near Alice in the Eastern Cape. Here, around Hogsback and Stutterheim, fairly substantial patches of forest occur. Again there is a long gap – until Engcobo in the former Transkei where some pristine natural forest areas still manage to survive. Added together, these patches amount to another 60,000 hectares (148,260 acres). A few forest patches still occur along some of the mountains and in the valleys of KwaZulu-Natal, but much has been exploited and

little remains of the former glory of these indigenous forest areas. Indigenous forest appears in small patches along the escarpment edge overlooking the lowveld in Mpumalanga, but the total area of these forest remnants does not amount to much more than 2400 hectares (5930 acres). In total, South Africa's natural forest areas cover less than 25 per cent of the country's surface. This paucity is a combined result of the country's limited rainfall and the ruthless exploitation by the woodcutters of the past of these limited forests – the beautiful timber was sacrificed for furniture, building materials and trade.

Dense evergreen subtropical forests occur along a coastal strip that extends from south of East London to the Mozambique border in the north. Rainfall along this strip averages around 1270 millimetres (50 inches). In the north the rainfall is greater and this, combined with the influence of the tropical climate which extends down the Mozambique plain, results in the coastal forest becoming more extensive and less penetrable. Many of the original coastal forests, with their valuable wood and bush, have been removed – especially in KwaZulu-Natal – to make way for monotonous and seemingly endless fields of sugarcane and exotic softwood plantations.

BELOW *This dense, evergreen subtropical forest, straddling the Mkambati River in an amphitheatre-like gorge in the Mkambati Game Reserve, is an example of the coastal evergreen forests that once dominated the lower reaches of most rivers flowing into the Indian Ocean between East London and the Mozambique border. Over the years, many of these forests have been severely plundered for the hardwood trees that they contain and, today, it is only in coastal reserves, such as at Mkambati, that their magnificence can be admired.*

Mixed woodlands and savannas

Mixed woodlands and savannas occur in an uneven inverted 'U', starting along the Botswana border in the west and then sweeping across the Northern Province, north of Pretoria, continuing along the low-lying areas of Mpumalanga and Swaziland in the east and into the lowlands of KwaZulu-Natal. Woodlands are stratified deciduous plant communities which have an open tree layer with crowns less than one tree diameter apart, positioned so that they do not overlap. Scattered shrubs are a common feature and there is normally a relatively thick undergrowth of tufted grasses. Savannas are plant communities with a discontinuous layer of woody species spaced more than one crown diameter apart with a dense ground layer of grasses and forbs (a term for any herbaceous plant that is not a grass). The woody species include both deciduous trees and shrubs. The grasses are either tall-grass savannas, which are tufted and long, or short-grass savannas. It is this vegetation type, together with the rolling landscape that was sculpted by the erosion cycles of the Miocene period, that is most commonly associated in the public mind with the African continent. This is probably because savanna provides both grazing and browsing for vast herds of wildlife, which are always associated with Africa.

Grasslands

On the interior plateau grasslands are the dominant vegetation type. During summer – and depending on the extent of the summer rains – grasses grow quickly and the flat, gently rolling highveld is transformed into various shades of green. But the aerial parts of these grasses are soon killed by winter frosts and they rapidly die back, turning the green plains to austere swathes of brown.

Grasses are conveniently classified into two broad categories described as 'sweet' and 'sour'. Sour grasses have a wiry appearance and a high fibre content and are only palatable in spring and summer when the nutrients are contained in the stem. However, in order to survive the lack of rain and the rigours of winter, the nutrients are drawn back down into the roots, leaving the grasses rank, sour and valueless as a fodder. These grasses, of which *Cymbopogon*, *Andropogon* and *Trachypogon* are characteristic species, are normally found on highly leached soils in areas of high rainfall. Sweet grasses are generally shorter and have a softer appearance due to their lower fibre content. They retain nutrients in their stems throughout the dormant winter period. They are typical of the drier regions and normally occur in clayey and brackish soils; Rooigras, or 'red grass' (*Themeda* spp.), is a prominent species. The line between sweet and sour grasses is very indistinct and ill-defined – indeed, throughout many of South Africa's grassland areas they frequently occur together.

TOP *Mixed woodlands, a dominant feature of the natural vegetation in South Africa's northeastern regions, comprise tiered, deciduous plant communities that change from green during summer to rich yellows and gold in autumn.*

CENTRE *Open spaces dominated by grasslands and widely dispersed trees give African savannas a distinctive character. Before the white hunters arrived in the last century, the savanna plains of southern Africa would have been full of wild animals, some grazing on the grasses and others browsing on shrubs and branches.*

RIGHT *South Africa's interior is dominated by a high undulating inland plateau that gradually descends westward from the eastern escarpment rim. Due to a combination of altitude and an extreme continental climate, the rolling grasslands that cover the plateau are green in summer and brown in winter. Remnant herds of Black Wildebeest (Connochaetes gnou) can be seen.*

Shrub-karoo

West of the grasslands and the Kalahari thornveld (also part of mixed woodland), semidesert – dwarf evergreen scrub (which is also described as shrub-karoo) – predominates. Although this region is characterized by a low, extremely variable mean annual rainfall, it nevertheless has a rich and distinct flora. In the south it has many affinities with Cape flora, but this reduces northwards. In this arid, or semidesert, region the vegetation shows a high degree of variation in its structure and form. In an attempt to adapt to their rugged environment, the plants have assumed many strange shapes in their struggle for survival. Patches of evergreen and deciduous trees are confined to the banks of watercourses. In shallow depressions where seasonal run-offs concentrate into evanescent pans, deciduous thorn shrubs and low trees grow. Evergreen succulent shrublands are characteristic of the southern areas that border Cape flora. In the north, open savanna-like grasslands are common on the sandy soils and on pan floors.

ABOVE *The Karoo's relatively harsh environment gives rise to a vegetation cover of xerophytic plants. These are plants which have developed specialized mechanisms and physiological adaptations that enable them to withstand drought conditions. Bushes are often thorny or spiny, thereby reducing the water loss that normally occurs through leaves. Most Karoo shrubs have small, stiff or leathery leaves that are covered with hairs or wax and incorporate resins and gums which help to reduce water loss. Succulents are common in the Karoo, and are characterized by large fleshy areas in their structure in which water is stored in juice form. Also commonly found are geophytes, which are bulbous plants that have underground storage organs in the form of corms, bulbs, tubers, swollen roots, or stems.*

RIGHT *A mature Quiver Tree* (Aloe dichotoma) *has multiple candelabra-like branch structures that point to the heavens and terminate in flowers resembling spiky crowns. The tree, which is protected in South Africa, dominates the barren landscapes of South Africa's arid desert areas and, when silhouetted against the setting sun, it creates an image of great beauty in an otherwise harsh place.*

Succulent-karoo

West of the shrub-karoo, the succulent-karoo takes over as the dominant vegetation type. Covering the most arid parts of the western sections of the vast Karoo region, it stretches from St Helena in the south to Namibia in the north. This region is characterized by rainless periods – often for successive years – and, as a result, many areas are totally devoid of any form of vegetation. However, nature has used its techniques of specialization and adaptation to create many interesting plant species that can withstand the demands of this hostile environment. Decorating the desert with its candelabra-like form, the Kokerboom, or Quiver Tree (*Aloe dichotoma*), for example, is able to survive in stony desert areas where temperatures reach blistering highs during the day but drop to freezing point at night. The Halfmens (*Pachypodium namaquanum*), its name derived from its half-man, half-plant appearance, only grows in the desert areas of the Richtersveld and southern Namibia. Water and nutrients are stored in its trunklike stem, which grows up to 5 metres (16 feet) in length. It has a corolla that always follows the sun, thereby eliminating the need for leaves or any other appendages that are necessary for capturing the sun's energy. Along the river valleys the Camel-thorn (*Acacia giraffae*) marks the dried-out watercourses and waits patiently for those infrequent moments when the river comes crashing down in flood and replenishes precious water reserves in the desert's burning sands.

Cape fynbos

In the southwestern Cape, stretching from Vanrhynsdorp in the northwest, north to the Olifants River and east to the vicinity of Humansdorp, is the Cape Floral Kingdom in which *fynbos* is the predominant vegetation type. Coined by the Dutch, the name 'fynbos' is derived from the fine-leaved form of many of the shrubs together with the bushy structure of the vegetation type that is peculiar to South Africa's southwestern and southern Cape. *Fynbos* is characterized by four growth forms which occur with variable frequency in any given landscape, namely tall protea shrubs with large leaves (proteoids); heathlike shrubs (ericoids); wiry plants which are reedlike (restioids) and bulbous herbal plants (geophytes). While proteoids and ericoids do not occur in all *fynbos* landscapes and geophytes normally only appear during the winter months, restioids are always present, and form the unique distinguishing feature of *fynbos*. The location and distribution of *fynbos* is determined by four factors: summer drought, low soil nutrients, and recurring fire and wind. It is in defiance of these collective adversities that nature has created one of the richest species-diverse vegetation types in the world.

Constituting about 80 per cent of the Cape Floral Kingdom, *fynbos* covers an area of less than 90,000 square kilometres (34,740 square miles). Defined by a high rate of endemism and immense species diversity, *fynbos* gives definition to the Cape Floral Kingdom, which also includes *renosterveld*, subtropical thicket, succulent-karoo and afromontane forest. The remarkable features of the Cape Floral Kingdom led botanists to declare it one of the six floral kingdoms of the world. The other kingdoms – Palaeotropic, Neotropic, Boreal, Australasian and Antarctic – all cover vast areas that often span two or more continents. By way of comparison, it is revealing to note that the realm of the Boreal Kingdom, for example, covers all of the northern continents (some 40 per cent of the earth's total surface), whereas the Cape Floral Kingdom covers a mere 0.04 per cent of the earth's surface.

ABOVE *The folded Kogelberg Mountains provide a rugged backdrop to the fynbos-covered, rock-strewn slopes that descend from their rocky summits. In terms of area, fynbos, or 'fine bush', is the smallest floral kingdom in the world, yet it has the largest number of plant species. It is this vast diversity that has inspired and intrigued many generations of botanists and that provides endless fascination for those who take time to explore its inner mysteries.*

BELOW *The beauty of fynbos is dependent on the heat of periodic fires to regenerate and ensure its continued life. The* Helichrysum, *with its striking white flowers, is known as a 'fire ephemeral' because it appears after a fire. It lasts for a few years, during which time it produces seeds which drop into the soil where they lie dormant until the next fire stimulates a new cycle of life.*

ABOVE *The Pondo Coconut* (Jubaeopsis caffra) *is very rare in South Africa, and occurs only on the north banks of the Mtentu and Msikaba rivers in the Eastern Province. Its fruit has a fibrous coating and resembles a small coconut.*

BELOW *The Umbrella-thorn* (Acacia tortilis) *is widespread in the low altitude, dry areas of the eastern and northwestern regions of the country. It has both hooked and straight thorns, and tightly knitted and twisted seed pods.*

ABOVE   *Grasslands and forest patches cover much of the southeastern coastal belt, which is characterized by shallow soils and high water tables. A variety of plants dot the grasslands with colourful patches during the flowering season.*

BELOW   *In the Karoo, a conical hill, carved and created by the erosive forces of nature, illustrates the layers of deposition which took place over billions of years, when Africa was still part of the supercontinent.*

ANIMAL LIFE

The great variety of habitats provided by South Africa's diverse topography, vegetation and climate has favoured the development of a varied and abundant fauna that includes no less than 360 species of land mammals, some 900 species of birds and almost 400 reptile species. The mammalian fauna is characterized by a wide variety of antelope; the presence of 'living fossils' such as Elephant, Giraffe, Rhinoceros, Hippopotamus and the secretive Aardvark; vast herds of Buffalo; and Zebra. Many of these animals are prey to a diverse range of carnivores, both large and small, which together form an essential component in the food chain.

Antelope

A total of 85 species of antelope occur in Africa – the word antelope, meaning 'bright-eyed', is used to cover all species which belong to the Bovid family. When this number is compared to the Americas – where there are no true Bovids except for the Prong-horned Antelope and the Bison – or to the few species that occur in Asia, it is possible to appreciate why Africa has gained international recognition for its richly diverse and abundant fauna.

In Africa antelope are found in almost every possible habitat, from deserts to grasslands, due to their ability to exploit a wide range of plant material, ranging from grasses through herbs and fresh and dry leaves to barks, fruits and berries. Some species can even dig out underground bulbs using their hooves. Over time antelope have developed specialized eating habits: some browse on the leaves of trees while others graze on only long or short grasses. These diverse eating preferences enable many species to live in the same habitat without undue competition.

Two species, the Quagga and Cape Blue Buck, have become extinct since the advent of European settlement on the subcontinent, while the Black Wildebeest, the Bontebok (*Damaliscus dorcas dorcas*) and the White Rhino (*Ceratotherium simum*) have been brought to the very edge of extinction through indiscriminate hunting. Many species are verging on endangered in their South African range because they have become exceedingly rare and their numbers are steadily declining. This is due to their isolation from other groups of the same species (thus limiting their genetic vigour) and to the loss or degradation of their natural habitat as a result of the impact of humankind.

The distribution of antelope in their natural state largely coincides with the different vegetation types that occur in southern Africa, with each type supporting a typical range of antelope. Some species, however, such as Buffalo, can survive in a range of habitats. In the desert and semidesert areas of the Northern Cape, Botswana and Namibia, where rainfall is erratic – varying between 100 and 400 millimetres (4 to 16 inches) per annum – and there is no surface water, and where the vegetation is typically composed of small bushes and sparse tufts of grass, the dominant species are Gemsbok (*Oryx gazella*), Springbok (*Antidorcas marsupialis*), Dik-Dik (Damaraland) (*Madoqua kirki*) and Red Hartebeest (*Alcelaphus buselaphus*). Gemsbok and Red Hartebeest also occur in the arid grassland and thornveld areas in the North West and Northern provinces where rainfall is slightly more reliable (approximately 400 millimetres, or 16 inches, per annum) and surface water occurs occasionally. In the dry woodland areas of Mpumalanga and northeastern KwaZulu-Natal, which are composed of grasslands with an open canopy of trees and characterized by their parklike appearance, the dominant antelope species are Tsessebe (*Damaliscus lunatus*), Kudu (*Tragelaphus strepsiceros*), Roan (*Hippotragus equinus*), Sable (*Hippotragus niger*), Impala (*Aepyceros melampus*), Blue Wildebeest (*Connochaetes taurinus*), and Grey Duiker (*Sylvicarpa grimmia*). In the evergreen forests that are made up of the coastal forests of the eastern littoral (extending as far south as Knysna) and the montane forests in the mountainous areas of the Drakensberg, the characteristic antelope species include Blue Duiker (*Cephalophus*

ABOVE *Well adapted to life in arid regions, these Gemsbok* (Oryx gazella) *drink from the Nossob River in the Kalahari Gemsbok National Park, which only flows briefly after periodic rains.*

ABOVE *Springbok* (Antidorcas marsupialis) *are gregarious and gather in large herds on open, dry plains, such that their distribution is restricted to the drier western regions of the country.*

ABOVE *Once widespread throughout southern Africa, Blue Wildebeest* (Connochaetes taurinus) *migrate seasonally in search of better grazing and water; they need to drink frequently.*

monticola) and Bushbuck (*Tragelaphus scriptus*); Nyala (*Tragelaphus angasi*) and Red Duiker (*Cephalophus natalensis*) occur in the northeastern tropical lowland areas. In the highveld grassland areas that cover much of the central interior of South Africa, rainfall varies between 500 and 1000 millimetres (20 and 40 inches) per annum and species include Blesbok (*Damaliscus dorcas phillipsi*), Vaal Rhebok (*Pelea capreolus*) and Black Wildebeest. The Cape Grysbok (*Raphicerus melanotis*) occurs in the winter-rainfall Cape *fynbos* areas. In the swamps of the Okavango Delta and on the floodplains of the Zambezi and its tributaries, where the dominant habitats are papyrus and reed swamps with riverine forests on the banks and higher ground, Lechwe (*Kobus leche*), Sitatunga (*Tragelaphus spekei*) and Puku (*Kobus vardoni*) are the dominant species.

Some antelope species are not restricted by vegetation type and climatic considerations, but rather by topography. Notable among these is the Klipspringer (*Oreotragus oreotragus*) which is found throughout southern Africa on rocky hills and mountain slopes.

Elephant

The African Elephant is the largest land mammal in the world. The male reaches a shoulder height of between 3 and 4 metres (10 and 13 feet) and a mass of between 5000 and 6500 kilograms (11,025 and 14,333 pounds). An important feature of the Elephant is its large ears, which not only serve as a display function but also assist in cooling the animal's huge body. The back of each ear is crisscrossed by numerous blood vessels and as the ears are flapped, the vessels are cooled by the moving air and the animal's blood temperature is thus reduced.

BELOW *African Elephants once occurred throughout the entire southern Africa region, but their distribution is now restricted to game reserves in the northern and eastern regions of the country and the Addo Elephant Park in the Eastern Cape.*

At waterholes Elephants squirt their bodies using their trunks, which also helps to cool their bodies. The trunk is used, too, for collecting food and water, for smelling, defence and a wide variety of other tasks. Tusks are another characteristic of most Elephants, although some individuals and even isolated populations are tuskless. An Elephant's tusks continue to grow throughout its life and they are useful tools for food foraging and protection.

Due to extremely broad habitat tolerance, Elephants were once widely distributed throughout South Africa. Today, apart from a small and isolated population at Addo Elephant National Park and the one or two that roam the Knysna forests, they are restricted to the game reserves situated in the northern and eastern parts of the country. Elephants are highly intelligent, social animals and usually live in small well-ordered family groups, each led by an older cow or matriarch. Adult bulls usually remain apart from the family groups, joining them only when the females are ready to breed. During oestrus a cow may mate with several bulls. After mating the bulls rejoin their bachelor groups, which are well structured with an ordered hierarchy based on physical strength and skill in combat. Fighting, which can become aggressive, is ritualized and based on the two combatants pushing head to head with the area of contact being in the vicinity of the tusks. The objective is for the Elephant to push his opponent's head down.

Elephants are herbivores and although they are not specialized feeders, they do show preferences for certain species of food, such as green grass after rains and the pods of the Camel-thorn (*Acacia erioloba*). Because of the often destructive behaviour of Elephants, the huge volumes of food they require in order to survive, and the limited amount of land available for game reserves, Elephant populations have to be controlled. This is usually done by culling, which has become an increasingly controversial management tool in recent times. As a result, alternative techniques such as contraception are presently being tested.

Giraffe

The Giraffe (*Giraffa camelopardalis*) is the tallest animal in the world. Males reach an average height of 5 metres (16 feet) and a shoulder height of over 3 metres (10 feet). With their extraordinarily long necks, long legs and distinctive lattice-patterned markings, Giraffes are easy to identify. Although not an absolute rule, many observers believe that the older the animal the darker its markings. This is particularly noticeable with old bulls, which are often very dark.

All Giraffe have short knoblike horns on the top of their heads, although they are usually more pronounced in adult bulls. Fighting, which is not uncommon among the males, appears awkward and leisurely. The two animals stand alongside each other and take it in turns to strike each other with their heads.

ABOVE *Giraffe are selective browsers that use their long, prehensile tongue to strip the leaves off trees. Here a pair feeds on the small leaves of the Knob-thorn* (Acacia nigrescens).

BELOW *A typically small group of Giraffe browses on Fever Trees* (Acacia xanthophloea) *on the banks of Nyamithi Pan in the Ndumo Game Reserve.*

This involves the Giraffe swinging its head under the neck of its opponent and then striking the opponent's flank with its horns. Giraffe are the preferred prey of Lion and their defence against these and other predators is usually a kick with the forelegs – they are known to be able to deliver devastating blows.

Giraffe live in dry savanna woodland, particularly in areas dominated by acacia species such as Knob-thorn (*Acacia nigrescens*), Delagoa-thorn (*Acacia welwitchii*) and Umbrella-thorn. Once common throughout South Africa, they are now restricted to game reserves in the country's northern and eastern regions. These mainly silent, gentle giants are browsers and their long necks and legs enable them to feed on the leaves at the tops of trees and tall shrubs which other browsers are unable to reach. Although Giraffe feed from a fairly wide range of trees, they are nevertheless selective feeders. They use their lips and their prehensile tongue, which can stretch out chameleon-like for some 45 centimetres (18 inches), to strip the leaves off twigs and small branches which are then eaten. They are active feeders throughout the day – except during the hot midday period when they rest in the shade – and they continue feeding at night.

Giraffe range over extensive areas varying in size from 20 square kilometres (8 square miles) to up to as much as 85 square kilometres (33 square miles), but they are not at all territorial and therefore do not defend their areas. They are semi-gregarious by nature and usually live in groups ranging from four to 40 individuals, the latter usually occurring as a result of a restricted or favoured food resource rather than because of any social ties. These groupings are consequently unstable and, as a result, there is a constant cycle of breaking up and regrouping. Bulls only associate with females temporarily – usually only when they are in oestrus. The gestation period is 15 months after which one calf is usually born. Within a few hours of birth the young animal is strong and agile enough to be able to follow its mother. The life span of Giraffe ranges between 20 and 30 years.

Perhaps because they do not conflict with other animals in their search for food, Giraffe tend to be sociable and are often seen in the company of Impala, Wildebeest, Zebra, Kudu and even Baboons.

Black, or Hook-lipped, Rhinoceros

To call the Black Rhino (*Diceros bicornis*) black is a misnomer, since it is usually dark grey with slightly lighter underparts. Indeed its body colour is often influenced by its habit of wallowing in dust and mud. For this reason its less frequently used name, Hook-lipped Rhinoceros, is more accurate. The characteristic triangular-shaped prehensile upper lip is used like a hook to strip off leaves, flowers, fruits and the smaller twigs of trees and shrubs. Rhinos have a shoulder height of 1.6 metres (5.2 feet) and an adult mass of 800 to 1100 kilograms (1764 to 2426 pounds).

Black Rhino are solitary browsers that prefer densely wooded thickets with shrubs and trees reaching to a height of about four metres (13 feet). Adult bulls occupy discrete territories which they mark by urinating on bushes and defaecating at established middens located at particular points throughout their territory. They spread out their dung and drag their feet through their middens, thereby impregnating them with their scent which is then carried along all the paths and trails they use. This reinforces the animal's exclusive occupation of the territory.

Black Rhino have two horns situated one behind the other with the longer one in front; the record length in South Africa is just over a metre (3 feet). Rhino horn is made up of numerous matted, hairlike but very hard filaments that are attached to the animal's skin as opposed to its skull. White Rhino have similar horns, except they are usually longer. The horns, the rhino's

ABOVE *A Black Rhinoceros bull in the Mkuzi Game Reserve listens intently for sounds that will enable him to determine the direction of his perceived enemy; the animal is extremely short-sighted.*

ABOVE *Because of their square lips and close-cropping front teeth, White, or Square-lipped, Rhinoceros graze on short grasses. More sociable than Black Rhino, they often congregate in small groups.*

weapons of defence and aggression, are ironically what make the animal vulnerable to human predators. Rhino poaching has become a scourge throughout Africa and a curtain of extinction has moved steadily southwards, as these mammals are being killed in their thousands to satisfy the demand for traditional oriental medicines and ornamental dagger handles.

Black Rhino are both aggressive and pugnacious animals which will not hesitate to attack humans and other real or perceived predators. They use their upward-curved horns to impale the enemy and with their massive strength, toss the victim into the air with an upward, hooking action. Both White and Black Rhino have poor eyesight and rely on their acute senses of smell and hearing to locate the position of potential threats.

Mating follows a period of spirited courtship during which the bull and cow spar with each other, sometimes quite aggressively, to the accompaniment of much snorting and a strange growling sound. The gestation period lasts for about 15 months and a single calf is born weighing between 30 to 40 kilograms (66 to 88 pounds). The calf suckles for up to two years, although it also feeds on vegetation from the age of about three months. While the calf is small the mother is alert and highly protective and will not hesitate to charge intruders. Interestingly, when on the move the Black Rhino cow leads and the calf follows, whereas with White Rhino the order is reversed.

White, or Square-lipped, Rhinoceros

Adult White Rhino (*Ceratotherium simum*) are larger than Black Rhino; an adult male has a shoulder height of around 1.8 metres (6 feet) and a body mass of between 2000 and 2300 kilograms (4410 and 5072 pounds). Like the Black Rhino, the White, or Square-lipped, Rhino does not get its common name from the colour of its skin but rather from a corruption of the Dutch word *wijd* meaning 'wide' or 'broad' – in reference to its wide, or square, lips. White Rhino have a large distinctive hump above the neck and an elongated head that is carried low – often only a few centimetres above the ground. Like the Black Rhino, the White Rhino has two horns, the front longer than the back. The record length for a White Rhino horn in South Africa is 1.58 metres (5 feet).

In southern Africa at the turn of the century the White Rhino had been all but exterminated by hunters, with the exception of some 35 animals that were restricted to the Umfolozi Game Reserve in KwaZulu-Natal. Through being protected, their numbers slowly increased until they spread into the adjoining Hluhluwe Game Reserve. By 1961 their numbers had increased to such an extent (some 700 animals) that a major capture and translocation programme was introduced known as Operation Rhino in which White Rhino were removed to game parks throughout Africa. To date over 4000 animals have been successfully relocated and the rhino populations at Hluhluwe–Umfolozi have been stabilized at 1200 White Rhino and 300 Black Rhino.

White Rhino are grazers and show a distinct preference for short-grassed areas within thick woodlands with access to water nearby. They are more sociable than their cantankerous cousins, the Black Rhino, and family groups ranging from two to five individuals are common. Sometimes larger groups come together for short periods, particularly around waterholes and mud wallows. White Rhino have a well-organized social structure based on the territory they occupy, which is suitably demarcated, patrolled and defended by a single territorial bull. It is interesting to note that the territorial bull will allow other bulls, both adult and subadult, to live within this territory providing they exhibit submissive behaviour patterns in his presence. White territorial bulls mark out their territory in the same way as Black Rhino bulls, as already described above. Cows and their calves do not belong to any particular bull's territory, but when they leave one to go to another the territorial bull in the territory they presently occupy may attempt to prevent them from leaving. Like White Rhinos, they feed in the cooler hours of early morning and late afternoon and rest in the shade during the heat of the day, lying on their brisket. While dozing, their ears constantly move about like radio antennae, listening for impending danger signals.

White Rhino are relatively slow breeders. Sexual maturity is reached at about five to six years of age and cows can reproduce every three to four years. The gestation period is around 16 months, and the new-born calf weighs between 40 and 50 kilograms (88 and 110 pounds).

Hippopotamus

The Hippopotamus (*Hippopotamus amphibius*) is a large, rather rotund animal with a broad-muzzled head, bulbous eyes, small ears, short legs and a smooth, hairless body. The shoulder height of an adult is 1.5 metres (5 feet) and fully grown males weigh up to 2000 kilograms (4410 pounds). These animals are nocturnal and semi-aquatic, spending most of the day submerged in water with just their nose and eyes sticking out above the surface. At night they emerge from the water to graze, preferably on short grasses. Their broad, flat lips enable them to crop the grass at ground level, thereby creating a lawnlike effect – particularly in those areas where creeping grass species, such as *Cynodon dactylon*, are common. During the winter months, or on cool summer days, hippos come out of the water and sleep in the sun on warm sandbanks. They are sociable animals and gather in schools of up to 15 individuals, which are usually composed of cows and calves with a dominant territorial bull in overall control. Territories are marked out both in the water and on the land with demarcations being strongest within and near the water. The bull marks his territory by scattering his dung with a vigorous sideways flick of the tail onto rocks and bushes.

Hippos are vociferous animals while in water and their deep-throated grunts are an evocative call from primeval Africa. Their apparently lazy and lethargic disposition belies an unpredictable, aggressive streak that makes veterans of Africa very wary of these animals; they have taken more human lives than any other animal on the subcontinent. Hippos have very few natural enemies, although Lions have been known to attack single adults and Hyena and Crocodiles prey on young calves.

BELOW *Hippopotami spend most of the day submerged in water, especially during hot spells. Although usually sociable, solitary bulls are often aggressive and can be very dangerous.*

Aardvark

The Aardvark (*Orycteropus afer*) is an unusual animal that looks something like a cross between a pig and a kangaroo. It has a long piglike snout, long tubular ears, a kangaroolike tail, and short powerful legs that end in panlike feet with long nails. Covered with short, light, sand-coloured hair, its body is approximately 140 to 160 centimetres (55 to 63 inches) long, between 45 and 60 centimetres (18 and 24 inches) tall and it weighs between 40 and 70 kilograms (88 and 154 pounds). It is a secretive, nocturnal animal that shelters during the day in burrows that it digs just before retiring at daybreak and from which it emerges at nightfall. Its staple foods are termites during the rainy season and ants during the dry season. Aardvark will travel long distances in a zigzag fashion in search of these insects, either returning to their original warren or digging a new one. Ecologists point out that the disused warrens have considerable ecological significance as they provide shelter and breeding sites for a wide number of other animals, such as Warthog, Hyena, Jackal, Wild Dog, snakes, bats, mongooses and even birds.

An Aardvark uses its acute sense of smell to locate prey underground and to determine its exact location before digging commences. Once it has located an ant or termite colony, it rips it open with its large front claws and uses its long sticky tongue to pick up the prey and its eggs.

Carnivores

Carnivorous animals were once numerous throughout southern Africa – indeed they were found wherever there was plentiful prey. Because of their predisposition to prey on domestic livestock and their inherent threat to humans, they were hunted ruthlessly and their distribution today is restricted to proclaimed game reserves only. Exceptions include occasional reports of Leopards being seen in remote places outside game reserves, and rogue Lion or Hyena breaking out of reserves and moving into another area.

ABOVE *The Antbear, or Aardvark as it is more com-monly known, is a nocturnal animal with a long, piglike snout, long tubular ears and a kangaroo-like tail. It has a unique appearance and does not resemble any other animal that occurs in southern Africa.*

Lion

Lion (*Panthera leo*) are the largest of the African cats. They range in colour from reddish-gold to a tawny and pale grey. In the Tshokwane area of the Lowveld, where genetic variation with strongly reduced pigmentation occurs from time to time, near-white Lions are sometimes seen. Male Lions vary in total length from 2.5 to 3.3 metres (8ft to 10ft 8in) with a shoulder height of approximately a metre (three feet) and a body mass that varies from 150 to 220 kilograms (330 to 485 pounds). Lion cubs are faintly spotted, but as they mature all distinct markings disappear with the exception of a dark patch on the tip of the tail. All body hair is short except for the adult male's mane of long hair that extends from the side of the face on to the neck, shoulders and chest. The colour of the mane varies from light tawny to black.

Of all the cats, the Lion is the most social, living in prides which consist of one or two males, between two and as many as eight females and up to 14 juveniles of varying ages. Lions are territorial animals and they defend their territory against neigh-bouring prides as well as against wandering single Lions. In order to do this the territory is regularly patrolled and defended and the boundaries scented. Proprietorial rights are advertised by roaring, which, on a still night, can carry for up to 8 kilometres (5 miles). Once they are about three years old, young Lions are forced out of the pride by the dominant males. They form nomadic prides and search for vacant land with sufficient game on which they can settle and establish their own territories.

Nomadic males, either singly or in pairs, also replace terri-torial males when the latter become too old to defend their territories and service their females. The nomadic males either kill the old male or drive him out and take over the pride. They usu-ally kill all the cubs of the former territorial male and this induces the females to come into oestrus, thus allowing the new males to father their own cubs.

Lions usually hunt cooperatively, mainly at night or in the early hours of the morning. The prey is stalked and careful strategies are employed, with the females doing most of the killing. This is usually done by breaking the prey's neck or suffocating it to death. Feeding is a group activity, but considerable competition, aggression and tension accompanies it as each animal tries to ensure a fair share of the kill. Often young Lions and cubs are unable to assert themselves and in times of scarcity this may result in minimal food reaching them and they may well starve to death. Lions' preferred prey consists of mammals, primarily ungulates, in more or less the following order of preference: Wildebeest, Impala, Zebra, Waterbuck, Kudu, Giraffe and Buffalo. However, when food is scarce they widen their range of prey from field mice to baby Elephants as well as to a wide range of non-mammalian prey.

Lions do not have a fixed breeding period. Litters consist of between two to six cubs, born after a gestation period of 110 days. Mating is a highly vocal and aggressive marathon event which takes place many times over a period of two to three days. The lioness gives birth to her young in a sheltered spot, suckles them and leaves them there when she goes out hunting. The cubs are weaned at six months and reach sexual maturity at 24 months.

Lions have the ability to tolerate a very wide range of habitats, from deserts to woodland and open savanna. Contrary to popular belief, Lions will seldom attack human beings, preferring to retreat if given the choice. If threatened, they will drop down into a crouching position, flatten their ears and emit grunts and threat-ening growls, while flicking their tail tips rapidly from side to side. Just before launching their attack, their tails will jerk.

BELOW *A young Lion licks the remains of a Burchell's Zebra killed earlier in the day. Lions observe a 'pecking order' in their feeding habits, usually enforced with a fair amount of aggression. The males have first choice and are followed by the females and then the younger lions. The cubs get the left-overs.*

Leopard

Once widespread throughout South Africa, Leopard (*Panthera pardus*) are only found along the mountain ranges of the Cape and in the game reserves and game ranches of the Bushveld and Lowveld. The total length of adult males varies between 1.6 and 2.1 metres (5 and 7 feet), with a shoulder height of between 70 and 80 centimetres (2 and 3 feet) and a body weight of between 20 and 90 kilograms (44 and 198 pounds).

These beautiful, secretive cats range in colour from almost white to a deep russet with black spots on their legs, hindquarters, flanks and head; the rest of the body is covered with black 'rosettes' which incorporate a deeper tone of the animal's basic colour. Leopard occupy various habitats, ranging from high mountains to coastal plains and from high rainfall to low rainfall areas. Their preferred habitat, however, is dense forest patches and riverine bush.

Leopard are solitary animals that only come together for a few days to mate, after which they go their separate ways. They are mainly active at night, although in isolated areas where they are unlikely to be disturbed, they may come out from their hiding places during the cooler daylight hours. Their hunting technique is to stalk their prey and then make a final dash in order to grab the animal and bite deeply into the back of its neck. The victim is then dragged to the top of a tree where it is cached, well out of the way of scavengers. The Leopard eats its victim leisurely over a period of a couple of days. It has a wide-ranging diet which includes insects, rodents, birds and medium-sized, and sometimes large, antelope. In mountainous areas dassies and baboons make up an important part of the Leopard's diet. It is also known to eat carrion, frogs and fish.

ABOVE *Leopard have the ability to adapt to a very wide range of habitats, from high mountains where temperatures are often low to coastal plains where temperatures are considerably higher. They are also found in both high and low rainfall areas. Water is not essential for their survival.*

Leopard are territorial animals that mark their territories with urine, droppings and tree-scratching points. The size of the territory largely depends on the availability of food, but may vary from 10 square kilometres (4 square miles) to several hundred square kilometres. They are mainly silent and stealthy animals, although they occasionally call with a strange rasping sound.

Female Leopards bear from one to three cubs after a gestation period of about 100 days. At birth the cubs are much darker than the adults and they are kept hidden in a secluded spot and suckled by the mother for about three months. They remain with her until they are able to fend for themselves, which is usually between a year and a half and two years. After this they leave their mother to find their own territory.

Cheetah

Cheetah (*Acinonyx jubatus*) are smaller than Leopard, with adult males ranging in length from 1.8 to 2.2 metres (6 to 7.2 feet), and having a shoulder height of between 60 and 80 centimetres (24 and 32 inches) and a body weight of between 40 and 60 kilograms (88 to 132 pounds). They are slender, streamlined animals capable of reaching speeds of up to 100 kilometres per hour (63 miles per hour) which they can sustain for limited distances in pursuit of their prey. They are lighter in colour when compared to Leopard and their spots are solid. They also have two 'tear streaks' which run from the inner corner of each eye to the corner of the mouth. The tail is ringed and has a white tip. The Cheetah is the only cat that does not have fully retractable claws and these can be clearly seen in the pug marks they leave in the sand. Cheetah used to be found throughout South Africa in a variety of habitats, but they have largely been hunted out except in the Bushveld and Lowveld where they still occur in small numbers as well as in the game parks of KwaZulu-Natal, where

ABOVE *Being secretive animals, cover is of paramount importance to Leopards and they frequently use trees as a place of refuge or to store surplus food.*

ABOVE *Cheetah use their tremendous speed and agility to track down their prey. After catching up with this Springbok ram, the Cheetah will knock it down and then bite deep into its throat before suffocating it to death.*

BELOW *While resting, Cheetah keep a constant watchful eye on what is happening around them. Although they are adept predators themselves, there can be no complacency in the African bush as predator easily becomes prey.*

they have been reintroduced. Cheetah tend to be solitary animals, but they are a lot more sociable than Leopard and as a result subadults often stay with the mother for longer periods, giving rise to the common sightings of groups of four to eight animals.

They generally prefer open woodland, savanna and open plains, avoiding where possible denser thickets and riverine habitats. Their preference for open areas is primarily because of their preferred method of hunting, which is based more on speed and agility than on stealth and ambush. Because they prefer to track down their prey, open plains and space in which to manoeuvre are more important to them. The Cheetah's hunting technique is to stalk its prey for a short distance and then to give chase at high speed. When it catches up to the victim it uses its front paw with its exposed claws to knock it off balance. This gives the Cheetah the opportunity to clamp its jaws on the throat of the victim and to suffocate it. The prey is usually eaten on the spot after disembowelment, although occasionally it may be dragged under nearby bushes for shelter. The preferred prey of Cheetah ranges from small to medium-sized ungulates, such as Impala, Duiker, Steenbok and Warthog, but when necessary they will also kill the young of Wildebeest, Sable, Tsessebe, Zebra and Kudu. Occasionally they lose their prey to larger and more aggressive predators, such as Hyena and Lion. Unlike Leopard, they are not carrion-feeders.

Cheetah are well known for their predilection for sitting on anthills and rocky outcrops and in the branches of trees, from which they can survey the surrounding countryside. These vantage points usually become a territorial prerogative and are marked by spray-urination.

From two to five cubs are born per litter and young animals are well hidden in order to provide them with a measure of security while the mother goes out hunting. Young cubs remain with the mother for about 18 months, or until they have learnt to hunt.

Spotted Hyena

Hyena characteristically have heavy forequarters which stand higher than their hindquarters. They are short-haired and fawn-yellow in colour with dark-brown spots that occur all over the body except on the head, throat and chest. The total length of the Spotted Hyena (*Crocuta crocuta*) ranges between 120 and 180 centimetres (47 and 70 inches), it has a shoulder height of 85 centimetres (33 inches) and a mass of between 60 and 80 kilograms (132 and 176 pounds). Spotted Hyena have rounded ears which stand permanently erect. Although the Spotted Hyena once roamed across most of South Africa, today it is restricted to the northern and eastern regions of the country. Its favourite habitat is open woodland.

Hyena live in family groups or clans numbering up to 18 animals and are normally led by a female. Strong social ties exist among clan members and this is vividly demonstrated when they greet one another – an elaborate ceremony is adhered to, involving much mutual sniffing of genitalia. The clan is territorial and its territory is mutually defended by its members. The animals forage nightly, either singly or in groups of two or three. They are highly vocal animals and have a varied repertoire of whooping, giggling and cackling calls.

Spotted Hyena have traditionally been viewed as cowardly scavengers, but after a series of scientific studies was done it was established that in addition to scavenging they are highly efficient and regular hunters. Their prey ranges from newly born antelope lambs to adult Kudu, Zebra and Wildebeest. They are rapacious eaters and will consume their victims virtually in their entirety – meat, offal, skin and bones. The Hyena's wide-ranging diet includes not only the animals they kill but also reptiles, rodents, insects, the faeces of other carnivores, birds, grass, aged or injured Lions, and also their own dead.

One to four cubs are usually born in summer after a gestation period of 110 days. They are dependent on their mother's milk for a period of about eight months and they are weaned after a year at which time they join their mothers on hunts.

Brown Hyena

Similar in size to the Spotted Hyena, the Brown Hyena (*Hyaena brunnea*) has a long shaggy coat with a dense mantle of hair on the back and shoulders. The mantle is lighter in colour and contrasts quite markedly against the overall dark-brown colour of the body. The Brown Hyena has a short, bushy tail. Its ears are sharp and pointed and are always erect. Like the Spotted Hyena, it has powerful jaws which enable it to crush bones.

Due to their wide habitat tolerance, Brown Hyena were once found throughout southern Africa, but due to human pressure on the land they are now found mainly in the drier western parts of the country – particularly in the Kalahari, as well as in Namibia and even along the extremely arid Namib Desert coastal belt. They are normally solitary animals that forage alone, although several animals who are believed to be part of an extended family will share the same territory as well as the burden of raising cubs. They are principally scavengers, eating the remains of any carcass they find as well as insects, fruits, birds and bird's eggs. Occasionally they hunt, but only tackle animals smaller than themselves – such as springhares and antelope lambs. They mark their territories by pasting secretions from their anal glands on grass stems. A curious custom observed by Brown Hyenas is ritualized fighting, when animals of the same sex from adjoining territories meet up with one another. Animals of the opposite sex are more tolerant towards one another.

The Brown Hyena is more nocturnal than the Spotted Hyena. During the day it generally rests in its den, which is usually underground in a disused Aardvark warren or deep within a dense thicket. It is capable of living independently of a permanent water supply, but will drink water when it is available.

Receptive females mate with wandering males rather than with the males of their own group. Two to three cubs are born after a gestation period of 90 days. They are born with their eyes closed and spend their first months in the den. Once they start taking solid food other members of the group will bring food to them. After about 15 months they are able to fend for themselves.

ABOVE *Feeding on a Giraffe carcass, a Spotted Hyena remains alert and wary as it constantly searches its immediate surroundings for potential danger. Note the difference between the hind- and forequarters.*

ABOVE *The Brown Hyena always looks dishevelled, unlike its spotted cousin. It is also smaller and more nocturnal than the Spotted Hyena, and is mainly restricted to the Kalahari. Today it is on the Endangered Species list.*

African Wild Dog

Heavily marked with white, yellow and brown coats, Wild Dog (*Lycaon pictus*) are about the same size as a German Shepherd. Slender in build and with long legs, they have rounded ears, a black muzzle and a black stripe between the eyes that extends over the head. They used to occur widely throughout Africa, but today are restricted to the larger reserves and to various isolated and uninhabited areas. In South Africa they only occur permanently in the savanna and woodland regions of the Skukuza, Pretoriuskop, Stolsnek and Malelane sections of the Kruger National Park, although they have recently been introduced to the Umfolozi-Hluhluwe Reserve Complex in KwaZulu-Natal. The Wild Dog is probably the rarest large carnivore in South Africa.

Wild Dog are specialized hunters that live in packs of between 10 and 15 animals. Predominantly diurnal, they prefer to hunt in the cooler hours of the early morning or late afternoon. Hunting is done by sight and once the pack has spotted a herd of prey it selects an individual and then slowly moves towards it, quickening its pace as the quarry starts to move off. The pack seldom deviates from its selected prey and will continue to chase it over several kilometres at speeds known to reach more than 50 kilometres per hour (31 miles per hour). If the prey is a small animal the dogs will pull it down immediately, but with larger prey they will bite and tear chunks of meat off it until the animal is weakened through shock and loss of blood and they are able to overpower it. Wild Dog are rapacious and frenzied feeders and it does not take long before their prey is ripped to pieces and

ABOVE *African Wild Dog are noted for their huge rounded ears which enable them to pick up not only low intensity sound but also very high frequency sounds. Pups, such as these, are normally born in the dry winter months when the grass is short and hunting conditions most favourable.*

quickly consumed. Probably because of this violent behaviour, Wild Dog have gained the reputation of being wanton killers. However, research done on Wild Dog in recent times has revealed that they only kill for immediate needs.

African Wild Dog are not territorial, preferring instead to range freely over very wide areas. The average home range in the Kruger National Park is about 450 square kilometres (174 square miles), but in arid areas the home ranges are estimated to run into thousands of square kilometres.

Pups are born in winter when the grass is short and the hunting conditions are best. Normally only one female comes into oestrus and she is covered by the dominant male. Between two and 10 pups are born after a gestation period of about 70 days. For the first three months of their lives the pups remain within the confines of the den, after which they are taken on hunts of increasing difficulty with the adult dogs. The cohesive social structure of Wild Dog is evidenced not only by their collaborative hunting but also in their breeding behaviour. For example, when pups begin to eat solids, adults returning from a hunt will regurgitate meat for their consumption as well as for those adults who remained behind to look after the pups or who were ill and could not go on the hunt.

REPTILES

Based on the findings obtained from research done on the earliest known reptile fossils (which were small lizardlike creatures found inside fossilized tree stumps), reptiles developed from amphibians during the Carboniferous period and date back some 315 million years. In subsequent periods of time reptiles evolved into a bewildering variety of forms, including the giant dinosaurs and their relatives which, for a period of 150 million years, dominated the earth. Today reptiles are either remnants of that period or they have evolved subsequently. Reptiles are divided into four orders: Order Chelonii, which includes turtles, tortoises and terrapins; Order Squamata, which includes snakes, lizards and amphisbaenians; Order Crocodylia, which includes crocodiles; and Order Rhynchocephalia, which includes the tuatara. Each of these orders is well represented in southern Africa, with the exception of the tuatara, which is only found on some of the islands on the north coast of New Zealand. In total there are some 400 reptile species in South Africa.

Chelonians are found in almost every environment – aquatic, oceanic and terrestrial – in both tropical and temperate climatic zones. Southern Africa has a very rich chelonian fauna, with five sea turtles in coastal waters, nine terrapins in freshwater rivers and vleis, and at least 12 land tortoises.

Turtles

The five species of marine turtle occurring in South African waters are the Loggerhead (*Caretta caretta*), Olive Ridley (*Lepidochelys olivacea*), Green (*Chelonia mydas*) and Hawksbill turtles (*Eretmochelys imbricata*), all of which belong to the Cheloniidae family, and the Leatherback (*Dermochelys coriacea*), which is the sole survivor of the Dermochelyidae family. Both families are of the suborder Cryptodira, which is one of the oldest reptilian orders that still survive today with a fossil history that goes back over 200 million years.

Over the many millions of years that sea turtles have been on earth, their numbers have contracted or expanded as competition between the different species has intensified during times of stress

ABOVE *A Leatherback Turtle buries itself in the sand before digging a flask-shaped hole into which it will lay its eggs. Turtles lay their eggs on the same beaches used by successive generations over the years.*

or waned during times of plenty. In the process some turtle species have disappeared altogether while others have increased in number in accordance with nature's unbending rule of 'survival of the fittest'. Along the coast of South Africa a remarkable degree of compatibility in the types of food eaten and the spatial relationships between the five species occurring here has been achieved. For example, in the shallow littoral zone, that is from the water's edge down to about 10 metres (33 feet) below the sea's surface, the Green Turtle predominates. It is carnivorous during the first six to 12 months of life, after which it is herbivorous, eating algae and various marine grasses (*Caulerpa filiformis*, *Gelidium cartilagineum*, *Codium manzii* and *C. dutheii*). The Hawksbill Turtle inhabits much the same part of the shallow littoral zone but also goes deeper, to about 20 metres (65 feet) below the sea's surface, and it feeds on sponges. Adult Loggerhead Turtles are found mainly in the subtidal zone – that is from 20 to 30 metres (65 to 100 feet) below the sea's surface – and their principal foods are molluscs, hermit crabs and echinoderms (sea urchins). Olive Ridley Turtles are found at the greatest depths along the South African coastline, from 30 to 50 metres (100 to 165 feet) below the sea's surface. They feed on crabs and prawns.

It is only on the surface of the sea where competition for food does exist and that is when turtle hatchlings first enter the sea and drift for up to two years along the ocean's currents. During this stage the food for all five species is made up of pleustonic fauna such as Bluebottles (*Physalia* spp.), most species of Jellyfish Medusae and Purple Storm Snails (*Janthina* spp.)

Adult turtles vary in size. Leatherbacks, which are the world's largest marine turtles and therefore the most spectacular, grow to a length of between 2.5 and 3 metres (8.2 and 10 feet) and weigh in excess of 900 kilograms (1985 pounds). Green Turtles, which are the most widespread throughout the southeast Indian Ocean area and the most numerous, vary in length from 1.2 to 1.5 metres (4 to 5 feet), with a maximum mass of 275 kilograms (606 pounds). Loggerhead Turtles, which are the second most common species to occur in the waters of southern Africa but the most frequent visitor to South African beaches, vary in length from a metre to 1.2 metres (3 to 4 feet) with a mass of 160 kilograms (353 pounds). The Hawksbill Turtle seldom reaches more than a metre (3 feet) in length and has a maximum mass of 135 kilograms (298 pounds). The Olive Ridley is the smallest and least common turtle in the southern African region with a maximum length of 80 centimetres (30 inches) and a mass of 46 kilograms (101 pounds).

All the turtle species that occur in the southern African region demonstrate similar reproductive behaviour, although it is mainly the Loggerheads and Leatherbacks that actually come ashore and nest along the beaches of Maputaland. The other species nest in the tropics on the beaches of Mozambique, Madagascar and the small tropical islands that lie in between.

Tortoises

Land tortoises belong to the suborder Cryptodira, which means 'hidden neck' and refers to the tortoise's ability to shorten its neck through an S-shaped flexure and so withdraw its head into its shell. Tortoises have adapted to terrestrial life and have ensured their continued existence through the provision of substantial self-protection. Their bodies are encased in thick domed shells, the tops of their heads are protected by a number of distinct shields and their feet are armoured. When threatened they are able to retract their heads and feet into their shells, which are impenetrable to virtually all enemies. Five genera and 12 species occur on the southern African subcontinent, of which three genera and 10 species are endemic.

ABOVE *The Leopard Tortoise* (Geochelone pardalis) *is the largest tortoise in South Africa; the adult normally weighs between 8 and 12 kilograms (18 and 26 pounds), except in the Eastern Cape where it grows much larger. Specimens weighing more than 40 kilograms (88 pounds) have been noted.*

Terrapins

These are unusual Chelonians which are named for having only three claws on each foot. Terrapins have flat, soft shells that allow for a measure of flexibility. These reptiles are fully aquatic and have long, extendable necks and a snorkel-like nose which together enable these active and shy animals to remain under the surface of the water for long periods. The Marsh, or Helmeted, Terrapin (*Pelomedusa subrufa*) is the most common in South Africa and is found throughout the country, with the exception of the Richtersveld region. Only four other species are found in South Africa, three of which occur solely in northern KwaZulu-Natal and one, the Pan Hinged Terrapin (*Pelusios subniger*), only in the Kruger National Park.

Snakes

Southern Africa has 130 species of snake, of which 35 have fangs and have sufficient venom to cause symptoms – which result from poisons ranging from a toxicity less than that of a bee sting to being highly lethal. Only 14 species, however, have caused human death on the subcontinent, including the five species of cobra (*Naja haje, N. melanoleuca, N. nivea, N. mossambica, N. nigricollis*), the two species of mamba (*Dendroaspis polylepis* and *D. angusticeps*), the Rinkhals (*Hemachatus haemachatus*), the Namibian Coral Snake (*Aspidelaps lubricus infuscatus*), the Puff Adder (*Bitis arietans*) and Gaboon Adder (*Bitis gabonica*), the Boomslang (*Dispholidus typus*), the Bird Snake (*Thelotornis capensis*), and the Rock Python (*Python sebae*). Snakes occur throughout South Africa and at least one venomous species occurs in all of the country's regions.

Crocodile

The Nile Crocodile (*Crocodylus niloticus*) is the only species of the Crocodylidae family that occurs in South Africa. When fully grown it can extend up to 6 metres (20 feet) in length and can weigh up to 1000 kilograms (2205 pounds). It has long, powerful jaws with prominent teeth. The eyes and valved nostrils are situated on top of the head and the skin is covered with scales or plates that are geometrically arranged, with those covering the head fused to the skull. The Crocodile's back feet are webbed to facilitate manoeuvring during mating and when positioning itself prior to ambushing its prey. Juvenile Crocodiles are greenish in colour with irregular markings along the back and sides, while the throat and underbelly are a uniform yellow. Adult Crocodiles change colour to a uniform olive or light grey with a lighter yellow or cream belly.

Nile Crocodile are found in the major rivers that drain to the east of the country as far south as the Thukela River; in earlier times they were found as far south as East London. Other favoured habitats include perennial pans, estuaries, wetlands and mangrove swamps. However, few viable populations exist outside formal game reserves and conservation areas. Nile Crocodile feed principally on fish, particularly Barbel, but they also ambush small antelope and other game when they come to the water to drink. There are many known instances of larger game such as Zebra and even Buffalo having been taken. The line is not drawn at humans and fatalities still occur. The prey is seized and dragged into the water where it is drowned. The Crocodile then softens the food by biting it. If it is too large to be swallowed whole, it rips pieces of flesh off before consuming them. In order to enhance its power to do this in water, the crocodile takes a full bite and then spins on its long axis, thereby adding centrifugal force to its purchase. The Nile Crocodile is known to store food under a bank so that it can be eaten over a period of time. Crocodiles are also carrion eaters. Although usually solitary hunters, cooperative behaviour in feeding and breaking up prey does occur among Crocodiles.

During the midday heat these reptiles come ashore and bask in the sun. When temperatures are particularly high they lie with mouths agape as this enables them to lose heat through evaporation. Crocodiles are able to swim effortlessly without breaking the surface of the water by using their broad, flattened tail as a large flexible 'paddle'. The life span of a crocodile is around 60 years in captivity, but very large wild specimens are likely to reach 100 years. Their principal enemy is man, although eggs and early juveniles are vulnerable to attack by leguaans and birds.

The breeding patterns of Nile Crocodile are well entrenched and both parents play an active role in the care and rearing of their offspring. The breeding season commences in May when the males develop a dominance hierarchy. Mating takes place in the water after an elaborate, if not awkward, courtship. Once fertilized, the female selects a suitable sunny bank – above the floodline and with both good cover and drainage – on which to establish her nest. During the month of November she will come out of the water at night and dig a 40-centimetre-deep (16-inch) hole at the nest site, into which she will lay between 16 and 80 white, hard-shelled eggs. The female does not feed during this period but remains at the nest in order to defend her eggs against predators and other Crocodiles, only leaving it briefly to drink water. Although the male remains in the vicinity, presumably on guard, the female does not allow it to come close to the nest site. Between 84 and 90 days later the hatchlings announce their readiness to discard their shells with high-pitched cheeps that can be heard 20 metres (65 feet) away. The female opens the nest and carries all the hatchlings to the water in her mouth where they are washed before being released. They remain close together in a nursery area for between six to eight weeks with the female in very close attendance. After that they are allowed to move further afield and begin to catch their own prey, which consists of insects, fish, terrapins, birds and small mammals. The sex of hatchlings is determined by ambient temperature during the period of incubation, with females produced at lower temperature (26 to 30°C, or 79 to 86°F) and males at higher temperatures (31 to 34°C, or 88 to 93°F).

ABOVE *Mole Snakes* (Pseudaspis cana) *are found throughout South Africa. They are normally large, averaging between 100 and 150 centimetres (40 and 60 inches) when fully grown; the longest recorded specimen was 210 centimetres (83 inches) from tip to tail. They are harmless yet useful snakes that live underground, mainly in abandoned animal burrows from where they prey on moles, rodents and other small animals.*

BELOW *The Egyptian Cobra* (Naja haje) *is predominantly found in bushveld and lowveld regions. Two races are found in southern Africa: N.h. anulifera, which is less aggressive and is found in an arc-shaped region stretching from northern KwaZulu-Natal through the lowveld in Mpumalanga to eastern Botswana; and the more aggressive N.h. anchietae which is found in western Botswana, Namibia and northwest Zimbabwe.*

BELOW *On hot days the Nile Crocodile comes ashore to bask in the warm sun. If the temperature gets too high, the crocodile has to open its mouth in order to lose excess heat through evaporation.*

BELOW *The Flap-neck Chameleon* (Chamaeleo dilepis) *obtains its name from the flap of skin at the top of the neck, just above the shoulders. It is a large chameleon, averaging in length between 20 and 25 centimetres (8 to 10 inches); the biggest specimen ever recorded was 35 centimetres (14 inches).*

ABOVE *The Tree Agama* (Agama atricollis) *is a beautiful lizard that is often seen clinging to a tree trunk while gently nodding its head. The top of the head of a breeding male is brightly coloured, varying from coppery-green to brilliant ultramarine; the sides of the head are blue-green and the throat a striking peacock blue. Its principal food is termites and flying ants. Contrary to popular belief, the Tree Agama's bite, although painful, is not poisonous. In South Africa it is only found in the subtropical coastal region of KwaZulu-Natal.*

BIRDLIFE

South Africa falls within the Ethiopian zoogeographical region and, with the exception of sugarbirds, all the birds occur in families that are widespread throughout the sub-Saharan region. Because of the varied habitats within the southern African sub-region (the subcontinent south of the Zambezi River), birdlife is prolific with an estimated 920 species (including seabirds) occurring in the subcontinent, of which 112 are endemic – primarily because they occur in habitats that are not common to other parts of the African subcontinent. These habitats are made up principally of the highveld, the increasingly arid environments to the west of the country, the high mountains of the east and the Cape Floral Kingdom in the southwest.

South Africa is richly endowed with birds of prey that range from the massive Lappetfaced Vulture (*Torgos tracheliotus*), one of the largest flying birds in the world, to the small Pygmy Falcon (*Polihierax semitorquatus*) and Little Sparrowhawk (*Accipiter minullus*). There are 51 resident species of raptor in South Africa and in the summer months this number is further augmented by 12 migrant raptors.

Twelve different species of owl occur in South Africa, ranging in size from the Giant Eagle-Owl (*Bubo lacteus*), the adult of which weighs 1.6 kilograms (3.5 pounds), to the diminutive Pearlspotted Owl (*Glaucidium perlatum*), which weighs a mere 70 to 85 grams (2.5 to 3 ounces).

ABOVE *The plumage of the Scops Owl* (Otus senegalensis) *is intended to resemble the bark of a tree, as camouflage is its principal form of defence during the day. Its plumage is commonly grey, but sometimes chocolate brown.*

Approximately 20 different species of seabird regularly breed along the South African coast. Of these the Cape Gannet (*Morus capensis*), Cape Cormorant (*Phalacrocorax capensis*) and the Jackass Penguin (*Spheniscus demersus*) are the most important numerically. In comparison with other parts of the world and taking into account the length – some 5000 kilometres (3107 miles) – and diversity of the South African coastline, this is not a large number of resident breeding species. However, this number is considerably augmented each summer by an influx of nonresident, non-breeding migrants from the northern hemisphere. The migrants are primarily waders, a group of shore birds that is poorly represented by resident species in South Africa. Also during the southern winter a number of seabirds migrate to South African waters from the Antarctic and sub-Antarctic islands.

In common with other southern hemisphere temperate lands South Africa is not rich in breeding species of ducks, geese and swans of the family Anatidae. Indeed there are only 16 indigenous breeding species in South Africa, which is not many when compared to Britain, for example, which has 47 species. However, South Africa has about 80 species of true waterbirds that belong to other families. The largest group is the herons, of which there are 17 species. The next most numerous are members of the Rallidae family, of which there are 11 species including rails, crakes, moorhens and coots. The eight species of plover are the next largest group of waterbirds, all of which are to be found along open shorelines, sandbanks, pans and marshes.

There are about 50 species of bird considered to be typical forest birds, some of which are widely distributed throughout South Africa while others are endemic to specific areas. A number of birds of prey are forest residents, including at least two owl species – the Wood Owl (*Strix woodfordii*) and the Barred Owl

ABOVE *Gurney's Sugarbird* (Promerops gurneyi) *is a common resident along South Africa's eastern escarpment slopes where it feeds on the nectar of proteas, aloes and red hot pokers* (Kniphofia *sp.*).

(*Glaucidium capense*). The magnificent Crowned Eagle (*Stephanoaetus coronatus*) is another denizen of the forest. It either perches on the lower branch of a tree and waits for its prey to pass beneath it or it uses its large wings and sharp eyes to manoeuvre skilfully through the forest to catch monkeys.

By far the majority of South Africa's bird species occur in mixed woodland habitats. Two main factors account for this. The first is the diversity of habitats, ranging from densely wooded parkland through to the arid scrubland bordering the Namib and Kalahari deserts. Different habitats ensure a diversity in bird species because of the wide-ranging environmental niches offered in each habitat. Secondly the extension of woodland from the tropics into South Africa means that many tropical bird species reach their southern limit inside South Africa.

A little over 100 species are resident in the rolling grassland and scrubland of South Africa. These birds are subdued in colour in order to blend in with the monochrome landscapes in which they are resident. Should they be brightly coloured they would become easy prey for their predators. This makes bird-watching in these regions difficult. Another complicating factor is that grassland birds fly less than their arboreal cousins. Their food consists of bulbs, seeds, insects, ground fruits, molluscs and other forms of small life, the search for which requires more walking and less flying.

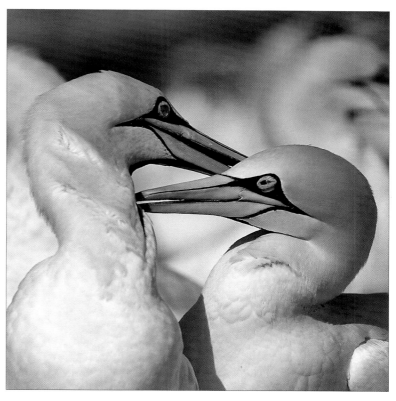

ABOVE *Cape Gannets are a common sight at Lamberts Bay on the Cape west coast where they gather in their thousands on offshore islands. Here a pair of birds engages in mutual preening.*

Life in the desert requires birds to be able to adapt to two major conditions. The first is the scarcity of water and the second is the heat of the desert. Desert birds meet the first condition by obtaining water from one or a combination of three sources: access to one of the limited waterholes or springs in the desert; extracting moisture from their prey; or producing 'metabolic water' through their own digestive processes. In respect of the second condition desert birds, like mammals, pant in order to lose excess body heat during hot desert days. But panting results in a loss of water and therefore desert birds need to develop a tolerance to overheating in order to be able to accommodate the fine balance between losing heat maximally and water loss minimally.

ABOVE *The Ground Hornbill* (Bucorvus leadbeateri) *is a black, turkey-sized, mainly terrestrial bird with a bright-red face and throat pouches. It produces a deep booming call, usually at dawn.*

ABOVE *The Lanner Falcon* (Falco biarmicus), *the largest falcon in South Africa, is identifiable at all ages by its rufous crown, which in juvenile birds is usually a paler colour. It is a fairly common, widespread resident.*

INSECTS

Insects are defined as those organisms that have six membranous, jointed legs and their mouth parts outside their mouths. The majority of insects live in or on the soil, but they are also found in water, in the air, in or on plants, in the sea or living as parasites either internally in the bodies of animals (including humans) or externally as bloodsuckers. By any measurement, whether it be in terms of diversity or abundance, insects are considered to be the most successful organism on earth. Some 70 per cent of all species in the animal kingdom are insects, which means that there are more insect species than all other species put together. It has been estimated that there are some three million insects in Africa alone. While insects represent a major threat to humankind's continued agricultural food resources, both during growth and storage, some insects have been enlisted by humans to help fight against imbalances in nature such as the invasion of exotic plants. In the Kruger National Park, for example, beetles have been introduced which attack invasive exotic weeds such as *Pistia*, *Eichhornia* and *Salvinia*.

One of the largest insect groups is made up of butterflies and moths, all of which belong to the order Lepidoptera. Worldwide there are more than 150,000 species, of which some 12,000 occur in southern Africa. Although distinction between butterflies and moths is not always clear-cut, as a group they differ from other insects in two fundamental ways: they have wings that are covered with microscopic dust-like scales which give colour and determine the patterns on the wings and sometimes the body as well; and they have a coiled proboscis or 'tongue' which is used to suck nectar out of a flower or moisture from damp ground.

BELOW *The larva of the Tiger Moth (Family Arctiidae) is covered in a dense coat of long hairs to repel predators. These hairs give the larva a 'woolly' appearance and give rise to the moth's other common name, woolly bear. These moths feed on grasses, herbaceous plants and lichens.*

ABOVE *Pyrgomorphids (Family Pyrgomorphidae) have the shape and build typical of grasshoppers. A characteristic feature of many species of this family of insects is their striking appearance due to their vividly contrasting coloration. These colours warn predators that they are poor-tasting and often poisonous.*

ABOVE *Distinctive features of damselflies of the suborder Zygoptera are their very thin and short antennae, and the fact that they do not hold their wings over their abdomens but rather at right angles to this part of the body while resting. Damselflies' bodies are normally very colourful and their wings have a metallic lustre which adds to their beauty.*

LEFT *Honeybees (Family Apidae) are highly socialized insects and live in communities where a division in labour is well developed, with the result that different segments of the community have specific tasks to perform. Various species of honeybee nest in trees, while others prefer to nest in rock crevices or in the hollow trunks of dead trees.*

BELOW *Numerous dung beetles belong to the subfamily Scarabaeinae, and range in size from a few millimetres to over 50 millimetres (2 inches). Several genera, for example* Scarabaeus *and* Kheper, *make balls of compacted dung and roll them to their nests, while others make their nests within the dung pad.*

BELOW *The African Monarch Butterfly (Danaus chrysippus aegyptius) is well known and widely distributed throughout the whole of southern Africa. It is also known as the Southern Milkweed Butterfly, in order to distinguish this subspecies from other subspecies that are also known as African Monarchs but are found elsewhere in Africa.*

WILD SOUTH AFRICA AT RISK

A common perception of Africa, fostered during the colonial era, is of a dark continent teeming with wild animals. While it is true that most of southern Africa was once 'darkened' from horizon to horizon with vast herds of antelope, Wildebeest, Buffalo and other wildlife, sadly this is no longer the case. Mankind has invaded and exploited this wilderness paradise and taken it over.

At first man came unobtrusively, hunting and gathering only what was needed to satisfy his immediate and simple needs. Living at one with nature, he left only bones, artefacts and his simple paintings on the walls of the caves he lived in. Above all, there was a respect for nature. This was reflected in early folklore and mythology, which was intimately tied to nature's caprice and its capacity to meet mankind's needs. With the passage of time, people discovered that iron could be extracted from certain rocks and that it could be used to fashion spears, which were used not only to assert authority over others but, increasingly, over certain aspects of nature. Natural forests and bush were cleared to make way for food crops, and animals – no longer hunted by small groups of men using primitive bows and arrows – were herded together and slaughtered in great numbers. Nevertheless, with nature's infinite capacity to repair damage and absorb mankind's excesses, a shaky modus vivendi existed between indigenous Iron Age populations and nature across the great plains of Africa.

This was the position until the voyages of discovery brought Europeans to African shores. Together with their sophisticated weaponry, these white men brought a different ethos – one that saw animals either as vermin or as artefacts of trade, and natural forests as a source of timber for building. From the moment explorers, hunters, traders and settlers invaded Africa's southern tip, the wildlife habitats of the subcontinent came under constant and ever increasing threat. As the settlers advanced northwards from their base in the Cape, they steadily rolled back the wild places which once covered vast reaches of southern Africa. In

sum, they decimated the wild animals 'whose numbers literally baffle computation', to quote the report of an early explorer. Elephant were hunted for their ivory and some animals were killed for the food they provided. In the first seven months of 1824 in the frontier town of Grahamstown alone some 22,700 kilograms (51,075 pounds) of ivory changed hands. In 1825 the export of 48,050 kilograms (105,950 pounds) of elephant tusks and hippo teeth through Algoa Bay (now Port Elizabeth) was only the beginning of the real trade in ivory which reached far greater proportions in Port Natal, or Durban. Vast herds of wild animals were also wantonly slaughtered in order to satisfy some primeval bloodlust that pulsated in the veins of men who found enjoyment in killing and a way to boost their self-esteem while heaping indiscriminate death upon the great plains of Africa.

The competition for space and resources between farmers and settlers and wildlife led to even further destruction of animal populations. Consider Archdeacon Merriman's observation in 1853 that: 'It will take a long time, however, thoroughly to stock these plains of the Orange River Sovereignty with cattle, instead of the vast troops of gnus, quaggas and antelopes of several kinds which now swarm like locusts, though they are beginning to give way a little before English dogs and guns which are incessantly at work amongst them.'

Over half a century later farmers and settlers exerted increasing pressure on the Natal authorities to throw open the hitherto disease-ridden northern areas of Zululand and Maputaland for cattle ranching and white settlement. Prior to this these areas were out of bounds for domestic cattle because of a deadly cattle disease known as *nagana*. In 1897 Surgeon-Major (later Sir) David Bruce found that the disease was caused by a parasite. Carrying out his research in a crude laboratory high up in the Ubombo

BELOW *Besides the early professional hunters, who slaughtered vast numbers of wild animals for commercial gain, mass hunting parties were also responsible for the wide-scale destruction of wild South Africa.*

ABOVE *No photographic records remain of the destruction brought about by European traders of the 17th, 18th and early 19th centuries to South Africa's hardwood forests. However, decimation of the country's few remaining natural forests still continues as subsistence farmers cut deeper into these areas, opening up more land for the cultivation of crops in order to ensure human survival.*

Mountains, Bruce discovered that wild animals (immune to the disease) were the host for *trypanosoma* parasites and that Tsetse Flies transmitted them from infected animals to healthy ones. The authorities believed that if they eliminated the wild animals they would be able to wipe out the deadly parasite and thereby open up large tracts of land for white settlement. In August 1917 the whole of the magisterial district of Ubombo was thrown open to hunters who were permitted to shoot anything except Rhino, Hippo and Nyala. As a result, thousands upon thousands of animals were wantonly destroyed in the name of civilization and progress. The Tsetse Fly, however, continued to transport the *trypanosoma* parasite in from other areas. In 1919 the Ingwavuma district was therefore thrown open to hunters and again there was an orgy of bloody destruction. In 1931 the administration decided to abolish the Mkuzi Game Reserve and 'to take steps to kill off all the game in a systematic and well organised manner', to quote the proclamation. Fortunately the reserve survived this lunacy. In the end, the senseless slaughter of Zululand's wild animals, which continued intermittently until 1943, achieved absolutely nothing other than the destruction of a precious heritage.

Vast tracts of natural forest and other vegetation were also destroyed after Europeans set foot on African soils. When Jan van Riebeeck arrived at the Cape in 1652 to establish a refreshment post, he ordered the felling of some trees that grew on the eastern slopes of Table Mountain in order to make way for a fort and housing. This triggered off a period of ruthless exploitation that continued for over two centuries, during which many natural forests in the Cape disappeared – never to be replenished. Early in the 18th century attention turned to the coastal forests in the George–Knysna area and a timber boom developed. Exploitation of the forests was highly wasteful and any form of control was

nonexistent. It has been estimated that well over 90 per cent of all timber that was felled at this time was left to rot in the forest, with only the choicest grades and sizes being removed. Fires, which were indiscriminately lit to burn the undergrowth and to chase away game, often got out of hand and burnt down large tracts of forest. On visiting the region in 1778, Governor Joachim von Plettenberg was alarmed at the extent of the damage. Johann Frederick Meeding, subsequently appointed as Resident at Plettenberg Bay, was assigned the challenging task of regulating the exploitation of the forests in the region. While Meeding did sterling work, exploitation continued unchecked in many places. By 1846 the situation had become so serious that the government closed all worked-out forests, divided them into agricultural lots and sold them off by auction. As a result, vast tracts of South Africa's hardwood forests became history.

In 1878, the Lieutenant-Governor of Natal, Sir Henry Bulwer, set up a commission of enquiry into the state of Natal's forests. Farmers in Natal were loading their wagons with once plentiful, but now precious, woods and trundling them over the Drakensberg to exchange them for sheep in the treeless Orange Free State. Indigenous forests represented capital in the hands of the woodcutters, who rapidly swarmed through the colony hacking down Red Milkwoods (*Mimusops caffra*), Stinkwood and Sneezewood (*Ptaeroxylon obliquum*), and the amber wood of the Yellowwood. Bulwer's Commission estimated that by 1878 over a third of Natal's natural forests had already disappeared.

The destruction of wild animals and natural forests were not the only inroads that were being made into the wild places of South Africa. In 1878 the Natal Legislative Assembly was presented with a Bill designed to try and prevent the overfishing that was taking place along the Natal coast. In support of the Bill the Colonial Treasurer stated that 'Destruction is going on wholesale and unless you do something about it there will not be a fish left in the waters of Natal'.

Another inevitable consequence of humankind's interference with nature was pollution, which raised its ugly head long before 1880 when a commission of inquiry was appointed to investigate the extent of contamination caused by the sugar mills pouring effluent into the streams, rivers and lagoons of Natal.

Fifteen years before the appointment of the Commission the problem of alien vegetation had already become such a serious one that a law aimed at eradicating the noxious Burr Weed (*Xanthium spinosum*) had been promulgated and passed. Little was done by the authorities to implement the law's enactment, however, and the weed became the precursor of a flood of alien vegetation which today threatens every single natural habitat in South Africa.

While the exploitation of South Africa's fauna and flora was widespread and self-indulgent, there was a realization right from the beginning that nature's bounty was not endless and that those natural resources which directly served the interests of the Dutch East India Company and its officials should not be overexploited. Within two years of landing at the Cape, Van Riebeeck issued an instruction that people were to have two meals per day instead of three and that they were to be limited to half a penguin per day per person (penguins, which were obtained principally from Robben Island, were an important part of the early settlers' diet). In 1657 a decree was issued prohibiting the shooting of birds and game animals, except by Company officials. In September 1658 Van Riebeeck's council took action to control the ivory trade and in October of the same year another decree was issued to control woodcutting. In 1702 it became an offence to damage a tree on public property – the penalty for which was a public flogging at the foot of the gallows.

In 1680 Simon van der Stel became the first governor to impose penalties for illegal hunting; he also introduced a licence system with an open season limited to two months. Punishment for infringement included fines, the confiscation of firearms and corporal punishment. Van der Stel wrote that '... unless steps are taken immediately, there will be nothing left of the indigenous species as these will be destroyed or driven away and the area ruined'. For the next hundred years or more the Dutch East India Company issued numerous *placaaten* (decrees) and regulations in an effort to control the hunting and exploitation of the Cape's fauna and flora, but despite all these rules the reality was that the Company did not have the capacity to enforce them and, worse still, the general public did not understand the need for their existence. When the English took over the administration of the Cape in 1806 and later when the Boers trekked into the distant corners of the subcontinent to set up their independent republics, the respective lawmakers continued to express their concern at the rapid destruction of those natural resources which were seen to be of direct beneficial value to their citizens. However, it is important to understand that their ethos was human survival and not the conservation of nature for its own sake.

In September 1858 the newly established Zuid-Afrikaanse Republiek (South African republic), realizing the consequences of the ruthless destruction of game, ruled that 'No person shall be entitled to destroy more game in any manner whatsoever than is absolutely necessary for his own consumption or can be loaded onto a wagon, or to kill game solely for hides'. In a period of 40 years, between 1850 and 1890, the Orange Free State Republic passed five important laws which were relevant to the conserva-

BELOW The statue of Paul Kruger in the Kruger National Park not only commemorates the naming of this world famous game reserve but, perhaps more importantly, the contribution Kruger made to conservation in South Africa.

tion of wildlife, the South African republic passed six laws and Natal four. But despite the passing of these laws the slaughter in the veld continued apace. The bills of lading in the ports of Cape Town and Durban showed escalating volumes in the export of wildlife products – elephant tusks, rhino horns, ostrich feathers, hides, skins, and bones. In 1866 a group of hunters operating in the Kroonstad district of the Orange Free State exported no less than 152,000 blesbok and wildebeest skins in that one year alone. And so while the hunting restriction laws were possibly irksome, they were certainly not a deterrent to men such as Sir Abe Bailey who reaped a fortune from the gold that nature had locked into the reefs of the Transvaal and leased huge farms for the sole purpose of hosting hunting parties which in a single day would bag hundreds of antelope and other game.

It was Paul Kruger, President of the South African republic (which later became the Transvaal), who first acknowledged the fact that the existing laws were inadequate to save South Africa's wildlife from total destruction. He realized that conservation of the Republic's wildlife heritage could only be achieved if specific areas of the country were set aside for the exclusive use of wild animals. In 1884, the year after he was elected president of the near-bankrupt Republic, Kruger expanded to an impassive *Volksraad* (council) his concept of establishing a game reserve in which animals could find refuge from the omnipotent onslaught on the veld. But these were men of wide open spaces, where animals were part of the landscape and had been freely provided by a benevolent God, and thus the thought of spending the Republic's precious money on protecting animals was anathema. In 1889, after the discovery of gold and an influx of foreigners into the country (adding to the pressures on the country's wildlife resources), Kruger reintroduced his ideas to the *Volksraad*. After careful persuasion he managed to get an amendment passed to Act 10 of 1870, which prohibited all forms of hunting on state lands. The amended law did go some way to reducing the destruction of the Republic's animals, but Kruger knew that he did not have the means of enforcing it and therefore his efforts were largely stillborn. The idea of creating a game reserve never left him, however, and he eventually managed to persuade the *Volksraad* to set aside a portion of land for this purpose. In August 1889 Proclamation R8009/89 was passed in terms of which certain farms in the bushveld situated between the Swaziland border, the Lebombo Mountains and the Pongolo River were proclaimed as a Government Game Reserve. And so, on 13 June 1894, the first game reserve in Africa came into being, consisting of farms totalling 17,400 hectares (42,995 acres), and Africa's first game ranger, a Dutch immigrant called Frederick van Oordt, was appointed. Within the reserve's boundaries 'all hunting, shooting, searching for, or in any manner taking possession of or trying to take possession of, chasing, driving away, or disturbing game in any manner whatsoever' was prohibited.

On 26 March 1898, just 18 months before the outbreak of the Anglo-Boer War, the Sabie Game Reserve – situated between the Sabie and Crocodile rivers on the eastern border of the South African Republic – was proclaimed. During the war, however, many animals were caught in the crossfire, used as moving targets, or slaughtered by soldiers who were forced to live off the land. Furthermore the disruption and hardship caused by war put the protection of wild animals far down on the list of government priorities and it remained so for many years after the conclusion of hostilities. However, the Sabie Game Reserve survived and after considerable debate, it was extended along the Transvaal's border with Mozambique right up to the Limpopo River, South Africa's northern border. Its name was changed to the Kruger National Park, in honour of the man who realized that the only

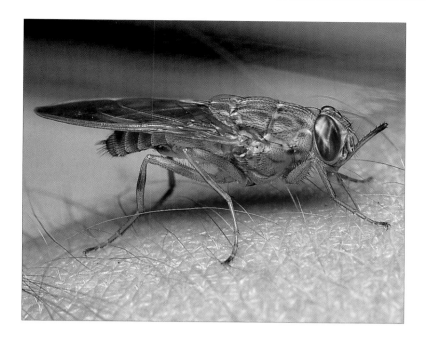

ABOVE *The Tsetse Fly, the curse of early pioneers, played an important role in holding back the avalanche of potential settlers who sought new lands to farm and areas on which they could graze their cattle.*

CONSERVATION IN SOUTH AFRICA

Of the 10 forms of conservation that are internationally recognized, the national park is probably the best known. International criteria governing the selection of areas for national parks are based on three principles: the protection of a national park must be entrusted to central government; each park must be of a viable size; and the public must have access to it.

The essential purpose of national parks is not only to preserve the plants and animals that live there but also the processes that govern their existence and their ability to adapt to a changing environment. This means that the central mission of national parks is to conserve ecosystems rather than species. In comparison to the total land area of the country, the land area that has been set aside for conservation in South Africa does not fare favourably. South Africa has 17 major national parks, yet only about two per cent of the country's total land mass has been allocated to nature conservation; many countries which have neither South Africa's financial resources nor its wide natural diversity have allocated up to five times more land area for this purpose.

An important objective among conservationists is for a national park to be proclaimed for each of the country's diverse ecosystems. However, with the new political dispensation's drive for massive upliftment of the rural poor for example, other priorities always seem to take precedence. Unsustainable population growth and rapidly rising land prices are just two of the problems that impact on the allocation of land for the purpose of establishing national parks. Another obstacle facing conservation is the multiplicity of authorities responsible for conservation control and management in South Africa. With the breakdown of the apartheid political system – in terms of which every so-called national state had its own conservation authority – a number of difficulties have arisen relating to the amalgamation of the separate nature conservation authorities in various regions and their restructuring into single entities.

South Africa's wild areas fall into three broad divisions: national parks; game reserves controlled at a national, provincial or municipal level; and lodge-based game reserves that are privately owned and controlled. According to the 4th VISION annual, the latest report of the Endangered Wild Life Trust, there are 39 national parks and nature reserves in South Africa, all of which are controlled and managed at either a central government or provincial level. There are also privately owned game management and safari areas that allow for a certain level of exploitation, such as subsistence fishing, ecotourism and trophy hunting. The legal status of each category differs with national parks enjoying the highest level of legal protection. Here human activities are very strictly controlled and exploitation, except for management purposes, is absolutely forbidden. Game reserves are controlled in terms of specific rules and regulations promulgated by the control authority for that area, for example the responsible provincial authority. Municipal and privately owned reserves may be proclaimed relatively easily in terms of specific ordinances, but they can equally easily be deproclaimed and so their long-term tenure is vulnerable.

In the final analysis it is only when both politicians and the public alike understand the essential role that nature conservation plays in securing mankind's continued existence on earth, that its future can be more or less assured. South Africa faces a particular challenge in trying to balance the needs of nature and the needs of rapid development. Rhetoric, however, is easy to mouth and while verbal commitment to a process of conservation-based community development may sound good on political platforms and at conferences, its translation into practical action is another matter. Only the future will tell whether the country's leaders have the vision and wisdom to meet the challenges involved.

real hope for South Africa's wild heritage was to preserve it in places from which mankind could be excluded. The management and control of the park was put in the hands of an independent National Parks Board created in terms of the National Parks Act, which was passed in parliament on 31 May 1926. And since that time the National Parks Board has played both a pioneering and consolidating role in establishing and managing South Africa's wild places.

In Natal five areas were demarcated and set aside for wildlife in 1895, and in 1897 four were proclaimed official game reserves. These were the Umdhletshe Reserve, situated adjacent to False Bay in Lake St Lucia and which was subsequently deproclaimed in 1907; the Hluhluwe Valley which is now the Hluhluwe Game Reserve; the Umfolozi Junction, lying at the junction of the Black and White Umfolozi rivers and which today comprises the Umfolozi Game Reserve; and St Lucia Game Reserve, comprising the water and islands of Lake St Lucia. The impact of white settlers, who wanted to settle in the conquered territories of Zululand, together with the notion that the only way to overcome the impact of the dreaded *nagana* disease was to destroy all the wild animals, nearly resulted in the destruction of all game in Zululand and the deproclamation of all game reserve areas. Thankfully sanity eventually prevailed and the already proclaimed game reserves survived and new ones have since been created. After careful nurturing by the Natal Parks Board, which was established shortly after World War II, the badly decimated game stocks have recovered – but only in proclaimed game reserves.

Human population growth and development have pushed the wild places of South Africa into the country's remotest corners. It is no longer men driven by a lust for blood or a desire to make money that threatens their existence. Poor people, driven by the ravages of poverty, are plundering the country's remaining wilderness areas in their search for open land on which they can grow their crops, graze their animals and build their houses. The wealthy, on the other hand, are constantly pushing for economic development and expansion, which also represents a major danger to many of South Africa's wild places.

NEW CHALLENGES FACING WILD SOUTH AFRICA

Throughout Africa wildlife and its conservation is under increasing threat as a result of greed, ignorance, political instability and the aforementioned unsustainable population growth. There are, however, other equally important, although less obvious, contributing factors. To begin with, wildlife sanctuaries are generally surrounded by areas of extreme rural poverty. As the level of deprivation increases so competition for land intensifies. There is also a perception among the rural poor that any land set aside for conservation has been taken from them, resulting in feelings of exclusion and resentment. The reasons for this date back to the colonial era when, throughout colonial Africa, European settler regimes introduced the concept of the 'King's Game', meaning that all wildlife on communal lands that once belonged to the local people automatically became the property of the king, or the state. For the indigenous residents on these lands, wildlife was no longer a common property resource but something that belonged to someone, the king. Since wild animals now belonged to the state and not to the people, and were perceived as being separate from their environment, they were only tolerated by the people if they could be poached. Furthermore, with the proclamation of game reserves, government representatives from newly established departments of nature conservation began to enforce state ownership of wildlife, thereby simultaneously reinforcing the process of alienation and creating hostile relationships with the local community.

The disparity between pristine national parks, which are in ecological balance, and the consistently overutilized areas in which rural populations have to live accentuates the bitterness and resentment that the people feel towards conservation. The reality is that in their daily struggle for survival, rural people cannot afford to take a long-term view on wildlife. Their interest and focus centres on their immediate circumstances and, without the means to counter poverty, overexploitation of natural resources must escalate. The problem of rapid and unsustainable population growth further intensifies this overexploitation. Communication programmes targeted at nonliterate audiences, which are designed to explain the need for conservation of wildlife and the need for all people to achieve a workable relationship with their natural environment, are scarce; those that are available are not sufficiently widespread to make a notable impact on the problem.

Formal management of South Africa's wild places has to become directly relevant to the rural poor, and this must be done through a holistic approach to conservation that links wildlife management with relevant social development. Indeed, the message from leading conservationists is that conservation has to move beyond the indulgent protection of endangered species, such as rhinos, and the establishment and maintenance of national parks. Dr John Hanks of the Peace Parks Foundation calls for the need to put the conservation of nature into the context of increasing human need and misery. Conservation and environmentalism must now be concerned with human survival, quality of life and sustainable development.

In the escalating crisis of survival, the remaining vestiges of wildlife – those wild places that are either inaccessible or locked away behind Parks Board fences – will come under increasing threat. Wildlife managers can either defend their areas of conservation against the erosive forces of endemic poverty (by building bigger fences or arming themselves with more guns) or they can be instrumental in helping to uplift the quality of life of their impoverished neighbours. In South Africa's rural areas, game parks are often the only tangible assets and therefore they provide the only possible vehicle for creating wealth and a base for further development in the region. If local communities can be empowered, for example, by including them in park planning and management, they can address some of the critical issues that face them. It is clear that wildlife management in a Third World environment has no future if it attempts to distance itself from the escalating rural poverty that surrounds its borders by adopting the 'fences and arms' approach.

The humanized approach to wildlife management strives to achieve a practical symbiosis between the mainly rural poor and the environment in terms which will benefit both. It is however only in recent times that this new approach has been given some sense of direction. In 1980 the World Conservation Strategy emphasized the importance of linking protected area management with the economic activities of local communities. The need to include local people in park planning and management was adopted enthusiastically by wildlife managers at the 1982 World Congress on National Parks in Bali. The congress called for increased support for communities living adjacent to parks through measures such as education, revenue sharing, participation in decision-making, compatible development schemes near or even inside protected areas and, where compatible with the protected area's objectives, access to resources. What the World Bank calls Integrated Conservation Development Projects (ICDPs) originated directly from this evolution in thinking.

The need for reconciliation

The unsustainable growth in human population that is such a prominent feature of the 20th century has created enormous economic and political pressure for making 'productive' use of the world's remaining natural ecosystems. This has placed an enormous strain on the environment at all levels - from massive natural resource exploitation by rich and powerful multinational

ABOVE *Game rangers play a new and vital role in wild South Africa today. They no longer simply patrol fences and keep poachers at bay, but rather have to win the hearts and minds of all those who are affected by conservation.*

corporations to the aforementioned erosive exploitation by the rural poor. Conservationists have to somehow resolve the fundamental conflict between increasing need and decreasing resources in order to reconcile humankind with the environment. Just as the early pioneers took the initiative in declaring certain places as conservation areas and fought against the pressures of rapacious greed, indifference and careless development, so modern conservationists must broaden their involvement in community development in order to reach out to their neighbours through a programme of proactive community upliftment. Sadly, despite the desperate need to link conservation with development, it seems to be an elusive goal that lies more in the realm of rhetoric than action.

It is important to remember that white hunters and settlers were responsible for the wholesale destruction of animals and the vast clearing of land for commercial farming in South Africa. Secondly, without detracting from its successes, early protectionist legislation in South Africa was promulgated by white politicians and administrators. The indigenous people were therefore neither considered nor consulted in either the destruction of nature's bounty nor in its subsequent protection. They, for their part, had a different, almost reverent, view of nature, attributing to it certain mystical qualities which had to be respected through the observance of rituals and taboos. It is true that indigenous human population densities were low, but then so too were those of the colonizers and yet this did not stop them from doing enormous damage to the environment in a very short period of time. In 1854, the immortal words of Native American Chief Seattle, in response to a request to sell his land, sums up the difference that existed between white settlers and indigenous people worldwide in their respective approaches to nature:

'*How can you buy or sell the sky, the warmth of the land? The idea is strange to us. Every part of this earth is sacred to my people … every clearing and humming insect is holy in the memory and experience of the red man. The sap which courses through the trees carries the memories of the red man. This we know. The earth does not belong to man; man belongs to the earth*'.

Although wildlife managers are aware of all these issues, the problem is how to deal with them. In 1980 the International Union for the Conservation of Nature (IUCN) published the World Conservation strategy. This was a major milestone in the conservation movement, since it represented the triumph of the pragmatists over the romantics. The IUCN gave the word 'conservation' new meaning, namely 'the management of human use of the biosphere so that it may yield the greatest sustainable benefit to present generations while maintaining its potential to meet the needs and aspirations of future generations'. The concept of conservation may indeed include the sustainable utilization of natural resources for the benefit of people, but it remains to be seen to what extent the utilization of natural resources available from game parks will benefit local neighbours and to what extent it has changed the attitudes of local people towards formal conservation areas and game parks.

Different perceptions towards the benefits of conservation also complicate the issue. For example, some conservation authorities believe that providing access to certain resources within protected areas (such as thatching grass, firewood, reeds, and barks) on a sustainable basis is sufficient to gain the support of local communities for conservation. In contrast, the perception of the local residents is that natural resources have always been common property and that they should therefore always have had the right to harvest them freely.

ABOVE *Unsustainable population growth is undoubtedly one of the greatest challenges facing South Africa. Land and resources have a maximum carrying capacity and, when that is exceeded, the result is increasing poverty.*

Another problem is the contrary perception held by many people living in poverty along the borders of well-stocked, pristine game reserves, namely that demand will not outstrip supply. They tend to believe that utilization of natural resources by adjacent communities is prevented because the conservation authorities (more specifically, the government) want all the resources in the game reserve for themselves.

The distribution of benefits is another important factor that serves to keep conservation and people apart. In many instances, for example, the dividends earned from ecotourism go directly into the government's coffers. The local community, who through the loss of access to traditional natural resources pays a heavy price for having a national park or conservation area established in its vicinity, is excluded from the transaction and therefore receives no obvious and direct benefit. Should the community not perceive any direct benefit for itself from the park's existence, there is obvious resentment.

Perspective is also important when considering the actual physical amount of benefit the utilization of natural resources can possibly bring to local communities. For example, if, in a good year, all the meat from animals culled in the Kruger National Park were given to the local communities living along the western boundary of the park, each person would receive less than one kilogram (just over two pounds). The park is unable to provide firewood, as it has to import its own requirements from Mozambique, and it uses all the thatching grass available in the park for the maintenance of its own buildings. Therefore, the issue of linking conservation, or natural resource utilization, and community development goes beyond sharing surplus or unwanted products of conservation with the local people. Instead, the conservation authorities need to examine the variables, which collectively comprise the value of wildlife and wild places, and the rights which attain to those values. The identification of methodologies, which will appropriate these values to the benefit of the local communities on a basis that is sustainable, should also be investigated.

Perhaps one of the most contentious and intractable issues to deal with in social development and the maintenance of the environmental integrity of wild places is the matter of unsustainable human population growth. The right to bear a child, or not, is considered to be one of the most fundamental of human freedoms. And yet underlying virtually every social problem, certainly in the developing world, is the tension created by a population growth rate that is not compatible with the resource base upon which that population has to depend. The result is overexploitation of that resource base and a resultant rapid deterioration of the environment and quality of life of the people. The circle is a vicious one, because overpopulation and poor quality of life are synergistic – the one sustains the other in a rapid spiral of increasing hopelessness. It would therefore be extremely unwise for environmental planners and their political masters to ignore this reality in any programme aimed at trying to ensure the integrity of wild places, social development and political stability.

To put the situation in South Africa in context, Africa has the dubious distinction of having some of the highest population growth rates in the world. It has been estimated that the population size could explode from the present 570 million to an overwhelming 870 million in less than two decades. Famine is already threatening over 150 million people and per capita agricultural production has decreased by 13 per cent over the last 15 years. As a consequence of rising population growth and decreasing production, more than 50 per cent of the people living in sub-Saharan Africa live in abject poverty. In Ethiopia and the Sahel region of West Africa, for example, frightening famines have gripped these regions twice in the last decade because their food supplies have simply run out. International famine relief has been a temporary palliative, but death on a large scale has been – and will continue to be – the ultimate solution.

The problems in South Africa are no less acute than those of the rest of Africa. Experts have warned that at the current population growth rate, within a mere two generations, the country's natural resources and socio-economic capability will not be sufficient for its population. This is likely to result in rapidly escalating social disintegration, unemployment, poverty

and relentless misery which could become unmanageable even in the best constitutional dispensation.

The politics of population growth in southern Africa have been skewed by the conflict between black and white. In the struggle for power, both sides have seen population growth as a political weapon - forgetting, perhaps, what Pyrrhic victory the use of that weapon can bring.

Political commitment to the process of linking conservation with community development is influenced by a number of factors. The first is the reality that in the immediacy of the daily cut and thrust of political survival, politicians are strongly inclined to relegate environmental issues to the backburner because of their long-term nature. In developed countries, people are beginning to place political value on such issues as clean water, clean air and an aesthetically pleasing environment. But in the developing world, where simply surviving each day at a time is a major preoccupation for the largest proportion of the population, clean air and water and a healthy environment are not political issues that poor people can physically afford to concern them-

selves with, other than possibly in some vague, ephemeral way. And so there is little pressure for politicians to concern themselves with these issues either.

In South Africa and most other countries, conservation management is a function of government and therefore part of the bureaucracy. While this gives natural resource management the authority it needs to carry out its tasks, it often limits the scope of its activities and reduces the flexibility that linking natural resource management with community development requires. The nature of bureaucracy also tends to stifle new ideas and innovative approaches to conservation management.

WILD SOUTH AFRICA: THE FUTURE

Humankind has come a long way, and the word 'ecology' is no longer just an academic term with no relevance to ordinary people's daily lives. Today, more and more people are beginning to understand the need for biodiversity and ecological balance and consequently there is an increasing awareness at certain levels of society for the need to conserve precious natural resources. While this bodes well for South Africa's few remaining truly wild places, their only real security in the future rests in expanding this understanding to all levels of society and by being able to demonstrate in practical and pragmatic terms what dividends wild places can render to humankind.

This is beginning to happen, albeit somewhat hesitantly. Firstly, most of the conservation authorities in the country have accepted the need to implement conservation-based community development strategies and while successes achieved so far are limited and sporadic, they do nevertheless point in the right direction. Secondly, the Government of National Unity has accepted the critical need to restore much of the country's indigenous habitats as part of a water-enhancement programme involving the rehabilitation of stream catchment areas through the removal of alien vegetation. The benefits of this programme are twofold: improved water supplies and practical demonstration of the role ecological balance plays in improving quality of life and large-scale job creation. Thirdly, wild places are South Africa's prime tourist attractions and tourism is proving to be one of the country's most important growth industries. Tourism does not come without a cost however. In many ways the growth and promotion of tourism is anathema to the notion of wilderness and wild places since its very purpose is to open up wild places and to expose them to as many people as possible. For tourism to be profitable it needs people, but people en masse and wild places are largely antipathic. Both necessity and reality therefore prescribe the need for compromise and it is within the balance of this compromise, combined with an understanding of the ecological value of nature's processes and the rendition of tangible benefit at a local community level, that the future of South Africa's wild places rests.

LEFT *South Africa still has many pristine areas which are there for all to enjoy. However, it is in their rational use that the future of these areas lies. With mounting population pressures, the preservation of such areas will become increasingly difficult to achieve. The solution to this impasse lies in education, communication and practical action.*

OVERLEAF *Increasingly, as population pressures mount, the need for some sort of accommodation between South Africa's wild places and local communities becomes more and more imperative.*

Focus on
THE EASTERN COASTAL PLAIN

The eastern seaboard of Africa is characterized by a broad coastal plain that sweeps down from Somalia in the north to St Lucia in South Africa's KwaZulu-Natal in the south. The southernmost tip of this plain, known today as Maputaland, is roughly triangular-shaped and covers a total area of about 8000 square kilometres (3088 square miles). Its diverse habitats and fascinating variety of fauna and flora make it one of South Africa's most exciting wild places.

Today Maputaland, or Tongaland as it was once called, is made up of the magisterial districts of Ubombo and Ingwavuma in KwaZulu-Natal. The name, Maputaland, is both disputed and disapproved of by some, but it has become a convenient appellation for the flat coastal plain that is bounded by the foothills of the Lebombo Mountains in the west, the St Lucia lake system in the south, and the Indian Ocean in the east. The northern boundary

has no basis in geology or geography, but was formed as a result of the political compromise reached between two European colonial powers, Britain and Portugal, who, in 1875 took their territorial dispute to the French President, Marshall MacMahon, for arbitration. Sitting in his office in far-off Paris, he settled the colonial row by simply drawing a straight-line boundary from the confluence of the Usutu and Pongolo rivers to the sea.

The Zulus call Maputaland *uMhlabawalingana*, which means 'the earth that is flat' and it would be difficult to find a more descriptive name for this low-lying area which has an altitude that seldom extends more than 100 metres (328 feet) above sea level; the Lebombo Mountains, which rise up to 700 metres (2297 feet) in places, are an exception. The soils in this region are generally sandy and have little agricultural potential, except along the floodplains of the Pongolo River, which meanders across the vast, flat plains of Maputaland. Although the region is too far south to be in the tropics, a rich diversity of tropical fauna and flora predominates due to the combined influence of the warm southward-flowing Mozambique Current and the continuity of a tropical climate along the low-lying Mozambique Plain.

The fascinating interplay between Maputaland's ecological foundations, its birds, animals and plants, and the intricate web of human involvement within that environment, provides an absorbing story about one of Africa's most beautiful, yet almost forgotten, wilderness areas. Largely bypassed by the forces of human conflict that ebbed and flowed across most of the land, Maputaland escaped much of the bloodshed and strife that accompanied the settlement of some parts of southern Africa. Tsetse Fly, Mosquitoes and other disease-bearing insects formed a protective barrier, ensuring that the area remained relatively sparsely populated. As a result, Maputaland has retained much of its natural integrity and wild character.

The Maputaland region consists of six interlocking ecological zones that run from north to south parallel to the coastline. While each zone has its own distinctive features, collectively they form a kaleidoscope of constantly changing environments. The Coastal Zone includes the dune forests, the intertidal zone and, offshore, a marine wonderland alive with brilliantly coloured corals and their associated reef life. Situated just inland of the dunes is the Coastal Lake Zone, which embraces the intricate Kosi estuary and lake system in the north, the St Lucia estuary and lake system in the south, and Lake Sibaya in the middle. To the west of the Coastal Lake Zone is the Mozi Swamp and Palm-belt Zone, the major feature of which is the wetland remnants of an ancient river system that terminated just south of Maputo Bay in the north. The Sand Forest Zone of Sihangwane runs roughly along two

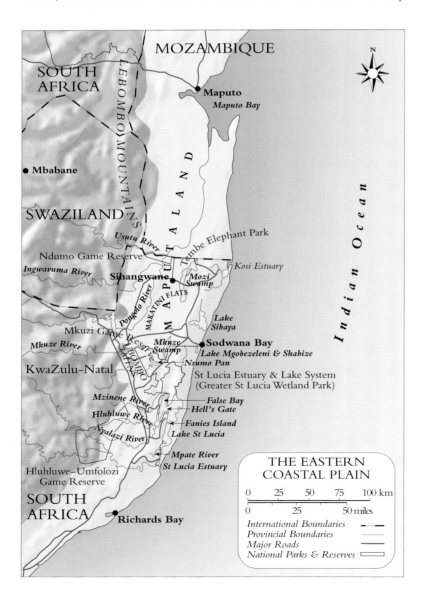

Opposite *The Goliath Heron* (Ardea goliath) *is found along the Eastern Coastal Plain and in the Northern and North West provinces; it is not a common resident. Because of its size, and its attractive combination of slate-grey and rufous colouring, it is a striking bird with an almost regal bearing.*

parallel dune lines east of the Pongolo Zone. The Pongolo Zone lies at the foot of the Lebombo Mountains and encompasses the floodplains and extensive pan system of the Pongolo River. The Lebombo Zone, which stretches along the Lebombo Mountains, makes up the western ecological zone of Maputaland.

For most of its length, Maputaland's Coastal Zone is pristine. Restless waters still crash onto virtually uninterrupted golden beaches that are little changed from those that Middle Stone Age man (circa 180,000BC) and early explorers and settlers found when they chanced upon this wonderland. The beaches and the adjacent sea have been proclaimed a marine reserve. Besides being a marine wilderness of infinite beauty, the reefs in the reserve are a vital link in the coastal food web of southeast Africa, providing a variety of foods and attracting, among others, commercially important migratory fish such as Kingfish (*Carangoides* spp.), Mackerel (*Scomberomorus* spp.) and Tuna (*Thunnus* spp.).

Maputaland's beaches are characterized by a rigid straightness that is relieved by occasional shallow asymmetric indentations. Between the beach and the huge barrier dunes that dominate the area and effectively divide the Indian Ocean from the Coastal Lake Zone are smaller hummock dunes that are covered in places with a variety of plants, such as Scaevola (*Scaevola thunbergii*) and Gazanias (*Gazania* spp.), which are capable of withstanding the rigours of close contact with the sea.

The barrier dunes form a permanent and integral part of the Coastal Zone. Towering above the hummock dunes, the seaward-facing slopes of these dunes are stabilized by dense thickets and forests that vary in height from a metre (3 feet) to between 5 and 10 metres (16 and 33 feet). This vegetation has the typical 'clipped edge' effect of sea-facing coastal bush and is very hardy as it has to cope with salt-laden winds as well as the mechanical blasting action of windblown sand. In the lee of the dunes, the influence of the sea and wind is reduced and the resultant vegetation is tall dune forests with an uneven canopy that varies in height from 6 to 18 metres (20 to 60 feet).

Created as a result of exposure to the northeast and southerly winds that prevail along the Maputaland coast, the barrier dunes exhibit an asymmetrical profile. From the Indian Ocean they ascend gradually to great heights – up to 150 metres (492 feet) near Lake St Lucia – before descending sharply on the other side. The dune range is broken in only two places along the entire length of the coast – where the rivers drain into the sea at Kosi Bay and at Sodwana Bay.

Immediately behind the forested dunes is the Coastal Lake Zone consisting of a chain of interlinking barrier lakes, lagoons and swamps set within broad open grasslands. These rolling grasslands are interspersed with lines of swamp and evergreen forests, thicket patches and heavily wooded savanna. The origin of the lakes and lagoons lies in Maputaland's ancient struggle with the sea. Once canyons on the floor of the ocean, they were carved out of an impermeable substrate by marine action. As the sea receded during the Pleistocene period (between 2,000,000BC and 10,000BC), the canyons were gradually exposed until they were subsequently sealed off on their seaward sides by sand barriers created as a result of longshore drift. These sand barriers were eventually built up by wind action into the immense parabolic dunes that line the seashore today.

Examples of this action include the four lakes of the Kosi system which are separated from the sea by a thin ribbon of land; Lake Sibaya, the largest freshwater lake in southern Africa, which is separated from the sea by a similar thin ribbon of land crowned by high parabolic dunes; Sodwana's Mgobezeleni lake system; and St Lucia, where South Africa's largest estuary system is locked behind some of the highest coastal dunes in the world.

The Mozi Swamp and Palm-belt Zone used to be a continuous shallow waterway that linked Delagoa Bay with St Lucia via the Mozi and Mkuze swamps. It is believed that this waterway was once an earlier coastline of the receding sea during the Pleistocene period. The swamps are fed by lateral subsoil drainage and in places, where the substrate is impermeable, pans and

ABOVE *Lining the beaches of Maputaland are large parabolic dunes, covered by hardy vegetation capable of withstanding the rigours of salt-laden onshore winds. The beaches of this region bear little evidence of human intrusion.*

ABOVE *The Coastal Zone of Maputaland is characterized by a string of lakes and wetlands, endowed with waterlilies (Nymphaea sp.), reeds (Phragmites sp.) and, in places, the mighty Kosi Palm (Raphia australis).*

ABOVE *The African Jacana* (Actophilornis africanus)*, or Lilytrotter, has extremely long toes and nails, enabling it to walk on lilies and other floating vegetation with impunity. Interestingly, the female is larger than the male.*

ABOVE *The Kosi swamp forest contains a variety of coastal and riverine forest trees, such as the Coast Coral* (Erythrina caffra)*, Tree Fuchsia* (Halleria lucida) *and Cape Beech* (Rapanea melanophloeos)*.*

wetlands have formed that contain numerous aquatic, herbaceous plant communities, including various grasses, sedges, herbs, lilies, and reeds. This zone is also characterized by evergreen thickets, consisting of species such as the Ironwood (*Vepris undulata*), Flat-crown (*Albizia adianthifolia*) and Silver Terminalia (*Terminalia sericea*); as well as termitaria thickets, of which the Jacket-plum (*Pappea capensis*), Magic Guarri (*Euclea divinorum*) and imposing Candelabra Tree (*Euphorbia ingens*) are important components.

But perhaps the most distinguishing feature of the Mozi Swamp and Palm-belt Zone is the predominance of the Ilala Palm (*Hyphaene natalensis*). A primary source of income for the local tribespeople is the highly nutritious wine or cider (known as *injemane* or *ubusulu* in Zulu) that is produced from its sap.

The Sand Forest Zone lies between the Pongolo floodplain and the Mozi Swamp and Palm-belt Zone. It is composed of gently undulating linear dunes, or ridges, the crests and slopes of which are accentuated by patches of sand forest. The dunes run parallel to the coastline from north to south with shallow troughs characterized by flat-floored sandy depressions situated in between. It is interesting to note that these dune lines were originally formed as a result of erosive shoreline and wind processes that followed the sea as it receded to its present position during the Pleistocene period. The highest of these ridges is a mere 143 metres (470 feet) above sea level, proving that height is a relative term on the plains of Maputaland.

ABOVE *The Thonga people tap the Ilala Palm for its sweet sap from which they make a low-alcohol palm wine that is an important source of nicotinic acid, vitamin C, potassium, and magnesium.*

Highly leached, whitish-grey acid sands predominate in the Sand Forest Zone. The only fertile soils – enriched mainly by humus and ash deposits from aeons of veld fires – occur in the surface layer, which is 10 to 20 centimetres (4 to 8 inches) deep. Because of the generally poor quality of the soils, the Sand Forest Zone has the lowest diversity of vegetation in Maputaland. Typical canopy trees found in these parts include the Lebombo Wattle (*Newtonia hildebrandtii*), which although it reaches a height of 25 metres (80 feet) elsewhere seldom reaches more than 12 metres (40 feet) in the Sand Forest Zone; the Bastard Tamboti (*Cleistanthus schlechteri*), which has a beautiful grain and is considered to be the hardest wood in Zululand; the Myrtle Bushwillow (*Pteleopsis myrtifolia*); the Torchwood (*Balanites maughamii*), a hardwood tree that reaches its southern limit in Maputaland; and the Sand Onionwood (*Cassipourea mossambicensis*). What the Sand Forest Zone lacks in diversity, however, it makes up for in other ways: this zone contains one of the finest examples of tropical dry forest in southern Africa.

Birds resident in the Sand Forest Zone are typical of those found in dry areas; common species include the Kurichane Thrush (*Turdus libonyana*), Brubru Shrike (*Nilaus afer*) and Dusky Flycatcher (*Muscicapa adusta*). The Yellow-spotted Nicator (*Nicator gularis*), Purplebanded Sunbird (*Nectarinia bifasciata*) and the African Broadbill (*Smithornis capensis*) are all rare species in southern Africa, and occur only in this zone of Maputaland. Numerous species of lizard and snake are widely distributed in the zone. Larger game animals are rare, however, their occurrence being restricted virtually entirely to the Tembe Elephant Park and Mkuzi Game Reserve, both of which fall within this zone.

BELOW *The Usutu River forms part of the northeast boundary between South Africa and Mozambique, as well as the northern boundary of the Ndumo Game Reserve. Red Cliffs, in Ndumo, affords a good view of the river as it meanders across the land between the Lebombo Mountains and the sea.*

The Pongolo Zone, the major part of which is situated along the base of the Lebombo Mountains, consists of deposits that were brought down by the rivers and streams that have drained these mountains since the beginning of time. The most important feature in this zone is the Pongolo River, which flows north on meeting the coastal plain after emerging from a gorge through the Lebombo Mountains. Most of the floodplain lies below the 50-metre (165-foot) contour from where it gradually descends to an altitude of 33 metres (108 feet) above sea level near its confluence with the Usutu River. The river meanders in a seemingly aimless fashion as it slowly makes its way to the sea, and has given birth to a series of oxbow lakes and pans that teem with birdlife and fish. In the river and pan waters

a total of 50 species of fish have been recorded, 40 of which do not occur south of the system. Each year these pans are replenished by the spreading waters of the Pongolo River as it floods its banks after the summer rains.

The Lebombo Zone comprises the Lebombo Mountains, which form the western boundary of Maputaland. Rising up from the Makhatini Flats, which average between 100 and 150 metres (330 and 500 feet) above sea level, the mountains ascend to a mean altitude of between 600 and 700 metres (1969 and 2297 feet) above sea level. The inland-facing, or western, slopes of the mountains are extremely steep, and almost precipitous in places. The seaward-facing, or eastern, slopes are deeply incised by valleys and gorges that give the mountains a rugged nature characterized by many almost inaccessible areas. Four large inland rivers cut through the mountains in spectacular gorges and flow seaward to the Indian Ocean. The largest river is the Usutu, which forms part of the northern boundary of Maputaland. The Pongolo, which rises near Wakkerstroom, is the second-largest river in the region. The remaining two rivers, the Mkuze in the south and the Ingwavuma, which lies between the Usutu and Pongolo rivers in the north, are no longer perennial.

BELOW *Standing on the Pongolapoort Dam wall, looking across the Makhatini Flats towards the sea, it is possible to understand why the Zulus call Maputaland* uMhlabawalingana, *meaning 'the earth which is flat'.*

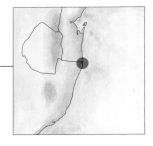

Kosi System

In the northeastern corner of Maputaland, just south of the Mozambique border, is the beautiful Kosi estuary which leads into a chain of interlinking barrier lakes, lagoons and swamps. Over 250 species of bird are known to occur in the area – of which about one-third are associated with water – and fish life is still abundant in the system.

The Kosi lakes cover an area of about 37 square kilometres (14 square miles) and the total system drains a catchment area of approximately 500 square kilometres (193 square miles). The soils in the catchment area are mainly leached acid sands, which means that there is virtually no erosion of soil into the lake system when it rains. The result is that the waters of the Kosi system are silt-free and this sets the estuary apart from most of the other estuaries along the eastern seaboard of South Africa, which are generally notoriously silt-laden and turbid.

In addition to the prolific and diverse birdlife and the many fish found in the Kosi estuary and in the coastal lakes of Sibaya and Mgobezeleni, the plant life of the area is also rich and varied. There are six different plant communities in total, ranging from mangroves to swamp forests, which combine to create a most fascinating biotic diversity. Mammals, which were once plentiful and diverse, are now restricted to Vervet and Samango Monkeys (*Cercopithecus aethiops* and *C. mitis*), the Thick-tailed Galago or Bushbaby (*Otolemur crassicaudatus*), both Red and Grey Duiker, the occasional Reedbuck, and a few Bushbuck.

An interesting feature of the Kosi lake system is the maze of intricately woven fish traps that are to be found there. For many centuries the people of Maputaland have been using these traps as a means of catching fish. Early Portuguese records, written in 1554, make reference to these traps, which are still used in the same way today as they were used then.

BELOW *For many centuries the people of Maputaland have fished in the Kosi estuary using permanent fish traps – these comprise guide fences constructed at right angles to the flow of water and to the shoreline so that they are able to trap fish as they migrate in and out of the estuary and lakes of the Kosi system.*

ABOVE *With its haunting call, the African Fish Eagle* (Haliaeetus vocifer) *is a quintessential element of the Kosi Bay system. This majestic bird is quite unmistakable with its white head and breast, chestnut belly and forewings, black wings and white tail.*

BELOW *The Thick-tailed Bushbaby, sometimes known as the Greater Bushbaby, looks a bit like a cat when it is on the ground. It is a nocturnal animal and gets its name from its loud scream which can be likened to that of a baby in distress. It feeds on insects, Tree Frogs and fruit.*

ABOVE *Detailed research has revealed that less than five per cent of the fish that migrate in and out of the Kosi estuary and lakes are actually caught in these traditional fish traps. This form of fishing therefore has no detrimental effect on the fish population in the system.*

ABOVE *Where patches of sunlight reach the forest floor, groups of Oxalis sp. grow prolifically. Oxalis flower from March to May, and attain a height of between 10 and 15 centimetres (4 to 6 inches).*

LEFT *The dune forests support a great diversity of vegetation, ranging from magnificent dense evergreen forests to grasslands. Within the forest there is also a wealth of botanical gems – from delicate orchids to creepers, climbers and bushes.*

BELOW *The swamp-dwelling Kosi Palm has special 'breathing roots' that grow upwards above the water level. It is a monocarpic species, meaning that it bears fruit once and then dies.*

ABOVE *Waterlilies are widespread throughout the wetlands, pans and in the far, still reaches of the waterways in the Coastal Zone. The plant has a thick prostrate rhizome with many small, fleshy roots that anchor it to the mud floor. The under surfaces of the leaves vary in colour, from a deep rich crimson to purple. The flowers open in the morning and close at midday.*

BELOW *In certain areas of the coastal forest, particularly where it is damp and light levels are low, Bracket Fungi (Polyporus sp.) frequently cluster in groups on rotting wood that accumulates on the forest floor. As with wood, the growth of fungi is registered in conspicuous growth rings.*

ABOVE *A beautiful member of the Amaryllidaceae Family is the* Crinum moorei, *which grows in inaccessible wetland areas and swampy forest margins. The stems grow to nearly a metre (3 feet) in height and it flowers in December.*

BELOW *Larvae, commonly known as Bagworms (Order Lepidoptera) live in self-constructed, silken bags to which they attach leaves or twigs, cut to size for protection. In this case the thorns of the White Acacia have been used. When it is fully grown, the larva pupates within its protective bag. After emerging the males fly off in search of females, who – peculiarly to the Family Psychidae – are wingless and remain within the bag. The male inserts his extensible abdomen and fertilizes the female. After this she lays her eggs and dies.*

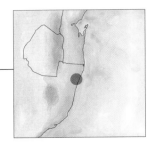

Lake Sibaya

Some 40 kilometres (25 miles) to the south of Kosi Bay along the Eastern Coastal Plain is a beautiful landlocked freshwater lake. Known as Lake Sibaya, it is extremely rich in wildlife. Some 280 species of bird have been observed on its waters and along its shores. The most numerous bird populations are the Reed and Whitebreasted Cormorants (*Phalacrocorax africanus* and *P. carbo*) that feed on small fish. Other important fish–eating species include the Pied and Malachite Kingfishers (*Ceryle rudis* and *C. cristata*) and the Fish Eagle, whose haunting call has always been so evocative of Africa's wild places. Hippopotamus, which are considered by many veterans of the African bush to be one of the most unpredictable and deadly of Africa's animals, live out their seemingly sleepy and placid lives in the waters of the lake. Other fauna closely associated with Lake Sibaya include 22 species of frog and eight reptile species, including the African Python (*Python sebae natalensis*), the Water Leguaan (*Varanus niloticus niloticus*) and the Nile Crocodile.

Narrowly separated from the sea by a range of high afforested coastal dunes, Lake Sibaya has a surface area of approximately 70 square kilometres (27 square miles) and an average depth of about 13 metres (43 feet). An interesting feature of the lake is that it is not fed by any river and nor does any river drain from it. Fresh water comes in from subterranean sources and drainage is by means of evaporation and seepage into the sea. The lake is home to some 18 species of fish, some of which, such as Gobiids (family Gobiidae), clearly reflect its marine origin. The other two principal fish types found in the lake are Cichlids (family Cichlidae) and Catfish (family Clarriidae).

BELOW *Lake Sibaya has an abundance of shallow, shoreline-based fish communities, but lacks a well-developed pelagic fish population due to the inadequate quantity of food available in open water. The fish fauna in the lake consists of 18 species, including Cichlids, Gobiids and Catfish.*

ABOVE *Nile Crocodiles are resident in virtually all large water bodies in Maputaland. The adults feed mainly on fish and play an important role as top predators in the aquatic ecosystem. This close-up picture of a crocodile's head shows some of the reptile's distinctive features – a long jaw and prominent teeth and geometrically arranged horny plates fused to the skull.*

RIGHT *Common in most freshwater lakes, pans and rivers in South Africa, the Malachite Kingfisher (Alcedo cristata) can be distinguished from the smaller Pygmy Kingfisher (Ispidina picta) by its turquoise- and black-barred crown which extends below the eye.*

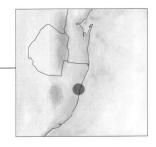

The Mgobezeleni Lake System

The Mgobezeleni Lake System is a small lake complex situated within the Coastal Lake Zone, a few kilometres inland from Sodwana Bay. The system comprises two lakes, Mgobezeleni itself and Shazibe, which lies two kilometres (6.5 miles) to the north. Lake Mgobezeleni is surrounded by steep banks with dense vegetation, the most prominent species being the Natal Wild Banana (*Strelitzia nicolai*). This alternates with low-lying swamp forest in which the predominant trees are the mighty Swamp Fig (*Ficus trichopoda*), the Coastal Hibiscus (*Hibiscus tiliaceus*), the Umdoni (*Syzygium cordata*) and the Quinine Tree (*Rauvolfia caffra*).

Around Lake Shazibe the vegetation is similar, except that the dominant trees are unusually tall. Much of the vegetation, however, has been drowned as a result of a high build-up of water in the mid-1970s when a bridge was built across the Shazibe River to the holiday resort at Sodwana Bay.

BELOW *The Mgobezeleni Lake System, situated a short distance inland from Sodwana Bay, comprises lakes Mgobezeleni (below) and Shazibe (opposite, bottom right) and an interconnecting river flowing into the sea at Sodwana.*

ABOVE AND BELOW   *Although small, the Mgobezeleni Lake System is important as it contains a variety of interesting plants and animals, most of which have tropical affinities. Together with the river that connects the two lakes to the sea, it forms an interesting estuarine system which has a number of unique attributes. Within the swamp forests, common trees include the Swamp Fig, Coastal Hibiscus, Umdoni and Quinine Tree* (Rauvolfia caffra). *The shores of both lakes are lined with grasses, reeds and sedges, including* Typha latifolia *subsp.* capensis, Phragmites mauritianus *and* Scirpus littoralis.

LEFT   *The Natal Wild Banana features very prominently at the foot of the steep, densely forested banks that surround Mgobezeleni.*

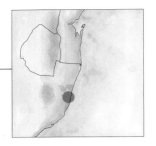

St Lucia Estuary

The most southern region of Maputaland comprises the fascinating St Lucia estuary and lake system. It is a place of wild beauty that reflects many of Africa's most poignant moods. Lake St Lucia, which was named by early Portuguese mariners who plied Africa's southeast coast, is the largest marine lake in Africa. It is approximately 60 kilometres (37.5 miles) long, and spreads northwards from the estuary mouth to the Mkuze River in Maputaland. Its width varies from 100 metres (330 feet) to a maximum of 21 kilometres (13 miles). The average depth of this 300-square-kilometre (116-square-mile) expanse of water is only about a metre (3 feet) and within its borders are several grass and reed-covered islands.

The shape of the lake can be compared roughly to the letter 'H'. The western and smaller leg of the H is known as False Bay; the cross-bar or straits between the two legs of the lake is called Hell's Gate and the eastern and longer leg is divided by a constriction into two sections at Fanies Island – Lake St Lucia North and Lake St Lucia South. Generally the eastern shore is marshy and reed-covered, while the western shore is steep and wooded.

Five rivers flow into Lake St Lucia: the Mkuze (which is the largest), Mzinene, Hluhluwe, Nyalazi, and Mpate. In addition to these major rivers there are a number of minor streams that drain from adjacent freshwater swamps. St Lucia can be likened to a vast natural workshop where the waters of the land meet the waters of the sea, and in this union a fascinating interplay between marine and freshwater life results. Great variances occur in the salinity of the water – from completely fresh to water saltier than the sea. In the less saline regions of the lake reeds and sedges grow in abundance, while in the more saline reaches mangrove swamps, Ruppia and Eel Grass are common. The vegetation provides food and shelter for a variety of marsh birds, various reptiles and small animals which live on the mud banks and on the trunks and roots of the mangroves. Detritus, which is made up mainly of rotting vegetation, provides the basic diet for aquatic organisms such as worms, shrimps, prawns, shellfish, Mullet and Mud Bream. These organisms, in turn, provide food for the larger game fish and for a large and diverse bird population. Being an estuarine system, St Lucia is also a valuable – but vulnerable – nursery for several marine species, such as fish and prawns, which both breed in the sea and then migrate to the lake to mature. The lake system is probably the most important prawn habitat in South Africa, the most common species being the White Prawn (*Penaeus indicus*).

Along the eastern shore, dividing the lake from the sea, is a plain of swampy ground with a number of freshwater pans. Bordering this plain in the east are the high parabolic dunes which dominate the full length of the Maputaland coastline. A great number of Hippos, estimated to be between 600 and 700, as well as numerous Crocodiles, live in these freshwater pans and in those areas in the lake where the salinity levels are moderate.

Lake St Lucia and its environs support 367 different bird species in 11 major habitats. There are only a few places in the whole of Africa that support such a high concentration of birdlife. Approximately one-third of the species are waterside birds inhabiting the mudflats, reedbeds, swamps and open waters of the lake. St Lucia has the only breeding colony in South Africa of the rare Pinkbacked Pelican (*Pelecanus refescens*), and when the plankton levels in the lake are high, it provides a home for enormous flocks of Flamingos (*Phoenicopterus minor* and *P. ruber*) and Pelicans (*Pelecanus sonocrotalus*).

BELOW *This magnificent aerial perspective of St Lucia clearly shows the Mapelane coastal dunes in the left foreground, the Umfolozi River mouth in the near-middle distance, the St Lucia estuary mouth in the far-middle distance and the St Lucia lake system in the far distance.*

TOP *St Lucia is well known for the congregations of Flamingos that gather on the lake when conditions are ideal. Both the Greater Flamingo (Phoenicopterus ruber), which has a large, black-tipped pink bill and is predominantly white with brilliant patches of red on the forewings, and the Lesser Flamingo (P. minor), which is smaller, more red in colour and has a very dark-red (almost black) black-tipped bill, can be seen foraging for food in St Lucia's shallow waters.*

ABOVE *The Purple-crested Loerie (Tauraco porphyreolophus) is normally very furtive and is usually only seen leaping from one branch or tree to another, during which the red colouring on its wings becomes conspicuous. Its principal habitat is evergreen coastal and riverine forests.*

ABOVE *St Lucia's western shore has much earlier origins than the rest of the lake, as it is actually an ancient marine shoreline. In many areas it is made up of cliff faces that rise up to 20 metres (66 feet) or more. The soils of the western shore are older, richer and more varied than those of the eastern shore, and the rainfall is lower and far more erratic than elsewhere in the St Lucia area. Over countless years, the complex interaction between soil types, rainfall, fire, and the grazing and browsing of herbivores has influenced the type of vegetation found in this part of St Lucia. As a result, the vegetation has characteristics that are typical of the bushveld. Acacias dominate, but there are also aloes and euphorbias.*

ABOVE *This view across St Lucia to Cape Vidal from Fanies Island illustrates the dominance of tall vegetated coastal dunes along the lake's eastern shores. Rising steeply from the sea, these dunes have been built and shaped by the wind over the past 25,000 years and reach over 200 metres (656 feet) in places, making them among the highest vegetated dune forests in the world. The dunes cause precipitation – over 1200 millimetres (47 inches) per annum – and consequently play an important role in water catchment for the St Lucia lake system. Made up entirely of wind-blown sands which have low concentrations of the nutrients required for plant growth, the vegetation has adapted to this environment by becoming efficient at collecting and gathering nutrients that are available.*

LEFT *There are about 700 Hippos in the St Lucia system, found mainly in the Narrows and along the eastern margins of the lake. In the water they are benign, unless disturbed. At night – when they are most dangerous – they feed on grass.*

RIGHT *Along the western shores, concretions (rocks with an onion-skin effect) are sometimes found together with fossils, which tell the ancient history of St Lucia. The fossils are of marine origin and include ammonites, clams and other sea shells, echinoderms and even the teeth of huge, indeed giant, sharks. These fossils date back to the Cretaceous era (about 140 million years ago) when the western shores were part of a marine environment. From a study of these deposits, scientists have been able to determine that the lake, the Mkuze swamps, the eastern shores, and the offshore coral reefs, are all of much more recent origin. These areas were formed during a second stage of development, brought about by a change in sea levels caused by the various ice ages and a combination of wet and dry periods over the past two million years.*

BELOW *Positioned between the Fever Tree in the foreground and False Bay Park in the background, False Bay was once a deeply incised river valley created by river scouring when there was a drop in the level of the sea. When the water level subsequently rose, this valley flooded and formed a large bay. From a study of fossils, scientists have also been able to determine that about 125,000 years ago, when the sea level was 2 metres (7 feet) above its present height, the bay was directly connected to the sea.*

Tembe Elephant Park

Separated from the Ndumo Game Reserve to the west by the Mbangweni Corridor, the 29,000-hectare (71,659-acre) Tembe Elephant Park is situated at Sihangwane. The northern boundary of the park follows the border between KwaZulu-Natal and Mozambique. Along its eastern border the park consists of a mosaic of sand forest, woodland, grassland and swampland. The unique sand forest vegetation – the largest tract of sand forest in South Africa – provides shelter for the endangered Suni Antelope (*Nesotragus moschatus*); both the sand forest and the Suni are protected within the park.

Tembe was proclaimed on 21 October 1983 primarily to provide protection for the last remaining unprotected herds of free-ranging Elephant in South Africa, which were originally part of a much bigger group of Elephant that used to migrate into the area from southern Mozambique. The proclamation of the park was surrounded by controversy, owing to the need to relocate people who were living in the area previously. This controversy was the result of a combination of three factors. Firstly, the resettlement of people in South Africa is a sensitive issue because of its association with apartheid. The movement of people out of the Sihangwane area was seen by some as an extension of that policy, and a strong sense of resentment was thus felt. At a more pragmatic level, people complained that they did not receive adequate compensation for the loss of access to the natural resources that were previously available to them and for the loss of crops that they had planted at their old homesteads. And thirdly, people felt alienated by the solar-powered electric fences that have been erected around the park in order to keep the elephants within the park boundaries. These fences are seen as a barrier that forcibly keeps people out of an area to which they previously had free access. This controversy is not unique and is symptomatic of the historical conflict that exists between man and animals wherever there is competition for natural resources.

BELOW *The Elephant in Tembe Elephant Park were the last free-ranging Elephant in South Africa. However, they inadvertently got caught up in the guerilla war that raged in adjacent southern Mozambique and, as a result, are extremely shy because they were constantly shot at. Many of these gentle creatures still carry bullets within them.*

ABOVE *The Suni Antelope is one of the rarest and most secretive antelopes in South Africa. It is chiefly nocturnal and is only found in the northeastern regions of South Africa, although it is widespread in Mozambique and the eastern areas of Zimbabwe. Its habitat is dry thickets and riverine woodland with dense underbrush.*

BELOW *The fruit of the Lebombo Raisin* (Grewia microthyrsa), *which occurs in the Sand Forest Zone, is eaten by birds, mammals and people. The plant's pear-shaped fruits, unlike any other Grewias, hang on curved stalks.*

BELOW *This intricately woven Orchid,* Microcoelia exilis, *found in the Tembe Elephant Park is only one of two leafless epiphyte Orchids found in South Africa. In the southern region this species is confined to northern KwaZulu-Natal only, but it has a wide-ranging distribution northwards, extending as far as Eritrea and westwards to Angola and Nigeria.*

ABOVE *The* Acridocarpus natalitius *is a handsome small shrub and climber that ranges in height from 2 to 10 metres (7 to 33 feet). Here is an early stage of bud formation, with each bud seemingly piled pyramidlike upon the other. An inquisitive ant can be seen searching for food.*

RIGHT *Endemic to northern KwaZulu-Natal, the* Acridocarpus natalitius *is normally found on the edge of forests and blooms prolifically between November and early December. The bright yellow flowers emerge from their buds sequentially, creating a roman candle effect of decreasing incandescence.*

BELOW RIGHT *The Olive Toad, also known as the Northern Mottled Toad, occurs in northern KwaZulu-Natal and the lowveld. Although it was also thought to occur in the northwestern regions of the country, scientists now believe the latter frog to be a separate species (Bufo poweri) – call differences between the two species have been noted and anatomical differences in the larynx have been found. Further research is still being conducted into this.*

BELOW *Fishing Spiders of the sub-family* Thalassinae *have long abdomens with white bands on either side. Another characteristic feature are their long legs with numerous spines, which it typically positions with one pair stretched forward and the other backward. They are usually found on or near water, some of the larger species catch tadpoles and even small fish.*

OPPOSITE *Although the soils of the Sand Forest Zone lack fertility, they support one of the finest examples of tropical dry forest in southern Africa.*

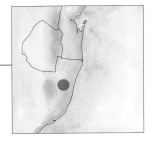

Mkuzi Game Reserve

Situated in the south of the Sand Forest Zone, and sandwiched between the Mkuze and Msunduze rivers and the Ubombo Mountains, is the Mkuzi Game Reserve – part of the Greater St Lucia Wetland Park. Established in 1925 and presently managed by the Natal Parks Board, the reserve encompasses more than 36,000 hectares (88,956 acres) of pristine bushveld vegetation – a variegation of woodland and thicket with small patches of sand forest and riverine forest evident along the watercourses.

Several seasonal pans are filled when the Mkuze River floods its banks and these pans provide a home to a wide variety of water birds. Game is abundant in the reserve and includes both Black and White Rhino as well as Giraffe and an exensive range of antelope. A few Leopards are present as well as Cheetah which were reintroduced in 1966. Black-backed Jackal (*Canis mesomelas*) are common in the area.

An important feature of the region is the Nsumo Pan, which lies on the Mkuze River floodplain at the eastern end of the reserve. Here a wide variety of water birds can be observed from hides built along the water's edge. The pan has a large population of Hippo. Crocodiles are also resident in the pan, although their numbers are somewhat restricted, and Leguaans can often be seen basking in the sun. Not far from the pan is a relatively small but dense forest of Sycamore Figs, with a number of trails meandering through it. Trumpeter Hornbills (*Bycanistes bucinator*) are common in the forest and their persistent plaintive cries add a feeling of solitude to a hike through the area.

Being situated in the Sand Forest Zone, termitaria thickets occur within the reserve. Here the major tree components are the Buffalo-thorn (*Ziziphus mucronata* subsp. *mucronata*); the Tamboti (*Spirostachys africana*), which is an important hardwood tree that emits a very poisonous latex but whose timber is highly sought after as it is almost indestructible; the Jacket-plum; the Dwarf Boer-bean (*Schotia capitata*); and the Transvaal Saffron (*Cassine transvaalensis*), which is a shrub or small bushy tree whose bark has a high tannin content and is used extensively in traditional medicine. In other areas where the sand mantle thins off and a prismatic sandy clay forms the subsoil, sand savanna trees predominate. Among these are the Silver Terminalia; the Marula (*Sclerocarya caffra*), which is an extremely important tree to the people of Maputaland; various Bushwillow Trees (*Combretum zeyheri*, *C. molle*, *C. collinum*); the Spineless and Green Monkey Orange trees (*Strychnos madagascariensis* and *S. spinosa*); the Black Monkey-thorn (*Acacia burkei*) and the Broad-leaved Resin Tree (*Ozoroa obovata*).

BELOW *Mkuzi Game Reserve has typical woodland with various species of acacia. Wildebeest, always inquisitive, turn to look at the intruder.*

ABOVE *The Crested Guineafowl (Guttera pucherani) is finely spotted with a tuft of feathers on its head resembling a crown. Restricted in its distribution to the northeast corner of KwaZulu-Natal, its preferred habitat is thick ever-green forests and broad-leaved woodland where there is dense undergrowth.*

RIGHT *Perhaps the most graceful of all antelope is the Kudu, its well-proportioned, grey-brown to rufous body and elegant spiralled horns not only giving this animal grace but also an air of regality. An antelope of wooded savanna, its distribution is limited to the northern and eastern parts of the country, with isolated populations in the Cape Province.*

BELOW *The Banded Mongoose (Mungos mungo) has dark-brown to black transverse bands on its back which extend from behind its shoulders to the base of the tail. The bushy tail becomes darker towards the tip.*

RIGHT *Trumpeter Hornbills are often mistaken for Silverycheeked Hornbills* (Bycanistes brevis), *but are distinguishable by the smaller and less obvious casque on top of their bills. The breast and underparts of this species are white and not solid black as in the case of the Silverycheeked Hornbill. The Trumpeter Hornbill is more widely distributed and found in evergreen, coastal and riverine forests where it feeds in the canopy of fruiting trees.*

BELOW *The female Warthog* (Phacochoerus aethiopicus) *is distinguished from the male by the presence of only one pair of warts situated just below the eyes. The males have two pairs of warts – one just below the eyes and the other midway down the animal's face – both of which are much bigger and more pronounced. Warthogs are grey in colour, sparsely haired and have the distinctive feature of holding their tails, which have a tuft of black hair on the tip, erect while running. They have a long mane that normally lies flat along the back, but rises up when the animal is under stress. The snout is typically piglike and the canine teeth of adults develop into long, curved tusks that can become very effective defensive weapons, especially in the case of boars where the tusks become quite large. Warthogs are normally found in open and lightly wooded savanna in a crescent-shaped region, stretching from the Eastern Coastal Plain through the Lowveld to the bushveld regions of North West. They are grazers and concentrate on short grasses and grass roots.*

ABOVE *A view of Hlonhlela Pan, looking across to the Ubombo Mountains on the western border of the Mkuzi Game Reserve. This pan is home to a wide variety of birds, mammals and reptiles which can be observed by visitors from the comfort of an exclusive bush lodge situated on its banks.*

BELOW *The Squacco Heron* (Ardeola ralloides) *is the smallest heron in the southern Africa region. It is found in well vegetated freshwater lakes and slow-moving rivers. Its habit is to skulk in reedbeds and in long grass where it will stand or sit motionless for hours.*

BELOW *The Mozambique Spitting Cobra* (Naja mossambica) *is a common resident in Maputaland. Found mainly in open grasslands, especially near swamps, it has the ability to spit venom with great accuracy for distances of up to 2 metres (6 feet). If the wind direction is right, it can spit even further.*

Ndumo Game Reserve

At the northern end of the low-lying Pongolo floodplain, on the border between KwaZulu-Natal and Mozambique, is the Ndumo Game Reserve. It is bounded by the Usutu River in the north and extends to the confluence of the Usutu and Pongolo rivers in the east. Ndumo's main feature is a series of floodplain pans that dominate the reserve. These pans, which are fed by the Usutu and Pongolo, are rich in nutrients and provide a habitat for large numbers of Hippo, fish, Crocodiles and birds.

Ndumo Game Reserve is only 10,000 hectares (24,710 acres) in extent, yet is remarkably rich in birdlife as a result of the number of diverse habitats that occur within its boundaries. The dry surrounding sand forests, riverine forests, reedbeds, sandveld, and woodlands are each favoured by a multitude of different bird species. The pans offer a unique aquatic environment that attracts such diverse bird species as Pelicans and Flamingos, large numbers of Whitefaced Ducks (*Dendrocygna viduata*), Eygptian Geese (*Alopochen aegyptiancus*), Blackheaded Herons (*Ardea melanocephala*), Saddlebilled Storks (*Ephippiorhynchus senegalensis*), Jacanas (*Actophilornis africanus* and *Microparra capensis*), and Fish Eagles.

In total, some 416 bird species have been recorded here. This figure is impressive when compared to the Kruger National Park, which is a little over 190 times larger than Ndumo Game Reserve but boasts only 89 species more. Some 83 per cent of the bird species found in Maputaland have been recorded at Ndumo; Maputaland, it should be noted, accounts for some 57 per cent of southern Africa's total number of species.

BELOW *The largest pan in the Ndumo Game Reserve is the Fever Tree-lined Nyamithi Pan. Surrounding the pan in its entirety is a 'carpet' of soft green grasses* (Cynodon dactylon *and* Echinochloa pyramidalis) *which can be seen in this photograph. As with all pans in the Pongolo River floodplain, Nyamithi is subject to periodic flooding in summer when these grasses become an important source of food for fish.*

ABOVE *The Green Mamba (Dendroaspis angusticeps) is a large slender snake, extending to 250 centimetres (98½ inches) in length when fully grown. It feeds on birds and small mammals and is shy and very seldom seen. Generally nonaggressive, the Green Mamba will only bite if cornered or visibly threatened. Its venom is neurotoxic, but less potent than the Black Mamba's, which causes paralysis and possible death in humans if not treated timeously.*

ABOVE RIGHT *The* Euphorbia grandicornis *is endemic to Maputaland and is a common plant in the Ndumo Game Reserve. It forms dense wide-spread thickets in dry thicket, scrub and woodland on predominantly red and grey sandy clay soils and it is also found in drainage lines. It is a low-growing plant, seldom reaching more than a metre or so in height.*

RIGHT *Although fairly conspicuous in this photograph, the eggs of the Water Dikkop (Burhinus vermiculatis) are normally extremely well camouflaged. These birds are to be found mainly at dusk on the banks of large rivers or lakes where there is fringing vegetation. They lie up in reedbeds or under overhanging vegetation during the day. The melancholy piping call of the Water Dikkop is usually heard at night.*

ABOVE *A common resident throughout southern Africa, the Blackheaded Heron is distinguishable from the equally ubiquitous Grey Heron (Ardea cinerea) by the black, or very dark-grey, head and back of its neck. It also has slate-grey legs, whereas the Grey Heron has yellow legs. It is usually found in grasslands rather than near water as is the case with the Grey Heron.*

BELOW LEFT *The Yellowbilled Stork (Mycteria ibis) has a long yellow bill with a noticeable, yet slight, downward curve. Found near lakes, large rivers and estuaries in the northern and eastern parts of the country, it is normally silent, except during the breeding season when it emits loud squeaks and hisses.*

BELOW *A White Pelican (Pelecanus onocrotalus) is a large white bird which assumes a pinkish flush while breeding It is a gregarious bird that gathers in flocks on coastal islands, estuaries, bays, lagoons, flood pans, and inland waters.*

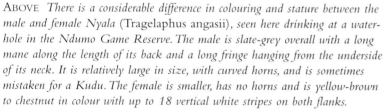

ABOVE *An African Leopard Butterfly* (Phalanta phalantha aethiopica) *rests on the heavily spiked stem of a* Euphorbia grandicornis, *which grows in profusion in various parts of the Ndumo Game Reserve. The African Leopard is widely distributed in the wetter eastern half of South Africa. Both male and female are orange in colour with delicate black markings on both wings. Restless and always on the move, this butterfly does not remain still even when it has settled, continuing to flap its wings every few seconds. In flight it constantly changes direction and height as a means of defence against predators.*

BELOW *Egyptian Geese are common residents throughout South Africa. They are raucous and very noisy in their social interactions. Both sexes look alike, but their calls are different with the females making a harsh honking sound and the males more of a wheezing hiss.*

FOLLOWING PAGES *Hippopotami are semi-aquatic animals that spend much of their day semi-submerged in the pans and rivers in the northern and eastern regions of southern Africa. During the winter months they spend less time in the water and lie up on mud or sand banks in the sun. They are normally found in schools of 10 to 15 animals, although larger schools are not uncommon. Schools normally comprise cows and young of various ages with a dominant bull in overall command.*

ABOVE *There is a considerable difference in colouring and stature between the male and female Nyala* (Tragelaphus angasii), *seen here drinking at a waterhole in the Ndumo Game Reserve. The male is slate-grey overall with a long mane along the length of its back and a long fringe hanging from the underside of its neck. It is relatively large in size, with curved horns, and is sometimes mistaken for a Kudu. The female is smaller, has no horns and is yellow-brown to chestnut in colour with up to 18 vertical white stripes on both flanks.*

Focus on
THE COAST

South Africa's coastline is more or less 'U'-shaped, with one side of the 'U' being totally different from the other due to differences in the temperature of the respective coastal waters. The eastern half is swept by the warm Agulhas Current and the western half by the cold Benguela Current, both of which have a major bearing on the nature of the marine fauna and flora that occurs along the respective coastlines.

The Agulhas Current originates in the tropics of the Indian Ocean where a huge anti-clockwise circulation of water, created by the prevailing equatorial wind systems, is deflected southwards by the African continent. The central core of this water mass follows the edge of the continental shelf where the relatively shallow waters abruptly become deeper.

Off the Eastern Cape coast, the continental shelf becomes wider and this results in the warm water of the Agulhas Current being deflected away from the continent allowing colder counterbalancing currents, coming up from the south, to penetrate along the immediate coastline. As a result, the south coast of South Africa – from about Port St Johns to Cape Point, or the bottom part of the eastern half of the 'U' shape – has a different set of marine animals and plants to those of KwaZulu-Natal and Mozambique, or, in other words, the top half of the eastern arm of the 'U'.

Along the west coast of South Africa an entirely different set of current systems prevails. Travelling from west to east in the sub-Antarctic Southern Ocean is a large current known as the West Wind Drift. Part of this current is deflected northwards where it passes along the west coast of the African subcontinent, forming the cold Benguela Current. The coldness of the current has a profound effect not only on the marine fauna and flora but also on the climate, because onshore winds that pass over the cold sea to the hot land do not yield their moisture in the form of precipitation. Consequently, the west coast of southern Africa is arid in the southern half of the western arm of the 'U', and becomes increasingly desertlike in the northern half. The combined effect of Coriolis forces and the prevailing southeasterly and southwesterly winds that blow along South Africa's west coast produce great upwellings of cold nutrient-rich waters, resulting in the west coast being one of the richest fishing grounds in the world. This in turn supports large colonies of seals and sea birds.

OPPOSITE *The South African coastline is noted for its widely diverse nature and beauty. Long beaches of white sands give way to hidden coves and rugged rocks against which the sea relentlessly hurls its energy. Along the Wild Coast there are many unspoilt beaches as yet undisturbed by humankind.*

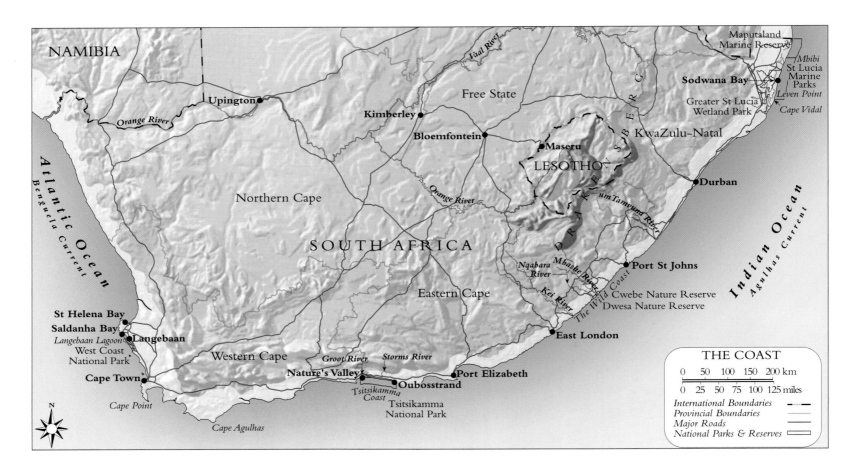

Although upwelling is a worldwide phenomenon, there are few places on earth where it occurs on the scale experienced along the west coast of southern Africa, which is characterized by large quantities of decaying animal and plant life constantly accumulating on the Atlantic Ocean floor. This process of decay yields huge quantities of organic nutrients. Brought to the surface through upwelling, this rich food source is distributed by the prevailing Benguela Current from the Cape waters all the way to Namibia and even beyond. When the concentrated nutrients rise up to within reach of the sun's rays in the euphotic zone (the ocean's upper layers), vast quantities of phytoplankton (minute forms of floating plant life) feed off the food and breed prolifically, resulting in their constant multiplication in number. The phytoplankton, in turn, provide food for zooplankton, which are floating animal forms structured in a seemingly endless variety of microscopic shapes and sizes. Mixed in with the zooplankton are the larvae of many larger animals, which drift in the currents of the oceans at this stage of their life cycle. Together they comprise the major food sources of the sea and the foundation for nature's greatest food web, which not only includes marine life but terrestrial life as well, of which humankind is the highest order. Of particular importance is the food provided for vast shoals of Sardines (*Sardinops sagax*) and Anchovies (*Engraulis japonicus*). These shoals provide food for pelagic predators as well as a variety of bivalve molluscs, which, in turn, provide food for higher level marine predators. Humankind predates at various levels of the food chain and, as a result, an active and diversified fishing industry has developed along the west coast of southern Africa, centring on the harbours of St Helena Bay, Saldanha Bay and Walvis Bay in Namibia.

In South Africa, the greatest concentration and variety of marine flora and fauna occurs in inshore waters where food is abundant, particularly along rocky shores – this is especially true of areas of upwelling. The rise and fall of the tides, however, combined with the incessant movement of water as waves wash back and forth, creates a highly stressful habitat to which marine life has adapted in various ways, depending on its location within the intertidal zone. For example, at the apex of the tidal zone (the maximum point where waves reach during high tide) marine plants and animals are subjected to long periods of exposure to the sun, with temperatures frequently rising to 40°C (104°F) or more; during the day, they can lose up to 70 per cent of their body water to the air. When the incoming tide reaches these creatures they become inundated and their ambient temperature decreases substantially. Organisms living under such extreme conditions require special mechanisms in order to survive and it is not surprising that only a relatively few plants and animals are able to achieve this. Further down the intertidal zone, the relative periods of exposure to the sun and inundation become inverted and an increasing number of organisms are able to survive there. This ability to adapt to the different conditions occurring along the rocky coastline results in discernible patterns of zonation.

On most rocky shores at least four distinct zones exist, based on relative depth. At the lowest level is the Infratidal Zone, which is dominated by algae beds. Above the Infratidal Zone is the second algae-dominated zone called the Balanoid Zone, which supports a different species of algae. The Balanoid Zone is usually subdivided between upper and lower subzones. In the Upper Balanoid Subzone animals dominate, with the predominant species being limpets, barnacles and winkles (along the KwaZulu-Natal coast this subzone also contains an oyster belt). In the Lower Balanoid Subzone the most predominant life forms are various species of algae, zoanthids, mussels, urchins and sponges. The uppermost, or Littorina, zone, is dominated by tiny littorinids (periwinkles) and other round-apertured gastropods. All are herbivorous and feed mainly on diatoms and microalgae. Although the division of the rocky shores into the four zones can be systematically applied along the entire South Africa coastline, there are regional variations in population species between the east, south and west coasts.

ABOVE *The Southern Elephant Seal* (Mirounga leonia) *is the largest of all living seals. The bulls have a short, bulbous proboscis that projects from just below the eye and hangs over the mouth. The Elephant Seal is a rare visitor to the shores of South Africa.*

ABOVE *Sea Goldies* (Anthias squamipinnis) *are small, brightly coloured fish that form a subfamily of the Rock Cods. Interestingly, most goldies begin their reproductive cycle as females. They gather in large harems where a dominant female is transformed into a male and then mates with the females.*

ABOVE *The Semicircle Angelfish* (Pomacanthus semicirculatus) *is one of the best-known angelfish in South African waters. It is a solitary species that gently makes its way along the edges of the reef in search of algae, sponges, various invertebrates and sea squirts, which make up the food choices of adults.*

ABOVE RIGHT *These Brown Mussels, clustered on the rocks along the Tsitsikamma Coast, belong to the second-largest molluscan class, Bivalvia, containing some 8000 species. As the name implies, all species in this class have a bivalved shell enclosing the body.*

Along the east coast, where the water is warmer and the sun's rays hottest, only a few species are hardy enough to be able to accommodate the harsh conditions experienced in the Littorina Zone. It is dominated by two snail species, the *Nodilittorina africana africana* and *Littorina glabrata*, and occasional tufts of *Bostrichia* alga. At the top of the Upper Balanoid Zone a dense band of Natal Rock Oysters (*Saccostrea cucullata*) encrust the rocks in many places. Below the oyster belt a mixed community of Brown Mussels (*Perna perna*), Barnacles (predominantly *Tetraclita squamosa rufotincta*, *Chthamalus dentatus* and *Octomeris angulosa*) and Limpets (particularly *Patella concolor* and *Cellana capensis*) occur. A characteristic feature of the Lower Balanoid Zone along the east coast is the density and variety of zoanthids which cover the rocks. In the Infratidal Zone the predominant algal species include *Hypnea spicifera*, *Spiridea*, *Calithamnion*. In those places where wave action is restricted, such as under overhangs or in holes in rocks, heads of coral can be found.

Along the south coast, only one species of littorinid occurs in the Littorina Zone, namely *Nodilittorina africana knysnaensis*. The Flat-bladed Alga, *Porphyra*, is common here as is the Shore Crab (*Cyclograpsus punctatus*). In the Upper Balanoid Zone the most commonly found Limpets include *Patella granularis* and *P. oculus* and the main species of Barnacles are *Octomeris angulosa* and *Tetraclita serrata*, while *Chthamalus dentatus* are found along the upper reaches of this zone. A common inhabitant of the rock pools along both the south and west coasts is the Winkle (*Oxystele variegata*), which uses its file-like radula to graze on microalgae and encrusting algae. The dominant algae in the Upper Balanoid Zone is the Sea Lettuce (*Ulva* spp.) and the Starred Cushion (*Iyengaria stellata*), which is found from Cape Point to Port St Johns. The Lower Balanoid Zone supports thick beds of algae, of which the most prominent are *Gigartina radula*, *G. stiriata* and *Gelidium pristoides*. Winkles, such as *Oxystele sinensis* and *O. tigrina*, and the Limpet *Patella longicosta* occur in various places in between the algae. In most pools along this sector of the coast-line Whelks (*Burnupena* spp.) scavenge for dead or dying animals,

and anemones are very common. Below the Lower Balanoid zone, an additional zone, which is not found along the east coast, occurs, known as the Cochlear Zone. The name is derived from the large presence of the Limpet *Patella cochlear*. Because of the dense populations of this Limpet there is no algae growth on this part of the rocky shore. Below the Cochlear zone, in the Infratidal Zone, Red Bait (*Pyura stolonifera*) is common, while comprehensive stands of various algae, such as corallines (the segments of which are impregnated with calcium as a deterrent to ward off grazers), are common. The most common algae include *Hypnea spicifera* and various species of *Plocamium* and *Laurencia* and *Bifurcaria brassicaeformis*, the latter having a preference for turbulent, wave-dominated waters. The Prickly-bladed Kelp (*Ecklonia biruncinata*) is another common resident here. Urchins (*Parechinus angulosus*) are found in protected areas between the rocks and, if their numbers increase beyond sustainable levels, their presence can have a detrimental effect on algae populations due to overgrazing and the *Lithothamnion* covering, which they leave behind on the rocks. Starfish are found in the Infratidal Zone, of which *Henricia ornata*, *Marthasterias glacialis* and the detritus feeder, *Patiria granifera*, probably occur in greatest number.

Zonation on the west coast is very similar to the south coast, with a noticeable exception being the presence of vast subtidal kelp beds, which line its entire length. The same species that occur in the Littorina Zone of the south coast also occur in this zone along the west coast. In the Upper Balanoid Zone there are far fewer Barnacles and, in addition to *Patella granularis*, *P. granatina* is another common Limpet resident here. The Lower Balanoid Zone supports a variety of algae – mostly Flat-bladed Red Algae such as *Iridea* and *Aeodes*, as well as *Aplachnidium*, commonly known as Dead Man's Fingers. The Tubeworm (*Gunnarea capensis*) also occurs here. The Cochlear Zone extends from the south coast to the west coast, where it includes an additional Limpet, *Patella argenvillei*, in great numbers. The Infratidal Zone has similar species to those occurring on the south coast, with vast banks of Red Bait and algae such as *Champia lumbricalis*.

Maputaland's Marine Reserves

From the South African border with Mozambique to a point one kilometre (half a mile) south of Cape Vidal, the Maputaland coastline comprises a string of proclaimed marine reserves, including the Maputaland Marine Reserve which stretches from the Mozambican border south to a point known as Mbibi 11 kilometres (7 miles) north of Sodwana Bay. Although geographically and ecologically the reserves are all part of the same thing, their nature varies due to different intentions and their times of proclamation.

Marine Reserve No. 1, which forms part of the Greater St Lucia Wetland Park, stretches from the southern boundary of Maputaland to Mbibi – a total distance of 79 kilometres (49 miles). The reserve extends from the low-water mark to an imaginary point three nautical miles out to sea. Here all activities, other than fishing with rod and line and spearfishing, are strictly prohibited. Marine Reserve No. 2, known as the Sanctuary, is situated within Marine Reserve No. 1, between Leven Point and Red Cliffs. Swimming is the only activity allowed here. North of Mbibi, in the Maputaland Marine Reserve, access to the beach is restricted and is only possible by four-wheel-drive vehicle at a very limited number of places due partly to the lack of roads in the area. More importantly, access is restricted because this short stretch of coastline is the only protected traditional breeding ground for turtles in Africa.

BELOW *Situated on the Maputaland coast, Black Rock was once part of an ancient sea cliff, but is now a series of jagged rocks that have been worn into a variety of contorted shapes. It is one of five rocky outcrops occurring along a coastline that stretches for some 200 kilometres (124 miles).*

Offshore, lying parallel to the coast, ancient dunes that were once part of the coastline but later submerged as the level of the sea rose during the Pleistocene period have been encrusted by beautiful coral reefs that provide a fascinating panorama of vivid colour. These coral reefs, which lie between 5 and 25 metres (16 and 82 feet) below the surface of the sea, are the only tropical coral reefs to occur in South African waters. They provide a productive environment for a rich diversity of tropical marine life as well as certain fish species indigenous to the colder waters of Europe, having reached Maputaland by migrating down Africa's west coast. Other fish common to these reefs have come from the cold Southern Ocean between Africa and the Antarctic. Some fish are endemic to Maputaland. As a result of this natural attraction to the area, over 1200 fish species have been recorded along the reefs of Maputaland which, together with the relatively unspoilt condition of the coral reefs, makes them an asset of immeasurable value. Maputaland also compares favourably with Australia's famous, species-rich Great Barrier Reef where only 300 more species are known to occur.

Along the isolated beaches of northern Maputaland a primeval ritual has been performed every year at the height of summer for at least the last 300,000 years. Giant Leatherback and Loggerhead Turtles emerge from the sea at night to lay their eggs in nests which they dig high up on the beaches. The nesting habits of turtles make a fascinating story. Once gravid, turtles return to the nesting beaches where they themselves were hatched despite the many thousands of kilometres they will have travelled since birth. This astounding ability to cross open oceans, travel vast distances – all of it done underwater in an environment where celestial navigational aids are not available – and return to the beaches on which they were hatched is one of the marvels of nature – a best-kept secret. Turtles' homing ability requires highly evolved guidance mechanisms which, despite extensive research, are not yet scientifically understood.

Nesting is a slow and laborious process and lasts for at least an hour. At high tide, the gravid turtle emerges from the sea and rests in the wash zone of the beach. Once satisfied that there is no danger, she advances up the beach in order to find a suitable site to lay her eggs. Here she digs herself in using her fore-flippers. Once settled, she carefully digs an egg cavity with her rear flippers to a depth of between 25 and 45 centimetres (10 and 18 inches) into which, after a short rest, she lays her eggs. She usually lays about 120 eggs at a time after which she gently sweeps sand over them, constantly feeling with her rear flippers until the hole is filled. Adding more sand, she kneads and presses the surface until it is packed hard. When satisfied, she then disguises the nest site by throwing sand vigorously around with her fore-flippers. Finally she returns, exhausted, to the sea. Loggerhead Turtles lay up to 500 eggs per season, while Leatherbacks lay up to 1000 eggs per season. During her lifetime, a female turtle may return to the nesting beaches in five separate seasons. Time intervals between seasons may vary from one to five years. It is interesting to know that the sex of the turtles is determined by the ambient temperature of the sand covering the eggs. If the sand is warm, females are born; if it is cool, males are born.

Between 50 and 70 days later, the hatchlings struggle out of their nest in the sand. Once they emerge above the surface of the sand, each matchbox-size hatchling faces the formidable task of finding the sea, which could be a few hundred metres away. The

run to the sea is a time of great risk as the hatchlings are exposed to many dangers – the predations of Ghost Crabs, Monitor Lizards, birds and dehydration from the sun if they are not quick enough. Having cleared the surf line, the hatchlings swim out into the open sea where they finally enter the Agulhas Current. They are swept down the east and south coasts of South Africa as far as the Atlantic Ocean. In the open sea, the young turtles are subject to continual risk through constant exposure to predators. It has been estimated that only one or two hatchlings out of every 1000 that enter the sea eventually reach maturity.

In time the surviving turtles are swept back into the southern Indian Ocean where they spend anything up to three years drifting, following the currents. During this time the young turtles feed on floating organisms such as Jellyfish, Bluebottles and Purple Storm Snails. After a number of years at sea, the ocean currents bring the young turtles back to the African and Madagascan coastlines where they start feeding on subtidal fauna such as molluscs and mussels. After this stage, the females are ready to be fertilized and the whole breeding cycle begins again.

BELOW *The laying procedure for Loggerhead Turtles is the same as that for Leatherback Turtles, except that they lay up to 500 eggs per season in batches of about 120 at a time at about 13- to 18-day intervals; Leatherbacks lay up to 1000 eggs per season at 10-day intervals.*

TOP LEFT *A Leatherback Turtle prepares a nesting site by first digging a body cavity into which she will settle before laying her eggs.*

TOP RIGHT *After she has dug a depression deep enough to hide her body, she commences the laborious process of digging an egg cavity with her rear flippers, which she uses like a spade. When this has been completed, she then deposits her eggs into the hole and covers them up, again using her rear flippers.*

ABOVE *Once she has laid her eggs, closed the hole into which she deposited them, sealed it by tramping the sand down gently using her rear flippers in a kneading action and then camouflaging her nesting site by scattering the sand around it, she returns to the sea, exhausted.*

The Wild Coast

Much further south of Maputaland, between the umTamvuna River in the north and the Kei River in the south, lies one of South Africa's wildest and least disturbed stretches of coastline. Few roads penetrate from the main towns in the interior down to the coast. As a result human settlements are relatively small and sparsely situated, ensuring that humankind's impact is limited and more or less restricted to specific parts of the coastline.

The waters washing the rocks and beaches along this sector of coast form part of a zone of transition, from the warmer sub-tropical waters of KwaZulu-Natal to the colder temperate waters of the Cape. Where they meet, they give life to a diverse combination of organisms that include tropical fish, which enter the area from the north, particularly in the summer months. Meanwhile, cold-water Cape fish are swept along the coast by the north-flowing countercurrent from the south. Notable among these are the vast shoals of Sardines that migrate north during winter, attracting seabirds and predatory fish in vast numbers. Offshore, Common and Bottlenose Dolphins (*Delphinus delphis* and *Tursiops truncatus*) can often be spotted playing in the waves and in the deeper waters Humpback (*Megaptera novaeangliae*), Minke (*Balaenoptera acutorostrata*) and Southern Right (*Balaena glacialis*) Whales are frequent visitors.

Rocky shores are a feature of this coastline, their nature varying according to the type of rock, from smooth terraces to jagged outcrops. In places the land drops dramatically into the ocean in the form of steep cliffs that resolutely face the sea's turbulent onslaught. Over time, however, they succumb gradually to the erosive strength of the waves and their strange, sculpted shapes add to the interest and attraction of the area.

Life on the rocks takes two principal forms. On those parts of the rocks exposed to the violence of the sea, filter-feeders extract minute organisms from the seawater that continually flows around them. These slow-moving animals have the ability to affix themselves firmly to the substrate so that they can resist the sea's incessant wave action. In the pools and crevices between the rocks a wide variety of micro-habitats exist, creating a multitude of natural aquariums in which a diverse range of marine creatures provide a kaleidoscope of colour, shapes, form and interest.

Interspersed between the rocky shores and headlands, small sandy bays and long stretches of open beaches are another typical characteristic of the Wild Coast. To the undiscerning eye it may seem that these areas are void of life. On the contrary, Ghost Crabs (*Ocypodidae* sp.), which are mainly nocturnal, and filter-feeders such as Sea Lice and Sand Mussels feed on the microscopic bacterial organisms the sea deposits on the sand every time a wave runs up the beach. Plough Snails (*Bullia* sp.) are scavengers that come up from their homes deep below the sands every time their sensory organs detect the smell of a dead creature on the beach. Each of these creatures is in turn prey to birds and other predators, ensuring the perpetuation of the beach's life cycle.

The Wild Coast contains some of southern Africa's largest and least disturbed pockets of coastal forest, many of which are conserved in nature reserves and state forests. As with the sea, these forests contain species typical of the temperate Cape and subtropical KwaZulu-Natal – although the latter tends to dominate. Soil type plays an important part in determining the actual tree species which grow in different parts of the coastal forests.

Along the Wild Coast, spectacular gorges and deep, forested ravines line the rivers that rise in the mountains of the southern Drakensberg. These rivers flow into the sea through wide estuaries when the river has reached a mature stage of development; more frequently, they are contained within deep valleys when they discharge their waters into the ocean. In some cases, such as at Waterfall Bluff, the rivers end in impressive waterfalls that spill over either sheer cliffs or down a series of rocky terraces before reaching the sea.

Between the forests, rivers and estuaries, rolling grasslands cover much of the coastal belt of the Wild Coast. These areas are characterized by shallow soils and a high water table and provide a productive habitat capable of supporting large populations of grazing animals. Adjacent to the sea the grasses are short – mainly *Stenotaphrum secundatum*, a highly palatable grass heavily utilized by herbivores – while further inland the grasses become less and less palatable with the taller *Themeda triandra* being the dominant vegetation. Where overgrazing is heaviest, the largely unpalatable *Aristrida junciformis* takes over. After the first rains in spring and during summer, a wide variety of beautiful lilies, orchids, Red-hot Pokers and irises colour the grasslands.

ABOVE *A colourful display of Mesembryanthemum flowers lines the interface between the coastal rocks and the grass-clad hills that drop steeply down to the sea along much of the Wild Coast.*

ABOVE *Much of the coastal evergreen forests, which have been ruthlessly exploited for their fine timbers elsewhere along the coast, remain in pristine condition at the Silaka Nature Reserve near Port St Johns.*

ABOVE *The flowers of the Pompom Tree* (Dais cotinifolia) *provide a shower of pinkish-mauve colour along the margins of the evergreen and riverine forests which occur at various places along the Wild Coast.*

LEFT *The Wild Coast has been heavily sculpted by the sea, with marine cliffs eroded into the sedimentary rock strata with which it interfaces. Hidden here by high tide, the sea bottom at the foot of the sea cliff has been widened by wave erosion to form a wave-cut terrace, which lies between the low-water mark and the highest level of wave erosion. Also cutting into the rock structure is a river that flows into the sea over a waterfall which will continue to cut back, eventually creating a deep river gorge and, one day, when the erosive processes of nature have been completed, a wide open delta.*

ABOVE *The rocks in the foreground are part of a wave-cut terrace cut out of cliffs that once stood above them – probably as impressive as those across the bay. These cliffs tried to withstand the sea's erosive power, but were steadily worn away, leaving the residual features visible today. The flat rock surfaces and rock pools created in this way are repeatedly inundated and exposed as the tides advance and recede, and they support a fascinating and diverse marine community.*

LEFT *Grasslands cover a large area of the Wild Coast's coastal belt, which is characterized by shallow soils and high water tables. The grasslands are highly productive, enabling them to support large populations of grazing animals. At the Mkambati Game Reserve Eland, among others, have been introduced.*

OVERLEAF *The Mkambati River is a beautiful river characterized by a series of crystal-clear pools and a number of gentle waterfalls, of which the Mkambati Falls, or Horseshoe Falls as they are also called, are the most impressive. Here the river splays out in an arc and drops down in a series of steps to a deep pool. The stream then tumbles over another waterfall before dropping several metres into the sea below.*

ABOVE *Widely distributed throughout the wetter, eastern half of South Africa, this lovely orchid (Disa polygonoides) is in flower in the Mkambati Game Reserve. Normally found in marshy places, or on damp slopes, it grows in scattered communities in both open grassy areas as well as near bush and on the fringes of forests.*

BELOW *Ocypode ryderi is one of three species of Ghost Crab found mainly on beaches in KwaZulu-Natal and along the northern beaches of the Eastern Cape where there are no kelp beds. These high-shore scavengers usually emerge at night as the tide falls.*

ABOVE *Along the Wild Coast, as well as the Cape south coast, the alternation of hard sandstones and softer shales causes a succession of capes and bays. The shales are less able to resist the erosive forces of the sea and so they give way more quickly than the sandstone, thereby creating bays that attract the sands carried by longshore drift. In this way, beaches are slowly formed. As the sandstone is more resistant to the sea's attack, it erodes more slowly, forming capes which ultimately protrude into the steadily advancing sea.*

BELOW *There are three species of Plough Snail: Bullia digitalis, common on the west coast; B. rhodostoma, common on the south coast; and B. natalensis, occurring on the beaches of KwaZulu-Natal. All three have similar habits and scavenge on dead or dying animals, which they absorb by means of their long proboscis.*

BELOW *Found along the coast and midlands of KwaZulu-Natal and the Drakensberg, the Pineapple Lily (Eucomis pallidiflora) has a remarkable inflorescence with a stout peduncle. The raceme is a column of six-petalled flowers, which have a purplish ovary in the centre. The coma of small leaves closely resembles a pineapple.*

ABOVE *The Black Mangrove* (Bruguiera gymnorrhiza) *is one of the most common trees found in mangrove communities along the coastline. The significance of mangroves is that they are a heterogeneous group of plants which have independently evolved mechanisms, enabling them to adapt to a normally hostile habitat. Being part of the intertidal zone, this habitat is inundated with sea water at high tide and exposed to the sun at low tide. In order to cope with constant tidal flooding and the high salinity level of the sea water, the trees have the ability to exclude much of the salt content in the water they absorb. The Black Mangrove's root structure emerges in knoblike loops above the substrate, enabling it to absorb oxygen and to discharge carbon dioxide.*

ABOVE *The Red Mangrove Crab* (Sesarma meinerti) *is the largest crab found in mangrove swamps along the coast. Cautious and shy, it digs permanent burrows in communal groups. These scavengers collect any organic material, although their main food is fallen leaves.*

BELOW *Many rivers rise in the Drakensberg and flow eastwards, discharging their waters along the Wild Coast. In places, rivers have cut spectacular gorges, or forested ravines, such as the Msikaba River Gorge in the Mkambati Game Reserve. Some rivers have not yet reached maturity and are characterized, instead, by wide floodplains by the time they reach their ocean destination.*

ABOVE *Bontebok occurred only in the Cape from Bredasdorp to Mossel Bay, where they were hunted to near extinction. Fortunately a reserve was set aside and the species was saved. Today they have been successfully introduced to other locations, including the Mkambati Game Reserve on the Wild Coast.*

BELOW *The Mkambati Nature Reserve is an 8000-hectare (19,768-acre) coastal reserve consisting mainly of grasslands. Along the coastline, and where rocks intercept the passage of grass fires, stands of Natal Wild Banana (Strelitzia nicolai) occur along with lichens, mosses, succulents and orchids.*

ABOVE *Blister Beetles (Family Meloidae) are attractively and brightly coloured in order to warn predators of their unpleasant taste. They contain cantharidin in their bodies, which is distasteful and irritating and, as their name implies, causes blistering of the skin. Adults are phytophagous and are often seen feeding on flowers. Female Blister Beetles deposit their eggs either on or in the ground, from which triungulins – tiny elongated larvae – emerge. They have well-developed legs and are unusual in that they are parasitic on locust and grasshopper eggs; they also parasitize the larvae and food stores of bees. Blister Beetles are widespread and occur not only in South Africa but in many other parts of Africa.*

Dwesa and Cwebe Nature Reserves

Although administratively the Dwesa and the Cwebe nature reserves are separate entities, ecologically they are part of the same system. The Dwesa Nature Reserve lies between the Mbashe River in the north and the Nqabara River in the south and is 5700 hectares (14,085 acres) in extent. North of the Mbashe River is the Cwebe Nature Reserve which covers an area of 2140 hectares (5288 acres).

Where the Mbashe and Nqabara rivers discharge into the sea, large estuaries have formed in which there are interesting mangrove communities. Within both reserves, numerous smaller rivers meander gently through forests to the sea where they form a series of pristine estuaries. It is possible to see the elusive African Finfoot (*Podica senegalensis*) and the rare Whitebacked Night Heron (*Gorsachius leuconotus*) on the banks of these estuaries. The Mbanyana River, within the Cwebe Nature Reserve, forms a beautiful lagoon before flowing into the sea. In the late afternoon and early evening the nocturnal, extremely shy Cape Clawless Otter (*Aonyx capensis*) can be seen swimming across the lagoon or foraging for food along its banks. During the day and evening, the evocative call of the African Fish Eagle often rings out over the lagoon, a favourite hunting ground.

Running the full length of both reserves is a chain of wide unpolluted beaches and secluded bays sandwiched between rocky outcrops which abound in undisturbed intertidal life. Here the African Black Oystercatcher (*Haematopus moquini*), which reaches its northern territorial limit at Dwesa, can be seen busily searching for oysters to eat, while the ubiquitous Turnstone (*Arenaria interpres*) laboriously turns over stones and shells seeking its prey hiding beneath them.

Covering the low hills rising from the shoreline are grasslands which provide grazing for Eland, Blesbok, Red Hartebeest and Blue Wildebeest, all of which have been reintroduced into the reserve. The grasslands are virtually enclosed by indigenous coastal forests which contain some fine specimens of large-leaved Guarri (*Euclea natalensis*) and Sneezewood (*Ptaeroxylon obliquum*) trees. A number of paths and trails lead through the forest and provide the observant visitor with the opportunity to see a wide variety of forest birds and secretive forest dwellers. Among these are the Samango Monkeys (*Cercopithecus mitis*) which, although noisy, are elusive and difficult to see, the Blue Duiker and a range of smaller mammals.

The variety of habitats from seashore and estuaries to grassland and indigenous coastal forest – all within a relatively confined area – makes the Dwesa and Cwebe nature reserves a birdwatcher's paradise. Over 300 bird species have been recorded in the area.

BELOW *The white-sand beaches that characterize Dwesa Nature Reserve's coastline rise up to hills that provide sweeping views across rolling grasslands, evergreen coastal forests, the streams and rivers which traverse the reserve, and the deep blue ocean beyond. Adding to the grace and beauty of this pristine region are animals such as Eland (*Taurotragus oryx*).*

TOP *Dwesa's rugged coastline is typical of the Wild Coast. The sea unleashes its fury on the sandstone cliffs, which steadily continue to erode until eventually headlands as mighty as these give way to the ocean's relentless power.*

ABOVE *The African Black Oystercatcher is easily identified by its jet-black body, bright-red bill and red eye ring. This wader occurs only along the coastline or in lagoons where oysters can be found, from Namibia in the west to Dwesa in the northeast.*

RIGHT *The Cape Clawless Otter has a dark-brown coat, which looks black when it is wet. Unlike other otters, the Cape Clawless can be seen away from water, where it ambles along with its back slightly arched. It is usually most active in the early morning or late afternoon and lies up under cover of heavy shade during the hot hours of the day. It feeds principally on freshwater mussels and crabs, as well as fish and frogs. It is also known to eat molluscs, small mammals, insects and birds.*

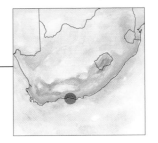

Tsitsikamma National Park

Situated on the Western Cape's southern coast, between Groot River at Nature's Valley in the south and Oubosstrand in the north, lies an 80-kilometre (50-mile) coastal strip of rugged and infinite beauty. In 1964 this area was proclaimed as two national parks – the Tsitsikamma Forest National Park and the Tsitsikamma Coastal National Park – but in 1987 the two parks were consolidated into a single park known as the Tsitsikamma National Park. The inland boundary more or less follows the 200-metre (656-foot) contour line, except in the southern Vasselot section at Nature's Valley where the boundary extends beyond this height and covers an area that reaches some 3.5 kilometres (2 miles) inland. The eastern boundary lies some 5.5 kilometres (3.4 miles) out to sea. The total land area amounts to 5373 hectares (13,277 acres). Throughout its entire length the park is crossed by clear streams that come down from inland mountains. In places these streams and rivers have incised deep kloofs through solid sandstone cliffs which buttress the sea. A good example of this is at Storms River where the river has cut a deep and precipitous-sided gorge through the surrounding sandstone. In other places, where they have been created in more recent geological times, the rivers cascade down a series of stepped waterfalls into the sea. Where the substrate is made of layers of softer shale wedged between rocky capes, the sea has carved out gentle bays while the rivers have created estuaries, some of which can be navigated for many kilometres. These estuaries and the navigable sections of the rivers leading from them offer some of the finest birdwatching and nature experiences in South Africa.

The fascination of the Tsitsikamma National Park lies in the wealth of fauna and flora in the two worlds it straddles – the terrestrial and the aquatic – and in their interaction. The terrestrial has two major components that compete for space. The first and most obvious is the rich variety of evergreen forest trees and shrubs located in the valleys and on the mountain slopes rising up from the shoreline. The second component comprises the fields of *fynbos* that are less conspicuous, but no less interesting, and which occur on the coastal plain and along the forest edges. According to scientific evidence, the *fynbos* has gradually gained the upper hand over the last millennia, increasing its territory as the climate along the Cape's southern coast has steadily become drier thus favouring *fynbos* rather than moisture-dependent evergreen forests. The forests support a variety of small terrestrial fauna, including the diminutive Blue Duiker, Chacma Baboon, Vervet Monkeys, Bushbuck, Bushpig and the Cape Clawless Otter.

The fauna and flora of Tsitsikamma's aquatic world is heavily influenced by the ruggedness of the coastline and the narrowness of the continental shelf at this point. The meeting between land and sea is often abrupt and violent due to the absence of sloping beaches and the moderating influence of the continental shelf on

BELOW *This view of the coastline along the Tsitsikamma National Park shows a wave-cut platform, formed as a result of wave erosion, with densely forested cliffs in the background. It is a wild and unspoilt stretch of rocky coast and is typical of almost the entire length of the Tsitsikamma National Park.*

incoming waves. Great energy is generated as waves build up over thousands of kilometres of open sea. When these waves reach the Tsitsikamma coast – virtually unhindered by the friction that is normally generated through contact with the sea floor – the water is released with full fury upon the rocks. This intense wave action restricts the growth of marine fauna and flora to those organisms which are capable of withstanding the vigour of the unbridled seas.

Another factor that affects the marine fauna and flora of this region is the influence of the transition between the warm waters of the east coast of South Africa and the cold waters of the west coast, since it is along the Cape's south coast where this transition is most marked.

Two of South Africa's most popular hiking trails traverse the Tsitsikamma National Park: the world-famous Otter Trail, which starts at Storms River and follows 41 kilometres (25 miles) of spectacular coastline to its conclusion at Nature's Valley; and the 61-kilometre (38-mile) Tsitsikamma Hiking Trail, which leads inland through the evergreen forests in the reverse direction – from Nature's Valley to Storms River.

ABOVE *A breathtaking perspective of Nature's Valley's seemingly endless sandy beach shows the Vasselot section of the Tsitsikamma Forest in the background. Although the beach seems to be devoid of marine life, on closer inspection it is almost as lively as that of a rocky shoreline, with the exception of the fact that the zoning is not as rigid and the animals and other organisms are minute and less colourful.*

ABOVE *The tall evergreen forests of Tsitsikamma (the Khoikhoi word for 'the place of sparkling waters') contain some of South Africa's largest trees, including massive Outeniqua Yellowwoods, Ironwoods, Stinkwoods, and a variety of indigenous ferns and climbers. The forests are home to the Knysna Loerie (Tauraco porphyreolophus) and Narina Trogon.*

OPPOSITE *This attractive waterfall is just one of many features to be viewed along the Otter Trail, one of South Africa's most scenic and popular hiking trails. The trail's popularity lies in its magnificent coastal scenery, the indigenous forests and mountain fynbos it passes through and the rich birdlife (210 bird species have been recorded so far) that can be observed. In addition large marine mammals, such as dolphins, seals and whales, come close inshore making very clear sightings possible.*

RIGHT *Fynbos dominates the seaward slopes of the mountains that dip into the sea along the Tsitsikamma Coast. Interestingly, the warm Agulhas Current, which bathes the southern fynbos coast, also supports the penetration of tropical vegetation into the temperate Tsitsikamma fynbos region and as a result, the Tsitsikamma coastal region is noted for its hardwood evergreen forests along the inland slopes and valleys of the coastal mountains, and fynbos along the seaward slopes.*

BELOW *A common resident of rocky outcrops throughout South Africa is the Rock Dassie, or Hyrax. From appearance it is easy to associate the Rock Dassie with rodents but, interestingly, their evolutionary relationships are more closely associated with the elephant and the dugong. They are small, stoutly built animals with short legs and no tails. Their ears are small and rounded and their colour varies from yellow-fawn to dark-brown. Rock Dassies are predominantly diurnal, but on warm moonlit nights they may come out of their places of hiding to feed. Normally they emerge after sunrise, but only become active once the day has warmed up. They spend a great deal of the day basking in the sun, while at least one dominant adult keeps watch for predators. If threatened, the watch sounds an alarm by emitting a sharp cry and all animals dash for safety. They are grazers and browsers and eat the leaves, bark and fruits of a wide range of plants. Most feeding is done in the morning and late afternoon. During the hottest part of the day they retreat into their shelters.*

BELOW *Arum Lilies* (Zantedeschia aethiopica) *grow in large groups, particularly where the ground is damp or swampy, either in open sun or semi-shade. Their distribution is widespread along South Africa's coastal regions, from the southwestern Cape to KwaZulu-Natal, where it extends to the midlands and the lower slopes of the Drakensberg Mountains. The Arum Lily, as with other species of the Araceae family, is characterized by small flowers crowded on a central fleshy spike, known as a spadix, which is enclosed in, or attached in some way, to a waxy white spathe (the colour of the spathe varies with different species).*

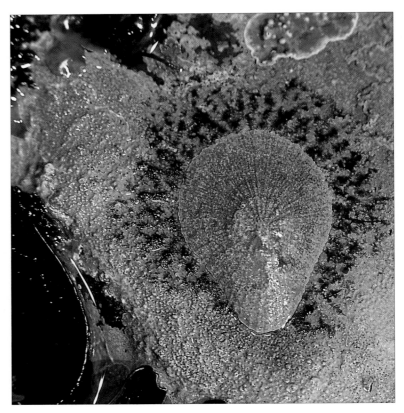

ABOVE *One of the joys of the Otter Trail is to watch schools of Indian Ocean Bottlenose Dolphins playing in the waves. Large schools pass by the Tsitsikamma coastline in their search for fish and squid to eat. Their bodies are robust and their snouts of a moderate length – with the bottom jaw protruding out further than the top one. They have a dark-grey back with paler grey sides and ventral area, and a thin pale line that runs from the eye to the flipper.*

BELOW *The Cape Wagtail (Motacilla flava) is common to the whole of South Africa. While its normal habitat is around lakes, dams, rivers and coastal lagoons, it has adapted to city parks and domestic gardens. It has greyish-brown upperparts with a narrow, black breast band and is distinguishable from the Longtailed Wagtail (Motacilla clara) by its shorter tail.*

ABOVE *Limpets graze on the small algal spores and diatoms that they can scrape from rock faces within the Upper Balanoid Zone of the seashore. Most Limpets are unable to handle the large seaweeds that occur in the Lower Balanoid Zone. One exception is the* Patella cochlear, *seen here with its surrounding 'algal garden'. The effect of Limpet colonies is such that where they occur, there is an abrupt change from dense algal growth to bare rock.*

BELOW *The Cape Robin (Cossypha caffra) is a common resident through-out South Africa, but is found in greatest number along the Southern Cape coast. It is distinguished by its white eyebrows, orange upper breast and greyish underparts. The Cape Robin has a rather pleasant and continuing call. Its habitat is principally montane river valley and scrub, but also includes evergreen forests and fynbos.*

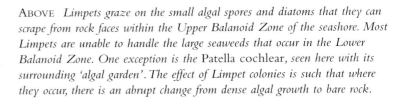

ABOVE *The tubular flower of the Wild Pomegranate contains copious nectar and birds frequently split open the petal tube near the base to obtain the sweet liquid.*

ABOVE RIGHT *Samango Monkeys are shy and rather secretive creatures. They are largely arboreal with a distinct preference for tall evergreen forest and riverine gallery forest. They may forage in open woodland, but always remain very close to the forest edge, to which they rapidly retreat at the first sign of danger. They are found in isolated pockets in the Eastern Cape, KwaZulu-Natal and Mpumalanga. They sometimes live in troops of up to 30 monkeys, although this is unusual — the normal troop size seldom consists of more than about 20. Like most monkeys they are highly vocal; the males frequently bark with a far-carrying single command followed by a strange rumble. In addition to this they have a wide range of other calls. Samango Monkeys feed on a diversity of plants, including seeds, tree leaves, fruits, flowers and gum. They also eat the barks of various trees and are quite notorious for this debarking activity, making them very unpopular with foresters. Occasionally they eat insects.*

RIGHT *During the Tertiary period, some two to 70 million years ago, the sea extended to the foot of the Tsitsikamma Mountains. The coastal plain between the sea and the mountain was shaped by wave action and this is possibly one of the best examples of a large wave-cut terrace in South Africa. Later, the land was lifted and the terrace was exposed, after which the rivers flowing from the Tsitsikamma Mountains carved deep, narrow gorges through it. A good example of this process is the gorge cut by the Storms River with its precipitous walls that tower some 300 metres (984 feet) above the water, just before it enters the sea at Storms River Mouth.*

OVERLEAF *The Wild Coast is well known for its dramatic seas and the huge waves which crash against its rocks, sending spray soaring into the sky. The reason for this can be seen in the profile of the continent's submarine floor. The continental shelf along the Wild Coast is narrow and, as a result, there is little friction from the sea's floor to reduce the energy of incoming swells. Some of these swells have gathered energy for thousands of kilometres, travelling from as far south as the reaches of Antarctica before unleashing their energy on the rocks of the Wild Coast in plunging breakers.*

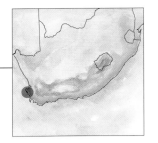

West Coast National Park

Washed by the cold waters of the Atlantic Ocean, the West Coast National Park lies on South Africa's arid west coast. Both Saldanha Bay and its extension, the Langebaan Lagoon, are unique in South Africa since they owe their origin to dramatic changes in the level of the sea that came about over many millions of years. With the successive advances and retreats of the sea resulting from alternate periods of earth warming and ice ages, barrier dunes built up along the coast. With the most recent advance of the sea, estimated to be about 9000 years ago, the sea broke through the dunes between the rocky headlands that flank the mouth of modern-day Saldanha Bay and filled the land behind the dunes – thereby creating Saldanha Bay and Langebaan Lagoon. Since no river feeds into it, the lagoon is not an estuary and therefore it does not have to cope with the stresses that result from a rise and drop in salinity levels due to drought and flooding. The lagoon has a highly productive and rich food web based on nutrients obtained from the salt marshes, dominated by those of the genus *Sarcocornia*, that surround its shores. These plants grow to maturity quickly in spring and early summer and then die back forming beds of decaying matter that are attacked by bacteria and converted to food for a wide variety of marine species which, in turn, become food for the many and varied waders that can be seen in the shallow waters around the lagoon.

Ecologically Langebaan is most significant for the huge bird populations that it supports. Many thousands of aquatic birds are resident here and in summer their numbers swell as Arctic migrants leave their breeding grounds in the Arctic Circle and make their way to the warmth, food and security Langebaan offers – particularly on the several islands lying at the entrance to the bay where over a quarter of a million birds find predator-free roosting and nesting grounds. An interesting separation between the different species exists on each island. One of the world's largest breeding colonies of Black-backed Gulls *(Larus dominicanus)* exists on Schaapen Island. On Marcus Island the largest single population of Black Oystercatchers congregate; they share the island with an estimated 10,000 Jackass Penguins, believed to be one of the densest penguin colonies in the world. Gannets and Cormorants favour Malgas Island, from which many thousands of tons of guano have been collected since 1845 when the commercial exploitation of this 'white gold' began in earnest.

The West Coast National Park also extends to the mainland surrounding the lagoon and the Donkergat Peninsula that divides it from the sea. The vegetation covering the land comprises the unique West Coast *strandveld,* made up of low bushes, sedges and succulents, which is brittle and barren in summer, but is transformed after the winter rains into carpets of wildflowers that cover the veld in a blaze of colour.

BELOW *The West Coast is characterized by cold, rich fishing waters. Cape Gannets have colonized Malgas Island, off the West Coast National Park, and an estimated 60,000 birds, or about a quarter of the total Cape Gannet population, breeds there annually.*

ABOVE *No rivers flow in or out of Langebaan Lagoon and therefore water levels are solely influenced by high and low tides. At low tide, extensive salt marshes and mud flats are exposed, which attract a wide variety of waders and aquatic birds. Langebaan is the largest wetland on the West Coast and the biggest salt marsh in South Africa. Every year, huge flocks of Greater Flamingos gather there between April and August.*

OPPOSITE *The tranquil Langebaan Lagoon is the focal point of the West Coast National Park; it is 16 kilometres (10 miles) long, 4.5 kilometres (3 miles) wide and on average about 6 metres (18 feet) deep. It is connected to Saldanha Bay – rapidly becoming a burgeoning industrial sea port – by means of a narrow channel. There was a time when the Langebaan Lagoon also had vast colonies of oysters, but by a quirk of nature they died out and the bed of the lagoon is now covered with an estimated 30 million tons of shells.*

RIGHT *The Preekstoel (pulpit) dominates the foreground of the West Coast National Park, which was proclaimed on 30 August 1985 and originally encompassed the 5700-hectare (14,085-acre) Langebaan Lagoon and its marshlands, 40 hectares (99 acres) of adjacent land, four offshore islets (Jutten, Malgas, Marcus and Skaap) and two sections of Sixteen Mile Beach. Four privately owned farms and the sand dune area of De Hoek were subsequently added and in August 1987 the private nature reserve of Oude Post also became part of the park. It is a very important conservation area, as scientists have estimated that it provides a home, either permanently or seasonally, to 50 per cent of the world's population of Swift Terns (Sterna bergii), 25 per cent of the world's Cape Gannets, 15 per cent of the Crowned Cormorants (Phalacrocorax coronatus) and 12 per cent of the population of African Black Oystercatchers.*

ABOVE *The Angulate Tortoise* (Chersina angulata) *is a medium-sized tortoise found in the fynbos regions of the Western Cape and along the West Coast, where it is generally much larger. Its diet includes grasses, annuals and succulents. An interesting feature of this tortoise is its ability to drink in sandy soils by pushing its snout into moist sand and filtering water from it, which runs off its carapace and collects around the head.*

BELOW *The Hottentot's Cherry* (Maurocenia frangularia) *is a rigid shrub that can grow to 4 metres (12 feet), principally in kloofs or protected areas near the sea. It flowers between January to May and has a striking cherry-like fruit.*

BELOW CENTRE *The Lesser Doublecollared Sunbird* (Nectarina chalybea) *is distinguishable from the Greater Doublecollared species by its shorter bill and narrower red breast band. Its body is also deeper grey in colour. Its preferred habitat is coastal scrub and fynbos, and less mountainous areas. It is also found along forest margins.*

BELOW RIGHT *The Sandlelie* (Veltheimia capensis) *is a perennial herb that grows up to about 40 centimetres (16 inches) in height and has a bulbous root structure. The leaves are bluish-green in colour with wavy margins. The plant has interesting flowers that are purplish pink with green tips and fruits that are inflated. It is normally found in the drier parts of the south-western regions of the Western Cape.*

LEFT *The Fyn t'nouroebos* (Drosanthemum hispidum) *belongs to the Mesembryanthemaceae family and is a spreading perennial that often covers considerable areas of Namaqualand with sheets of pink and white. Each plant has a single flower on a short stalk.*

BELOW *Various antelope species, including the ponderous Eland were reintroduced into the West Coast National Park after the addition of some 6800 hectares (16,803 acres) of farm land in 1989. Today, the total area of the park is some 25,000 hectares (61,775 acres) and the park is registered as a wetland under the Ramsar Convention.*

Focus on
THE BUSHVELD

The term bushveld is generally used to describe a type of savanna characterized by relatively short trees, of which acacia and broad-leaved species are dominant. Bushveld, or mixed woodland as it is also known, generally occurs at altitudes below 1500 metres (4922 feet). In South Africa these woodlands extend in a giant sweep that starts north of Port Alfred and follows the coastal plain across KwaZulu-Natal and Swaziland and then opens up into a huge fan-shape which spreads out across the three provinces of Mpumalanga, Northern and North West, finally reaching into eastern Botswana in the west. Within this biome there is wide diversity in the ecological landscape which arises from a multitude of factors such as altitude, aspect, climatic influences, soil types, and human intrusion. As a result of a combination of these factors, three basic subdivisions can be made: lowveld, middleveld and thornveld.

The term lowveld, spelt with a lower case 'l', covers much of the arc that extends from northern KwaZulu-Natal through Swaziland and the low-lying plains that stretch from the foothills of the eastern escarpment in Mpumalanga to Mozambique and along the Limpopo valley to well west of Messina. The term Lowveld, spelt with an upper case 'L', is generally used to describe that part of the lowveld in Mpumalanga that lies between the foot of the escarpment and the South African border with Mozambique, along the Lebombo Mountains and between the Crocodile River in the south and the Letaba River in the north. Rainfall in the lowveld ranges between 400 and 800 millimetres (16 to 32 inches) per annum and occurs during the summer months; temperatures are distinctly tropical and, as a result, humidity and human discomfort levels are high. The presence of malaria and other tropical diseases meant that until the discovery of

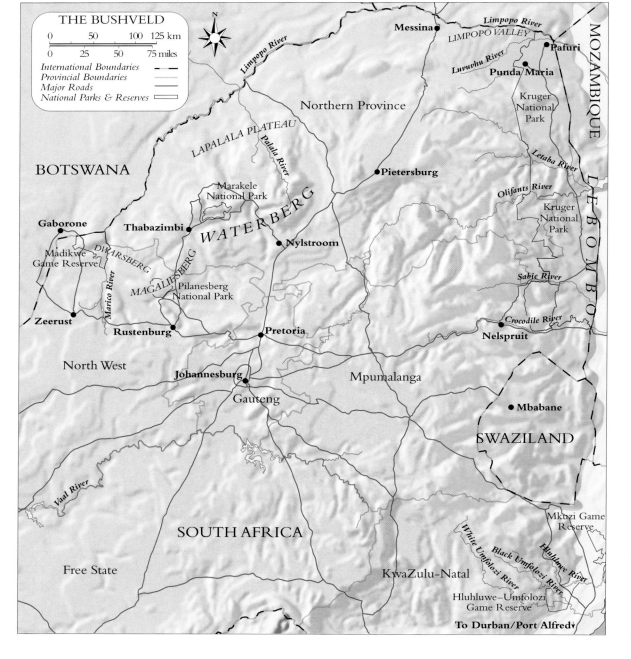

THE BUSHVELD

0   50   100 125 km

0   25   50   75 miles

International Boundaries
Provincial Boundaries
Major Roads
National Parks & Reserves

Limpopo River

Messina

LIMPOPO VALLEY

Pafuri

Luvuvhu River

Punda Maria

MOZAMBIQUE

Northern Province

Kruger National Park

LAPALALA PLATEAU

Palala River

Letaba River

LEBOMBO

BOTSWANA

Pietersburg

Olifants River

Marakele National Park

Kruger National Park

Gaborone

Thabazimbi

WATERBERG

Nylstroom

Madikwe Game Reserve

DWARSBERG

MAGALIESBERG

Marico River

Pilanesberg National Park

Sabie River

Zeerust

Rustenburg

Pretoria

Crocodile River

Nelspruit

North West

Johannesburg

Gauteng

Mpumalanga

Mbabane

Vaal River

SWAZILAND

SOUTH AFRICA

Mkuzi Game Reserve

Free State

KwaZulu-Natal

White Umfolozi River

Black Umfolozi River

Hluhluwe River

Hluhluwe–Umfolozi Game Reserve

To Durban/Port Alfred

OPPOSITE *The mood of the bushveld changes according to the time of day. At first light it is a hive of activity, but as the merciless sun climbs towards its zenith, life seems to come to a standstill, as virtually all the animals retreat into the bushveld's shadows. Sometimes the searing heat is relieved by a sudden thunderstorm, after which there seems to be a new lease on life. As the sun sets, a brooding silence descends over the veld, broken only by the evocative sounds of the night.*

suitable prophylaxes, human habitation was sparse and restricted in the main to the higher-lying areas which are cooler due to prevailing breezes. Tree cover is considerable and gives the lowveld a parklike appearance; the trees however are irregular in height and vary in stature from mere shrubs to grand specimens of 10 metres (33 feet) or more. Shrubs and tall grasses grow beneath the tree canopy. The grass is tufted and occurs in clumps that reach a metre (3 feet) or more in height during the summer rains. Tree species vary according to locality; in the wetter parts many of them belong to the Bauhinia family, and along river courses and wetlands, Fever Trees are a common sight, their distinctive pale-green or yellowish trunks and branches lending a sense of surrealism to the landscape.

In the northern, drier parts of the lowveld one of the most distinctive tree species is the Mopane. It is a medium to large deciduous tree that varies in height from 4 to 18 metres (13 to 60 feet), and covers large hot and low-lying areas in southern tropical Africa. Where conditions are adverse Mopanes remain stunted and become mopane scrub. The leaves provide important fodder

for many animals, while brightly coloured caterpillars – generally known as Mopane Worms – of a large greyish-brown moth (*Gonimbrasia belina*) also feed on the leaves. Rich in protein, they are considered a delicacy by local inhabitants. The worms are either roasted and eaten straight away or dried and stored for many months.

Another distinctive tree in the drier regions is the Baobab (*Adansonia digitata*). Evocative of ancient Africa, it has a fat tapering trunk that gives way to thin and tangled branches that look more like the tree's roots than its crown. Its strange appearance gave rise to the San legend that the Baobab once angered the Creator and as punishment he planted the tree upside down.

The middleveld, the second subdivision of bushveld and less tropical than the lowveld, occurs north of the Magaliesberg up to the 600-metre (200-foot) contour line. This is a summer rainfall area which varies between 500 and 750 millimetres (20 and 30 inches) per annum. During winter, the nights become very cold and frost occurs from time to time. Tree distribution is more uneven and patchy than in the lowveld and the trees are generally much shorter – seldom reaching more than 7 metres (23 feet) in height. The grass is also shorter but more continuous in cover. A wide variety of acacia trees grows here, most of which are characterized by flat or umbrella-shaped crowns.

In North West Province, rainfall decreases and conditions become dry resulting in a savanna type known as thornveld, which differs from that of the middleveld and lowveld. Large patches of soil are exposed in the thornveld due to the aridity of the region, resulting in an incomplete cover of the ground both by trees and a combination of grass and shrubs. The trees are generally small, seldom reaching more than 4 metres (13 feet) in height. A notable exception is the Camel-thorn, one of the main tree species in the arid thornveld, which attains heights of up to 16 metres (52 feet) in the region's deep, red sandy soils. Its pods form an important fodder and provide a delicacy for elephants. When dried and crushed, the pods are used by the Tswana people for curing headaches and discharging ears. The Silver Terminalia (*Terminalia sericea*) is a small to medium-sized, well-shaped tree that grows to between 4 and 6 metres (13 and 20 feet) in height, occasionally reaching 10 metres (33 feet). It is very common in the three subdivisions of the mixed woodlands. Among the indigenous African people a decoction of the roots of the tree is used to cure diarrhoea and to relieve colic. It is also used as an eyewash, while a hot infusion of the roots' outer layers is used as a cure for pneumonia. Tswana potters use the silky, silvery leaf hairs to make a glaze for their pottery wares.

RIGHT *The Knob-thorn Tree averages 8 to 10 metres (26 to 33 feet) in height, although in places it may grow up to 20 metres (66 feet) high. This deciduous tree occurs in low altitude woodland and wooded grassland, particularly near rivers and lakes. Its dark-brown bark has large knob-like prickles and it is this feature which gives the tree its common name. In older trees, the bark becomes deeply fissured and the knobs less conspicuous. The Knob-thorn is often found where sweet Rooigras grows; this is usually favourable ranching country.*

BELOW *This close-up perspective of the candle-like flowers of the Knob-thorn illustrates how the flowers appear before the leaves do. Because of their number and their full covering, the flowers make the tree highly conspicuous.*

Hluhluwe–Umfolozi Game Reserve

Situated in northern KwaZulu-Natal within a lowveld zone is the Hluhluwe–Umfolozi Game Reserve. It comprises two separately proclaimed game reserves, both of which date back to 1895, and a corridor of land between them which was given over relatively recently to conservation in order to link the two game reserves together. This was done when it was found that an option to mine the corridor for coal was not viable. Both game reserves rank among the oldest in Africa. Hluhluwe covers an area of 23,067 hectares (56,999 acres) and Umfolozi some 47,753 hectares (117,998 acres). Umfolozi was the traditional hunting ground of the Zulu kings and lies between the Black and White Umfolozi rivers. Hluhluwe consists primarily of steep, wooded hills, grass-covered slopes and riverine woodland along the Hluhluwe River and the other streams which drain the area. Abundant water and dense bush makes game-viewing at Hluhluwe fairly difficult, particularly in summer. Much of Umfolozi is also hilly with level floodplains along the White and Black Umfolozi rivers. Savanna woodland and thicket,

interspersed with open areas of grassland, cover large parts of the reserve. The Umfolozi Game Reserve is probably best known for the important role it played in saving the White Rhino from extinction and today both reserves serve as the last stronghold in Africa, and therefore the world, of both the White and Black Rhino. The Hluhluwe–Umfolozi Game Reserve complex is home to 84 mammal species, including Elephant, Buffalo, Giraffe, Kudu, Blue Wildebeest, Nyala, Hippopotamus, Impala, Waterbuck, Red Duiker and Burchell's Zebra. Predators are well represented by Lion, Leopard, Cheetah, Wild Dog and Spotted Hyena. Some 425 bird species have been recorded in the combined game reserve complex.

BELOW *Bush-covered hills in the Hluhluwe Game Reserve provide a home for an extraordinarily wide range of fauna and flora. The reserve, which is one of the oldest in Africa, still retains much of the feel of untrammelled Africa.*

OPPOSITE TOP *The Whitebellied Korhaan (Eupodotis cafra) is a fairly common resident in the drier, western parts of South Africa. Although it is a larger bird than the Redcrested Korhaan (Eupodotis ruficrista), it is relatively small in comparison to other korhaans. As the common name of this species suggests, a distinguishing feature is the white belly.*

OPPOSITE BOTTOM *The Greenbacked Heron (Butoides striatus) is small, dark grey and has a black crown and dark-green back with slightly paler underparts. Bright, orange-yellow legs and feet are a distinguishing feature of this bird. It also has a long, black nape plume, which only becomes obvious when it lifts its head on alighting. This secretive bird frequents a wide range of habitats, including mangrove swamps and coral reefs at low tide, freshwater dams, lakes and sluggish rivers – particularly those with overhanging trees.*

LEFT *Burchell's Zebra, once plentiful and distributed throughout South Africa, are today restricted to the game reserves in northern KwaZulu-Natal and the lowveld in Mpumalanga. Although different specimens vary widely in both their patterning and coloration, they all exhibit stripes that extend to their underparts – unlike the Cape Mountain Zebra (E. zebra zebra) and Hartmann's Mountain Zebra (E. zebra hartmannae), both of which have white underparts.*

BELOW *The Nile, or Water, Monitor (Varanus niloticus), or Water Leguaan as it is more commonly known, is the biggest African lizard and has a large body, powerful limbs and strong claws. It occurs in a wide range of habitats, including rivers, pans, dams and lakes throughout the eastern part of the region – as far south as the Gamtoos River. It is often seen on rocks or dead tree stumps, basking in the sun. In colder, temperate regions it is known to hibernate during the colder winter periods. The Nile Monitor's diet is varied and may comprise frogs, eggs, insects, fish, crabs, and mussels.*

Kruger National Park

The Kruger National Park is one of the great conservation areas of the world, and over 650,000 local and foreign visitors are attracted to its quintessential natural beauty every year. An astonishing 19,455 square kilometres (7510 square miles), or nearly 2 million hectares (4,9 million acres) in extent, from north to south the park is some 350 kilometres (218 miles) long and from east to west it is about 60 kilometres (37.5 miles) wide. To place this in perspective, the park covers an area larger than the country of Israel.

Situated within the Lowveld, this great swathe of grassland, thicket, woodland and riverine forest provides a spectacular array of landscapes and animal life which has, because of its sheer size and unspoilt quality, the ambience of primeval Africa. Its boundaries are natural on three sides: the Luvuvhu and Limpopo rivers in the north, the Crocodile River in the south and the Lebombo Mountains along the east where the park abuts Mozambique. In the west an unnatural boundary has been drawn and reinforced with fencing which cuts across the ancient migration routes of Wildebeest and Zebra, who in previous times sought better grazing nearer the wetter escarpment during winter.

The park can be loosely divided into four different vegetation regions, resulting from the combined effect of a decrease in rainfall towards the north and a broad geological division that runs along the park's north–south axis. On the western side of this axis the geological composition is largely heavily eroded granite while on the eastern side it is essentially basalt. Interspersed within each of these very broad and generalized divisions are riverine forest and sandveld areas, such as those around Punda Maria in the northwest and along the park's eastern boundary south of Pafuri; both support unique communities of flowering plants. Indeed 35 ecological landscapes have been identified within the Kruger National Park. In ecological terms, the word 'landscape' is used to describe a unique combination of climate, soil, topography, vegetation and the animals which live there, all of which combine to form an interactive unit. While a landscape is thus large enough to include several distinctly different plant communities and a number of different soil types, the essential thread that holds it together is the pattern of relationships between the landscape's constituent components.

The southwest is dominated by granite koppies that have been weathered by nature into dramatic natural castles on whose ramparts Klipspringers often stand in bold silhouette against the

BELOW *The Olifants River is one of only four perennial rivers that flow through the Kruger National Park. The river supports one of the major Hippo populations in the park, as well as 10 pairs of the very rare Pels Fishing Owl (Scotopelia peli). Unfortunately, pollution levels in the river are rather high.*

piercing blue skies that are so common over Kruger. In the fissures and crannies of nature's castles, lizards lurk waiting for their moment to bask in the sun or hunt their prey. Sitting very still, a Leopard may be silently surveying its surroundings in preparation for a pending hunt, or it may be resting, its camouflaged body blending perfectly into the background.

Over countless millennia, as the granite outcrops succumbed to nature's eroding onslaught, coarse quartz sands as well as fine clays were produced. The sands, being heavier, remained on the higher ridges, while the clay was steadily washed down into the valleys. As a result the ridge tops and higher ground have sandy, largely infertile soils which support large-leaved thornless trees, which include the Large-fruited Bushwillow (*Combretum zeyheri*) and tall but unpalatable grasses (generally known as 'sourveld'). Here animal life is stunted, but notwithstanding, graceful antelope, such as Sable and the ubiquitous Mountain Reedbuck, can be seen shading under the trees and adding interest to the landscape.

In the valleys the clayey soils support small-leaved, thorny acacia trees and the grasses are shorter but sweet and palatable. The leaves of these trees have less tannin than the broad-leafed trees and therefore they too are more palatable, although more difficult to eat because of the tree's array of protective thorns. It is thus in the valleys that the animals congregate in larger numbers – the grazers concentrating on the grasses and the browsers on the small leaves of the thorn trees. White Rhinoceros are found more frequently in the southwestern part of the park.

ABOVE RIGHT *The flowers of the Sickle Bush* (Dichrostachys cinerea) *provide the bushveld with splashes of colour between October and January. The flower is made up of two parts – the first being the long, slender, pink, sterile staminodes and the second the fertile, short catkin. The flower spike droops and hangs upside-down on the tree, resulting in the pink section being above the yellow. The 'sickle' effect that is created gives the tree its common name.*

RIGHT *A Kudu cow peers from behind a bush. The females are rufous in colour, unlike the males which are more grey, and their sides are clearly marked with six to 10 vertical white lines.*

BELOW *Chacma Baboons* (Papio ursinus) *spend a considerable part of their day grooming each other. Baboons are highly gregarious and social and live in troops of between 15 and 100 animals. In these established organizations, all males are dominant over females and are ranked in strict order.*

From the Sabie River to the Olifants River, which more or less bisects the Kruger National Park from west to east, the vegetation is largely open savanna in the east with large patches of Knob-thorn Acacia and fine individual specimens of Marula trees, whose fruits are favoured by wildlife and humans alike. Along the rivers and dry riverbeds which crisscross this area Leadwoods (*Combretum imberbe*), ranging in size from mere shrubs to large trees reaching up to 15 metres (50 feet) in height, grow in profusion. West of the geological divide are dry open woodlands in which Bushwillows, varying from shrubs along the dry riverbeds to trees 10 metres (33 feet) or more in height, tend to dominate. Although by no means restricted to this area of the park, Burchell's Zebra, Impala, Giraffe, Blue Wildebeest and Black Rhinoceros tend to favour this sector. Since Lions' favoured prey is Zebra and Wildebeest, these largest of all cats are most commonly found in this part of the park. North of the Olifants River, where the topography is predominantly low-lying and the climate tropical, Mopane woodland (or *Colophospermum* woodland) stretches out as far as the eye can see. Mopanes grow in two forms: a multi-stemmed shrub that grows up to about 3 metres (10 feet) in height and a tree which usually has one, but occasionally two or three, stems and grows up to 18 metres (60 feet) in height. More than half the Elephants in the Kruger are found in Mopane woodland since the Mopane not only provides a nutritious fodder but also has the ability to rejuvenate itself after being reduced by Elephant – much like grass after it has been grazed. Other notable animal species that are found predominantly in this part of the park are Roan Antelope, Tsessebe and Eland, while Nyala and Bushbuck are frequently seen in the riverine forests of this region. In the northeast of the park, where it is hotter and drier, the vegetation thins out revealing large uncovered open spaces. Here Baobabs, the monarchs of the African bush, make their regal appearance and keep an imperious surveillance over a landscape of rugged hills and ridges.

The Kruger National Park has the greatest number and widest terrestrial species diversity of all wild places in South Africa. In total it has the following species: 147 mammals; 505 birds; 118 reptiles; 34 amphibia (toads and frogs); 49 freshwater fish; 404 trees and shrubs; 224 grasses and 1275 other plants.

BELOW *Solid granite weathers along lines of weakness created by veins of feldspar, which is softer than granite. In the process, granite boulders and balancing rocks are left behind. Granite domes are formed by repeated heating and cooling. Over time, with the penetration of water, layer after layer of rock 'peels off', as can be seen in this photograph.*

ABOVE *Elephants are often playful and spar with each other, locking their trunks and butting their heads together. They live in small family groups and seldom show aggression towards each other, preferring to break their play should tempers rise.*

RIGHT *Leopards spend a good deal of their lives in trees and are thus excellent climbers. They are mainly active at night and are usually solitary animals, except when they come together to mate or when a mother has cubs. Males mark their territory against other males, although their territories may overlap with a number of female territories.*

BELOW *A young male Lion rests during the hot hours of the day. Lions usually lie up in the shade of a tree or under the overhang of rocks. They hunt mainly at night and in the cool hours of the day, often covering huge distances in search of food.*

ABOVE LEFT *Formicine Ants (subfamily Formicinae), seen caring for their pupae, are the most advanced and specialized ants in terms of their structure and habits. Several species have become very sophisticated in the art of food collecting. Some species, mainly those which feed on honeydew and other insect secretions, have developed 'herding' techniques in which they control certain aphids and coccids, protecting these insects from predators and parasites and even going to the extent of constructing shelters around them. In winter they often collect the aphid's and coccid's eggs and carry them back to the shelter in order to ensure their continued survival.*

ABOVE *The Flap-neck Chameleon's diet consists mainly of insects, particularly beetles and grasshoppers. When threatened, it inflates its body, distends its throat, raises the occipital flaps and opens its mouth wide, exposing its red-orange mouth lining. Although it is not poisonous, it is feared by many tribal people and is the subject of considerable folk legend and myths.*

LEFT *The Pangolin (Manis temminckii) is a distinctive mammal because of the large brown scales composed of agglutinated hair that cover its upperparts, sides and tail. Smaller scales also cover the outer sides of the legs and top of the head. It has powerful hindlegs and a long heavy tail for balance. When threatened it rolls itself into a ball, encasing all its vulnerable parts within an armoury of razor-sharp scales.*

OPPOSITE BOTTOM *The Vine Snake (Thelotornis capensis), which is also known as a Bird or Twig Snake, is very thin with a lance-shaped head and large eyes. Extremely well camouflaged, it is able to move very fast when disturbed. It ambushes its prey – normally lizards and small birds – then kills it by envenomation, and finally swallows it whole. The Vine Snake's principal habitats are savanna and coastal forests.*

RIGHT *The Pearlspotted Owl (Glaucidium perlatum) is the smallest owl resident in the southern African region. Its notable features are a lack of ear 'tufts', a rounded head, and white spots on the back and tail. The Pearlspotted Owl has two black marks on the back of the neck that give the appearance of two eyes. It is relatively common and is found mainly in dry thornveld and broad-leafed woodlands.*

BELOW *The Yellow Pansy Butterfly (Junonia hierta cebrene) is an easily recognizable species. It has bright orange and yellow patches on a base colour of black on both the fore- and hindwings and a distinguishing blue-violet spot on each hindwing, next to the costa. This species is typically found in the wetter eastern half of the country, but extends along the coast as far as Cape Town. It is seldom found in large numbers and tends to fly singly. It can often be seen sitting on the ground sunning itself. It relies on camouflage as a major strategy in its defence and, when threatened, it quickly closes its wings in order to allow the grey-brown underside to blend into its surroundings.*

BELOW RIGHT *The Impala Lily (Adenium obesum) is a thickset succulent shrub, or small tree, which seldom reaches more than 3 metres (9 feet) in height. It usually occurs at low altitudes in hot dry areas, often among rocks, but sometimes also in open sandy woodland. It has very bright white or pale pink flowers with bright pink to crimson borders. The lily also has toxic properties and was used in earlier times to poison arrows and fishing waters. Notwithstanding, it is heavily browsed by game and cattle.*

LEFT, CENTRE AND BOTTOM *This photographic sequence shows the birth of a Blue Wildebeest calf. A single calf weighing about 22 kilograms (48 pounds) is born after a gestation period of about 250 days. Mating normally takes place between March and June and most calves are dropped from mid-November to the end of December. Drought and unseasonal rains could affect this pattern. In order to be able to survive the rugged and ruthless dictates of the African bush, wildebeest calves are able to run with the mother within a few minutes after birth. Although wildebeest are well known for their huge migrations when they seek out new feeding grounds, bulls are nevertheless territorial in the sense that they may have between two to 150 cows under their control. The cows may, however, move through the territorial areas of control of other bulls and mate with them. Outside of the breeding season the large cow herds move freely without being controlled by the territorial bull. Bachelor herds are usually found on the periphery of the main concentration of animals.*

OPPOSITE TOP LEFT *Watsonia (Iris family) are one of South Africa's loveliest floral treasures and are plentiful in the well-watered mountain districts of South Africa – from Clanwilliam in the Western Cape, along the southern and eastern coastline and across KwaZulu-Natal to Mpumalanga in the country's northeast. There are 77 species of Watsonia that are endemic to South Africa. An interesting feature of this plant is the way in which it retains or sheds its leaves, according to the prevailing rainfall. During winter, in summer-rainfall areas, it is dormant and loses its leaves, while in summer in winter-rainfall areas it also loses its leaves. The flowers come in a variety of colours, including shades of scarlet, pink, orange, mauve, purple, and white.*

OPPOSITE TOP RIGHT *A notable distinction of the Grey Hornbill (Tockus nasutus) is its dark bill. It is normally found in thornveld and broad-leafed woodland in the extreme north of the country. Another characteristic feature is its soft plaintive whistling call, unlike the raucous cacophony of some species.*

OPPOSITE BOTTOM LEFT *The Martial Eagle is one of South Africa's larger eagles and is relatively uncommon throughout the region. It frequents a wide range of habitats, ranging from deserts to mountains, but is most commonly found in thornveld.*

OPPOSITE BOTTOM RIGHT *The Tumbleweed Flower (Boophane distichia) is also known as the Red Posy and belongs to the Amaryllis family. There are only three or four species of Boophane in South Africa, of which B. distichia is the best known and most widely distributed. This striking flower emerges in spring, during September and October, from a subterranean bulb root in seemingly hard, bare ground. After flowering, the flower head turns brown, becomes loose from its bulbous root and rolls across the veld. Caught in the prevailing wind, it eventually comes to rest against a bush or rock where it drops its seed. The species grows in all the summer-rainfall areas of South Africa.*

FOLLOWING PAGES *Umbrella-thorns (Acacia tortilis) are usually round-crowned when they are still growing, but on maturity become flat-topped. They are widespread in low altitude, dry woodland areas. A distinguishing feature is their multiple spines, which have both a hook and a spike – hence the Afrikaans common name 'haak en steek' (meaning 'hook and stab'). Sitting on top of the tree are two Secretarybirds (Sagittarius serpentarius), which are large, long-legged grey and black birds that prey on snakes and other reptiles. They like to roost in the tops of trees and mature Umbrella Thorns provide an ideal setting for them.*

The Waterberg

The Waterberg consists of a range of mountains and a series of intervening plateaus and plains situated northwest of Nylstroom in the Northern Province. The area was once a giant lake which, over countless millennia, gradually dried up, with the mud of the lake being transformed into shales and sandstones. The whole region was subsequently subjected to cataclysmic volcanic action and the landscape was thrust up into escarpments to the south, north and east. Around 400 million years ago the area became part of a giant inland sea and further sediments were deposited. In due course this sea dried up and the sediments were hardened and became compressed into rock. Around 150 million years ago the region was subjected to tremendous tectonic forces and the sedimentary rocks were faulted and split into huge blocks with cliff sides and plateaus. These have steadily eroded to create the grand topography that characterizes the Waterberg today.

The Waterberg mountains are majestic and rugged and rise up to the central Lapalala plateau which covers about 15,000 square kilometres (5790 square miles). As far as the eye can see, African bushveld stretches in seemingly endless vistas which eventually disappear beyond the distant blue horizons. Within this vast wilderness there is a wide variety of habitats, ranging from dense Combretum-dominated sourveld to open grassland and woodland laced with thick riverine forest, especially along the banks of the Palala River.

The Waterberg region has been home to humankind for many centuries. The San people once roamed its vast open spaces and left their paintings in caves and overhangs throughout the area. Late-Iron Age man was there too and a number of smelting sites and artefacts bare testimony to his presence. When white colonialists crossed the Vaal River and settled in what eventually became the Republic of South Africa, large farms were demarcated in the Waterberg and were either given or sold cheaply to the settlers. At first cattle ranching was tried, but water shortages and sour grass made this unprofitable. Various forms of agriculture, including tobacco farming, were tried, but market conditions and a host of other factors made it difficult.

Only when the farmers realized that what nature had given them was their biggest asset – namely wilderness – did the Waterberg change from being perceived as a forsaken dumping ground into one of South Africa's prime wild areas. The flat open woodland and vegetated mountain slopes are perfect territory for Rhinoceros, Kudu, Buffalo, Gemsbok, Wildebeest, Eland, both

BELOW *This is a scenic view of the Matlabas River, running through the Marakele National Park. In the background the ruggedly eroded Waterberg Mountains can be seen receding into the distance. The Marakele National Park provides a home to an impressive variety of fauna and flora.*

Roan and Sable Antelope, Steenbok, Duiker, Klipspringer, Mountain Reedbuck and Warthog. Today over 400 game farms have been established, and offer exciting wilderness experiences or controlled hunting to people from all over the world. Many wilderness trails have been opened up; these can either be done on foot or on horseback, through remote and pristine country-side which, besides the footprints and hoofmarks left behind by the trailers, bears no other visible evidence of human presence.

Recently opened to the public is Marakele National Park, which is situated in Northern Province in the southwestern part of the Waterberg near Thabazimbi. It is presently about 45,000 hectares (111,195 acres) in extent with another planned 40,000 hectares (98,840 acres) to be added over the next five years. Marakele, which means 'sanctuary' in Tswana, is character-ized by deep valleys, majestic mountain landscapes and grass–clad hills. Much of the vegetation in the park is sweet acacia savanna which is suitable for a wide variety of antelope species, as well as other game such as White and Black Rhino and Giraffe. When the additional land is added, Elephant will be introduced as well as carnivores such as Lion, Cheetah, Hyena and Wild Dog. At present Marakele provides a home to an impressive diversity of animals including: Black and White Rhino, Tsessebe, Buffalo, Giraffe, Kudu, Impala, Eland, Red Hartebeest, Gemsbok, Burchell's Zebra, Blue Wildebeest, Bushbuck, Nyala, Brown Hyena, Leopard, Caracal, Duiker, Steenbok, Rhebok, Klipspringer and a number of smaller species. Some 275 bird species have been recorded so far and, as the park becomes fur-ther established, this is expected to increase to over 400 species. A total of 800 breeding pairs of the endangered Cape Vulture (*Gyps coprotheres*) are located here, making it the largest breeding colony of these birds in the world.

ABOVE *Jagged cliff faces have been cut by the Palala River through the sedi-mentary rocks which were laid down about 400 million years ago. About 150 million years ago they were split into huge blocks through mighty tectonic forces and have since been eroded by water and wind into these rough column-like cliffs which rise up vertically from the floor of the river.*

LEFT *The White Syringa (Kirkia acuminata) is deciduous and ranges in height from 6 to 15 metres (20 to 50 feet). It occurs in various types of wood-land at medium to low altitudes, very often on rocky ridges and outcrops. In autumn its leaves turn from green to light yellow and then to deep gold and eventually to a rich red, creating spectacular splashes of colour and great beauty. An interesting feature of this tree is that its roots swell up with water, which it later uses during dry winter periods. During times of drought, both animals and the local people dig these roots up for their stored water.*

ABOVE LEFT *The fruit of the Large-fruited Bushwillow has four wings that dry to a pale brown in winter and remain on the tree until the leaves have fallen off. As the wind blows they make a rustling sound and for this reason they are known in Afrikaans as 'Raasblaar bome' ('noisy-leaf trees'). Their presence is said to indicate the existence of sour grass, which is not palatable to game and domestic animals. From the fibrous roots of the tree local African people have traditionally woven baskets and fish traps. The leaves, when crushed and combined with certain vegetable oils, are used as an embrocation to ease backache; when water is added to this decoction it is used as an eye lotion.*

ABOVE *The fruit of the Red Bushwillow* (Combretum apiculatum) *is also four-winged, but is smaller than that of the Large-fruited Bushwillow. The fruits are reddish-brown when mature and they are covered in soft hairs, giving them a satinlike feel. The leaves of this tree are used by the Zulu people to make a decoction that is used as an enema to relieve stomach disorders.*

LEFT *Crested Barbets* (Trachyphonus vaillantii) *are very colourful birds, distinguishable by their orange face and erectile shaggy crest. They are the largest barbets found in the region and are totally unmistakable in appearance. Their habitat is varied and includes open broad-leafed woodland and riverine forest and thornveld. This bird is a common resident in the central, northern and eastern regions of South Africa.*

ABOVE *The Marakele National Park has been stocked, inter alia, with the uncommon Tsessebe. A characteristic feature of the Tsessebe is its higher shoulders and sloping back. It is a grazer and is typically found in open savanna woodland and adjacent grasslands. It tends to congregate near water, in small herds of five or six animals, although herds of up to 30 animals have been recorded. These antelope have a strong sense of territoriality, with single territorial bulls defending an area within which the cows and young animals live permanently. The Tsessebe is an attractive antelope, with a shorter face than the Hartebeest with which it is frequently confused. Its coat is dark chestnut in colour and has a distinctly purplish sheen.*

RIGHT *Brown hard ticks (Rhipicephalus sp.) belong to the family Ixodidae, and are responsible for transmitting most diseases affecting animals. They have a hard dorsal shield, or 'scutum', that covers the whole upper surface of the male; in females, it only covers a small area behind the capitulum. The scutum is patterned and is diagnostic for each species of tick. Sometimes the pattern is made up of pits, grooves and bumps, but on occasion the scutum bears a distinctive colour pattern. The rest of the body has a high measure of elasticity, which allows it to swell up enormously as it imbibes blood from a host animal.*

Pilanesberg National Park

Situated approximately 50 kilometres (30 miles) northeast of Rustenburg, Pilanesberg comprises a circular mountain mass – the weathered remains of several cycles of ancient volcanic eruptions, outpourings of lava, the collapse of craters, ring fracturing around the volcano, and the intrusion of magma into those fractures. It has a diameter of 27 kilometres (17 miles) and rises to a height of 600 metres (1 967 feet) above the surrounding flat bushveld. The jagged mountains that nature has carved out of the volcanic remains form six roughly concentric circles and contain some of the largest known outcrops of syenite – a rock similar to granite – in the world.

Pilanesberg has seven different habitats as a result of its situation within a transitional zone, between the wetter eastern and drier western regions of South Africa. It thus has vegetation typical of moist savanna regions on the hills, and scrubby thorn thickets typical of the arid Kalahari on the valley floors.

Ecologists have divided the vegetation of Pilanesberg into five divisions, of which the grasslands and savannas are the most dominant. Perhaps the most conspicuous to the visitor are the rolling grasslands covering the valley floors. These grasslands, although attractive in appearance, are not nutritious because they consist of sour grass species, including *Heteropogon contortus*, *Diheteropogon amplectens*, *Trachypogon spicatus*, *Eliomurus muticus*, and *Urelytrum squarrosum*. For this reason the animal carrying capacity of these seemingly luxuriant grasslands is very limited. The proliferation of sour grass species results from a combination of poor soils and a high water table in summer. This is due to many factors, including the presence of an impermeable substrate, heavy sheet erosion, frequent burning and overgrazing in the past.

Much of Pilanesberg is covered by savanna, which can be categorized into three broad types: valley savanna, which is dominated by acacias and includes Sweet-thorn (*Acacia karroo*), Umbrella-thorn, Leadwood (*Combretum imberbe*), Karree (*Rhees cancea*), Tamboti, and Buffalo-thorn (*Ziziplus mucronata*). Pediment savanna occurs on the acid pediment grasslands where waterlogging is reduced through runoff and the break-up of the impermeable substrates. Important tree species are Beechwood (*Faurea saligna*), Hook-thorn (*Acacia millifera*) and Sweet-thorn. Hill savannas, an important feature of Pilanesberg's vegetation, are divided into two types. Xerocline savannas, which occur on the drier northwestern, eastern and northern slopes and are characterized by more dense tree cover, consist mainly of the Red Bushwillow. Other species found here include Hook Thorn, the beautiful Large-fruited Bushwillow, the Live-long (*Lannea discolor*) with its lovely coppery-coloured bark, and the Wild Pear (*Dombeya rotundifolia*). The second type of hill savanna is composed of the less densely covered mesocline savannas, which occur on south-facing slopes and include such species as the ubiquitous Hook-thorn, Beechwood, Buffalo-thorn, Wild Pear, the Large-fruited Bushwillow, and the Mountain Cabbage Tree (*Cassonia paniculata*).

In the mid-1970s, the mountain mass and intervening valleys that make up the Pilanesberg were proclaimed a game reserve of some 500 square kilometres (193 square miles), or 58,000 hectares (14,332 acres). The reserve provides a spectacular setting for some 56 species of mammal, including the 'Big Five' (Lion, Elephant, Buffalo, Rhino and Leopard), and about 300 species of birds.

BELOW *A scenic view of the Pilanesberg National Park, showing the eroded mountains which once formed part of the ancient volcanic system that dominated the area. In the middle distance, lying in a natural basin formed by the mountains, is the Mankwe Lake. The grasslands that surround the lake provide grazing for a wide variety of grazers and during the hotter months, from October to March, the grasslands are laced with the large, tubular, white flowers of the Cape Primrose* (Thunbergia artriplicifolia).

ABOVE *Pilanesberg has the wooded savanna and hilly country with cover and access to water preferred by Kudu. The present Kudu population in the park exceeds 600. Kudu are browsers and eat a greater variety of plants than any other antelope in the region. Their favoured food is the leaves of* Acacia *and* Combretum *species in early spring. In summer, their preference is for the leaves of the Sickle Bush while in winter they tend to concentrate on the leaves of the Red Bushwillow.*

LEFT *Most of the Giraffe in the Pilanesberg National Park were introduced from Namibia and are predominantly lighter in colour than those often found elsewhere in South Africa. Giraffe are browsers, but because of their great height they have a distinct advantage over their food competitors as they are able to reach leaves which the others are not able to do. Giraffe are well adapted to arid environments and are able to cope with prolonged periods of drought. They are not territorially bound and are thus able to wander freely within suitable habitats.*

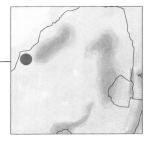

Madikwe Game Reserve

The Madikwe Game Reserve covers an area of 75,000 hectares (185,325 acres) and is bordered by Botswana in the north, the Marico River in the east, the Dwarsberg mountain range in the south and the Zeerust–Gaborone road in the west. Madikwe is a new reserve situated within the western thornveld sector of the bushveld region. It was once poorly developed farmland which had been abandoned after being purchased by the previous government as part of its homeland policy for incorporation into the erstwhile Bophuthatswana homeland. While unsuited for farming, Madikwe is perfect for wildlife as its highly productive sweet veld suits grazers, browsers and mixed feeders. Soon after the park's inception in 1992, it embarked on a four-year re-stocking programme known as Operation Phoenix. In terms of this programme bulk grazers (White Rhino, Hippo, Buffalo, Zebra and Waterbuck); concentrate grazers (Blue Wildebeest, Gemsbok, Red Hartebeest, Tsessebe, Common Reedbuck, Mountain Reedbuck, Springbok, and Warthog); mixed feeders (Elephant, Eland, Impala, Nyala, Bushbuck, and Ostrich); browsers (Giraffe and Kudu); and carnivores (Lion, Cheetah and Spotted Hyena) have been, or are to be, introduced. Leopard and a variety of small antelope already occur within the region, and Black Rhino, Sable and Roan Antelope are still to be introduced.

The rationale underlying the development of Madikwe is to create a major ecotourism asset which will be able to generate substantial funds, primarily for the socio-economic development of adjacent rural communities and to provide a number of job opportunities for local people.

ABOVE *A crimson and white throat, white forehead and squared tail are the distinguishing features of the Whitefronted Bee-eater (Merops bullockoides). These birds are usually found in pairs during the day, but they roost in flocks either in trees or on rock ledges along riverbanks at night. Their preferred habitat is wide, slow-moving rivers with steep sandbanks.*

BELOW *The Madikwe Game Reserve is situated in the dry North West, along part of the Botswana border. The perennial Marico River forms the border along much of the reserve's eastern boundary and in the south it is bordered by the Molatedi Dam.*

PREVIOUS PAGE *The Madikwe Game Reserve is a wild expanse of hills and bushveld that was until recently ranching country. Since its establishment in 1992, some 10,000 animals have been released in the reserve and it is now able to offer visitors superb animal and bird viewing. During the restocking programme, emphasis was placed on bulk grazer species due to the highly productive sweet veld with tall bunch grass species predominating — an ideal habitat for these species. Two luxury lodges and a bush camp have been established, which provide upmarket accommodation and offer conducted game drives and bush walks.*

ABOVE *African Elephants have been reintroduced into Madikwe in accordance with the park's stated policy of reintroducing those animals that were historically resident in the area. While Elephant populations have declined throughout Africa — as a result of hunting, poaching and exponential human population growth — those in game parks have steadily increased due to the security and protection offered in these environments. However, because of the finite size of game parks and the habitat destruction caused by Elephants as part of their feeding habits, there is a need to maintain an appropriate balance between population numbers and carrying capacity. To do this, culling is necessary. However, it has led to considerable debate in conservation circles since it is considered cruel and a controversial management tool. Experiments are currently being conducted in the Kruger National Park on contraception methods, to see if this could provide an alternative to culling.*

BELOW *The large tuber root of the* Adenia glauca *is greyish-green in colour, smooth-skinned and looks exactly like an elephant's foot — hence its common name. The plant's stems arise from the neck of the tuber and have glaucous leaves. Between August and January, the elephant's foot has numerous greenish-yellow, sweetly scented flowers. During October and November, it produces granadilla-like fruits that turn yellow-orange when ripe. It is endemic to a small area of North West Province and southeast Botswana.*

OPPOSITE BOTTOM *In keeping with the philosophy of reinstating the animals that were historically found in the Madikwe region, Lions have recently been reintroduced into the Madikwe Game Reserve.*

LEFT *The Spotted Bush Snake* (Philothamnus semivariegatus) *is very slender, with a distinct head and tail. The body is bright green to olive and characteristic markings include dark spots and bars on the forebody (although this is not common to all snakes of this species). These markings lighten to a bronze-grey towards the tail. The head is either a deep green or a bluish-green and the eyes have golden irises. This snake's prey includes geckos, chameleons and Tree Frogs and its hunting grounds are around shrubs and bushes growing on rocky ridges or along river banks. It is a speedy climber and is well camouflaged in foliage. It has a characteristic, but unusual, habit of undulating its head and neck sideways while keeping the rest of its body motionless. When threatened, its neck inflates, revealing bright-blue skin, and it may strike.*

LEFT CENTRE *The Rock, or White-throated, Monitor Lizard* (Varanus exanthematicus) *is a large, heavy lizard with strong, stocky limbs and sharp claws. It is covered with small beadlike scales, making its skin tough and difficult to penetrate. It has a rounded head with a bulbous snout, and its nostrils are two slits which are situated nearer the eyes than the end of the snout. The tail is longer than the body. It is a solitary animal and lives in a tunnel which it usually digs under a rock, or it may use a disused animal burrow, a hole in a tree, or a crack in the rocks which is not exposed. The lizard hibernates in its retreat, in a semi-dormant state, for most of winter. Its scientific name comes from the Greek word* exanthema, *meaning 'skin disorder', because of the lizard's leprous appearance. This results from the profusion of small ticks which cling to the soft skin around the eyes, nostrils and limb joints. Its diet mainly consists of invertebrates, such as snails, grasshoppers, beetles and millipedes. The Martial Eagle is the lizard's main predator. White-throated Monitors are found in savanna and arid areas throughout the subcontinent.*

Focus on
THE DESERTS

Although much of South Africa is arid, only true desert conditions are reached near the lower course of the Orange River and along the northern sectors of the Namaqualand coastline. South Africa becomes progressively drier westward due to the fact that the predominant winds blow from the southeast and lose most of their moisture along the southeastern coastline and eastern escarpment. South Africa's arid regions are thus located in the western half of the country and can be roughly divided into three areas: the *Kalahari Desert* which includes much of the Northern Cape north of the Orange River and the southwestern parts of North West Province (it continues into Botswana); the *Great Karoo* which extends from the Cape's folded mountains in the south and west to the Sneeuberg in the east, and the Orange River in the northeast until it meets the Kalahari Desert in the north; and *Namaqualand* which covers the area that stretches from the Orange River in the north to a line from the Olifants River mouth, through Vredendal and Vanrhynsdorp in the south, and from the Atlantic coast in the west to the Kalahari in the east.

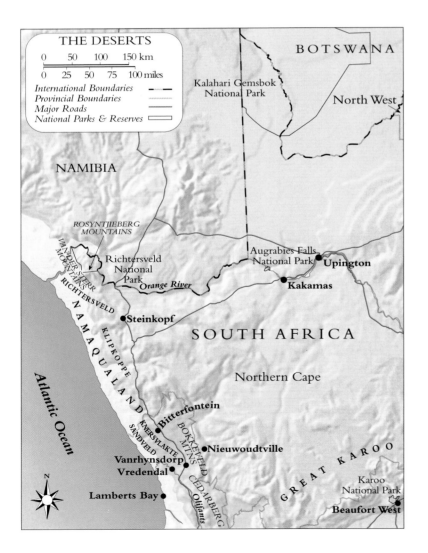

Kalahari Desert

The Kalahari is described as a desert, but it has little in common with the conventional notion of 'desert'. Its gently undulating sandy plains are, for the most part, surprisingly thickly vegetated, particularly in spring after the first hesitant rains have fallen, turning it into a gentle flowering wilderness. Should reasonable midsummer rains follow, the adaptable Kalahari has the ability to become a pastoral paradise with tall grass and leafy shrubs. But when the rains do not come, the Kalahari shows its other side and becomes a harsh lunarlike landscape of red sands shimmering under the sun's unrelenting heat and the searing blue metallic sky.

The Kalahari's sands are characterized by a red colour resulting from a thin film of red oxide which coats the actual grains. These sands provide what is probably the largest continuous sand surface in the world. Varying in thickness from less than three metres (10 feet) to over 100 metres (330 feet), the sands cover almost a third of the African subcontinent, making up an area of some 2.5 million square kilometres (965,000 square miles). They stretch from south of the Orange River in the south to Zaire in the north and from Etosha Pan (Namibia) in the west to Hwange (Zimbabwe) in the east. More specifically however, the name 'Kalahari' refers to the southern reaches of this gigantic tongue of land that covers the vast sandveld region of central and western Botswana and extends into eastern Namibia and the northern Cape. The sands of the Kalahari accumulated in a huge depression as a result of continental uplift more than 60 million years ago. While the surrounding highlands grew in height, the central area remained at this low level. During the period of extreme aridity that followed, in which diurnal temperature ranges were immense and winds were often violent, a good deal of the sedimentary rock in the basin was broken up and reduced to sand. This sand steadily collected in the valleys and hollows of the bedrock. Further climatic changes later initiated a wet period that lasted many millions of years, during which time the surrounding highlands were eroded by rivers and streams that poured into the basin from all sides, covering the low-lying areas with river gravels and soils rich in clay and lime. Again the climate changed and an-other period of aridity descended upon the land, causing all standing waters to evaporate, leaving behind a thick crust of surface limestone called calcrete. Where sedimentary rocks occurred, they were ground down to form a layer of sand over the calcrete. Most of the southern Kalahari is thus underlaid by sheets of calcrete and calcareous sandstone. Borehole drillings have revealed that the calcareous layer is over 100 metres (330 feet) thick in places.

RIGHT *The male Lions of the Kalahari Desert are renowned for their large black mane and their ability to go for long periods without water. The Kalahari Desert is part of the southern end of the largest expanse of sand on earth. These sand beds, which were created by violent winds many millions of years ago, once blanketed much of southern and western Africa. Today, the desert is restricted to parts of Botswana, South Africa, Zimbabwe and Namibia.*

The Kalahari is enigmatic and variable. On its northeastern fringes it embraces forest and swampland. Here the Okavango River spreads out in a huge delta and dies in a blaze of verdant glory in the Kalahari's pitiless sands while the Chobe River ploughs a path of riverine bush and lush grassland across its sands before joining the Zambezi on its journey to the sea. In the southeast the Kalahari combines tree and bush savanna with mopaneveld and bushveld, while in the southwest it is dominated by thornveld and arid scrub savanna. Across its plains great herds of wildlife, that have long disappeared elsewhere in southern Africa, still range according to the seasons. Here the timelessness of a primordial Africa is still embodied in the quintessence of the Kalahari's soul which has not yet been seduced and subdued by humankind's ruthless need to dominate.

Ironically, the absence of surface water was once one of the Kalahari's greatest assets since it discouraged permanent settlement and protected the sensitive semidesert ecosystem from being over-grazed by domestic animals. At the same time, in an almost perverse way, the Kalahari's inimical nature preserved the San and their way of life long after they were driven away from all the better-watered parts of the subcontinent. However, while the region's aridity delayed settlement, it did not prevent it when methods of tapping underground water supplies were developed. As these improved, so pastoralists were able to penetrate ever deeper into this vast thirstland. The result is that in modern times increasing areas have been opened up to domestic grazing and cattle ranching, and this has necessitated the erection of fences to check the spread of stock diseases. But these fences have cut across the migration routes of the great herds of game that used to roam freely, causing thousands of animals to die – either ensnared in the wires of the fences or from thirst as a result of being cut off from their traditional supplies of water.

Great Karoo

The Great Karoo accounts for almost a quarter of South Africa's land area. Of all the country's arid areas it is the best known since all the main roads and transport routes from South Africa's industrial centre, Gauteng, to the coast (excluding the KwaZulu-Natal coast) pass through it. For many, it is a drab, monotonous and barren part of the country that is best passed through as quickly as possible. For those who take time to stop and stare, and to learn the Karoo's secrets, it is a place of increasing fascination. Here nature has designed an intricate web of ecological relationships and mechanisms which enable plants and animals to survive the Karoo's harsh midday heat as well as its freezing winter nights,

BELOW *A characteristic feature of the Karoo are the dolerite sills which have provided protection for the sedimentary depositions beneath them, resulting in the flat-topped 'table' mountains and bell-like buttes throughout the region.*

and to survive long periods of devastating drought and the brief periods of strident rain when dry riverbeds are turned into raging torrents and the surrounding clayey soils imprison rain-water in surface pools and marshy plains.

It is interesting to see how the Karoo's vegetation has adapted to the region's unforgiving climate. Most of the vegetation is xerophytic, meaning that it has special mechanisms that enable the plants to retain water and thus survive in extremely dry conditions. Mesembryanthemums (Mesembryanthemaceae family) and Stapelias (for example, *Stapelia gemmiflora*), which have thick, rounded stems that are filled with moisture, predominate. Crassulas (such as *Crassula nodulosa* and *Kalanchoe* sp.) bring splashes of bright colour to the Karoo during spring and summer, and have tiny, leathery leaves that are able to catch the precious morning dew, when it comes, and to absorb it, allowing only the superfluous water that comes with heavy rain to run off. Some plants, such as members of the Liliaceae family, have moisture-filled bulbous roots which serve as the plant's water storage tanks during times of drought. Other plants have a waxy coating to their leaves which reduces water loss through transpiration.

BELOW *The Slangalwyn* (Aloe broomii), *also known as Bergalwyn, is a member of the Liliaceae family and is noted for its dominant single or branched inflorescence that is very densely multi-flowered.*

ABOVE *The monotony of the dull green and grey bushes of the Karoo is relieved in spring by the bright splashes of yellow that the flowers of the Wild Pomegranate* (Rhigozum obovatum) *bring to the landscape.*

BELOW *The delicate red flowers of the scrambling shrub, Swartstormbos* (Cadaba aphylla), *emerge somewhat incongruously in early summer from the branches of an unprepossessing Karoo bush and provide dashes of colour in what can be a drab landscape.*

Namaqualand

Namaqualand is a strangely schizophrenic region – hot, dry, barren and relentless in summer yet soft, beautiful and infinitely appealing in winter and spring when nature spreads out vast carpets of bright orange, yellow and white flowers across the usually harsh landscape. In order to adapt to the region's rigorous climate, the vegetation has had to develop special mechanisms of survival and the result is a unique and very interesting flora. Namaqualand is renowned for its variety of daisies, as well as for its many geophytes, dwarf shrubs and succulents. These vary from the creeping Rank-t'nouroe (*Cephalophyllum namaquanum*), which has delicate daisylike flowers that sparkle amid the plant's dull greyish-green succulent leaves to the stubby Botterboom (*Tylecodon paniculatus*) and the Quiver Tree.

Namaqualand can be divided into four discrete subregions according to the geographical nature of the surroundings: the Richtersveld, Klipkoppe (meaning 'rocky hills'), Sandveld and Knersvlakte. The Richtersveld was referred to by early explorers as the 'land that God created in a fury'. Covering some 40,000 square kilometres (15,440 square miles), it is South Africa's only true mountain desert. On first sight the Richtersveld is usually perceived as barren, stark and inhospitable with a moon landscape twisted by the anguish of a tormented earth – indeed, a land created in a fury. But gradually first impressions fade and steadily they give way to the realization that in the Richtersveld there is a fragile harmony between plant life and the harsh environment. For within the recesses of the region's restless landscape there is a rich variety of plant life that has learnt to conserve its energy and moderate its presentation in order to survive the vicissitudes of a hostile environment.

The Richtersveld has the greatest number of endemic succulent plants in the world. These plants have adapted to the extremely arid conditions in a number of ingenious ways, including the development of different root systems which penetrate to great depths in order to reach subterranean water, or the creation of superficial root structures which enable the plant to absorb dew. Most succulents have fleshy stems with limited or no branches and insignificant leaves so that they can reduce transpiration.

The Klipkoppe is an escarpment about 50 kilometres (30 miles) wide, wedged between the Sandveld in the west and the Bushmanland plateau in the east, and stretching from south of Steinkopf in the north to just south of Bitterfontein in the south. It is a desolate and arid area considered by many to be the true Namaqualand, distinguishable by its distinctive round, rocky, granite hills separated by sandy plains.

The Sandveld is a strip, about 30 kilometres (20 miles) wide, that stretches along the coast from the Orange River in the north to Lamberts Bay in the south. It is made up of loose white sand at the coast which gradually changes to red in the interior. Rainfall averages between 50 millimetres (two inches) at the Orange River to 150 millimetres (six inches) at Lamberts Bay. Vegetation seldom reaches more than a metre (three feet) in height with the predominant species being *vygie* bushes (Mesembryanthemaceae), with T'arra T'kooi (*Ruschia frutescens*) being the most common along the coast and the Skildpadbos (*Zygophyllum morgsana*) the most common inland.

The Knersvlakte lies between Bitterfontein in the north and Vanrhynsdorp in the south, the Sandveld in the west and the Bokkeveld Mountains near Nieuwoudtville in the east. It is an area of rolling hills with very saline soils covered in small, white quartz pebbles . Rainfall ranges between 100 and 200 millimetres (four and eight inches) and the vegetation, which is dominated by various species of the *vygie* family, is very low and varies in height from 10 to 50 centimetres (four to 20 inches). In places the vegetation gives way to large patches of red sand. Small-stock farming is practised extensively and gypsum is mined at a number of places.

BELOW LEFT *After good winter rains the fields of Namaqualand are covered with a variety of flowers, often in a combination of similar or matching species such as these* Felicia *and* Hirpicium *daisies.*

BELOW *Sambreeltjies* (Felicia australis) *are annual herbs with single flower heads on leafless stalks. The flower has an average of 25 mauvish-blue ray-florets, while the disc florets are a bright yellow. They occur in Namaqualand, the Clanwilliam district, in Paarl, and in the Great Karoo.*

ABOVE *During the wildflower season sheets of colourful daisies, such as* Ursinia *daisies, cover the fields of Namaqualand. In nature's wonderful restorative way, Namaqualand's daisies tend to congregate on land that has undergone some form of stress and are thus part of an ecological healing process.*

BELOW LEFT *The flowers of* Osteospermum *sp. daisies.*

BELOW Gazania *sp. are bright and colourful and occur throughout the region, as well as elsewhere in southern Africa.*

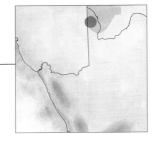

Kalahari Gemsbok National Park

Proclaimed in 1931, the Kalahari Gemsbok National Park covers a total area of 9600 square kilometres (3700 square miles), although plans are afoot to merge the park with Botswana's adjoining Gemsbok National Park to form one of the region's first Transfrontier Parks. Together these two parks, which uniquely straddle the common political boundary between two separate countries, will make up one of the largest game reserves in the world. To the lasting credit of the politicians and administrators of the time, they recognized the reality that wildlife and ecology observe physical and not political boundaries and they gave credence to this when the boundaries of the two parks were drawn up. The essential purpose for which the park was established was to protect what many people consider to be the prince of all antelope, the Gemsbok, or Oryx. These large graceful desert animals with their straight, pointed horns had been ruthlessly hunted for a century or more and were bordering on the brink of extinction at the time the park was established. Today the combined parks have 58 species of mammal (including the ebullient Springbok, the famous black-maned Kalahari Lion, Cheetah, Leopard, Hyena, Jackal, Eland, and Wildebeest to name a few) and 55 species of reptile. It also boasts more than 260 bird species as well as a diverse range of insect species.

An interesting feature of the Kalahari Gemsbok National Park is its topography, which on the South African side of the border is made up of wave after wave of red sand dunes created by prehistoric gales which raked the sands into more or less parallel north–south lines varying in height from 10 to 20 metres (33 to 65 feet). A lasting memory for many visitors to the park is the sight of a herd of Gemsbok slowly topping a dune, pausing at its summit to elegantly survey the surrounding scene and then slowly disappearing down the other side. Another is that of a herd of Springbok in full flight, effortlessly springing into the air to clear trees and shrubs of up to five metres (16 feet) and more in height. And in the stillness of the desert night little can be more evocative of a precious and passing Africa than the deep-throated roar of a Kalahari Lion on the hunt or the occasional chilling cry of the Brown Hyena in search of its prey.

OPPOSITE *Much of the central Kalahari is flat and grass-covered, but towards the drier regions in the west this cover gives way to intermittent but often large sand dunes, coloured red by a thin film of iron oxides that coat the sand grains.*

BELOW *Gemsbok are essentially a desert species and favour the sandy dunes with their sparse grass cover.*

LEFT *The Tsamma, or Karkoer (Citrullis lanatus), occurs principally in the warm arid parts of southern Africa. The well-known watermelon sold in shops is a developed form of this species, achieved through selection by plant breeders, and is now cultivated in many different parts of the world. Unlike the cultivated watermelon, Tsammas are bitter tasting and much smaller. An important quality of the Tsamma Melon is its ability to remain intact and retain its flesh and moisture for many months after abscission from the parent plant. Many wild animals use the Tsamma Melon as a source of water and food during the dry season. The San in the Kalahari Desert use it as their only source of food and a water resource for months on end. They mash the flesh to a watery pulp, after which it is half eaten and half drunk. It is also cooked and used in stews.*

RIGHT *The Ostrich is a common resident throughout southern Africa. The only wild Ostriches in the region are found in Namibia, the Kalahari and along the western and northern borders of the Northern Province. All Ostriches that occur predominantly in the drier western regions of the inland plateau, lowveld and southwestern Cape are a mixture of North African species, as a result of domestic stock breeding programmes.*

LEFT *The Ground Squirrel (Xerus inauris) is entirely terrestrial, but is typically squirrel-like in its looks and behaviour. It lives in an extensive burrow system and is easily identifiable by the white stripe that flanks its side. It is endemic to the arid areas of southern Africa and its preferred habitat is open areas with little cover and a hard substrate. These gregarious, diurnal animals congregate in groups ranging from five to 30. The females and young remain in a colony, but the males move from one colony to the next. They frequently stand on their hind legs in order to enhance their view of the surrounding countryside. Ground Squirrels feed on seeds, bulbs, roots, grass and insects — particularly termites. When feeding they cover their bodies with their bushy tails in order to provide an 'umbrella' against the harsh African sun. Interestingly, they often share their burrow systems with Suricates (Suricata suricatta) and Yellow Mongooses (Cynictis penicillata).*

ABOVE *Small populations of Blue Wildebeest occur along the Nossob River in the Kalahari Desert where subterranean water and the occasional flow of water in the river after rains provides moisture for limited grass cover. The Blue Wildebeest's preferred habitat is open savanna woodland and open grassland.*

BELOW *On reaching the age of three years, young male Lions are forced out of the pride by dominant older males, which have prominent manes.*

ABOVE *The Pygmy Falcon is small and often mistaken for a shrike. Its distinguishing features include its colouring – the male is grey above and white below and the female has a chestnut back – and the way in which it sits upright on an exposed branch. The Pygmy Falcon is found in dry thornveld and in semi-desert regions, principally in the Northern Cape Province, the southern Kalahari Desert and Namibia. Interestingly Pygmy Falcons are often found near the nests of Sociable Weavers (Philetairus socius). The falcon preys mainly on insects.*

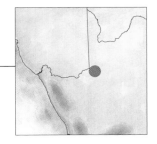

Augrabies Falls National Park

Situated some 40 kilometres (25 miles) northwest of the little town of Kakamas is the Augrabies Falls National Park. Here the mighty Orange River is forced through a narrow channel into a 250-metre-deep (820-foot) ravine hewn out of solid granite. The falls, known as the Augrabies, after passing through the narrow channel rage down a series of cataracts to finally plunge for 65 metres (210 feet) into the ravine. Immediately above the falls, the mighty Orange, together with small islands and waterways, achieves a width of some three kilometres (two miles). When the river is in flood and over 405 million litres (89.1 million gallons) of water tumble into the ravine every second, the river seeks out another 18 channels through which it forces its yellow, raging waters into the gorge, making it the sixth-largest waterfall in the world. In the process a great noise is generated. This gave rise to the Khoi name of *aukurabis*, meaning a 'place of great noise'. Over many millions of years the river has cut back some 15 kilometres (9.5 miles) through the granite-gneiss rock strata that underlie the geology of the region, thereby forming the earth's largest gorge eroded through granite. The ravine's smooth, polished and water-worn walls bear silent testimony to nature's inexorable power.

The Augrabies Falls form the central feature of the Augrabies Falls National Park. The park is 13,600 hectares (33,606 acres) in extent and encompasses some of the driest regions in South Africa, reflected in its lunarlike landscape. The vegetation is typical of the drier parts of the southern Kalahari with prominent species such as the Quiver Tree, which proudly rears its distinctive candelabra-like shape from rock-strewn hillsides and barren valleys and from whose bark the San have for centuries made pincushion quivers for their poisoned arrows. Other species found in the park are Karoo Boer-bean (*Schotia afra*), Cape Willow (*Salix mucronata*), Wild Olive, the hardy Liliaceae (*Haworthia tessellata*) and, for those who have the eye to find them, Lithops, the fascinating plants that survive predation by looking like stones.

BELOW *Over many millions of years the mighty Orange River has cut a 250-metre-deep (820-foot), 15-kilometre-long (9-mile) gorge through solid granite rock. Legend has it that diamonds have been washed down by the river and are trapped in the gravels that lie in the deep pool beneath the main falls.*

ABOVE *The lunarlike landscape of the Augrabies Falls National Park provides spectacular scenery in the early morning and late afternoon, when the sun's fiery furnace is subdued and the colour temperature of light is low, and thus able to capture shadows and enhance the deep reds and the various oranges and yellows of the rocks and sands of this extremely arid region. During most of the day the sun's harsh heat and searing light washes almost all the hues out of the rocks and countryside, leaving them colourless and one-dimensional.*

RIGHT *The Thorny-leafed Soetdoringbos (Codon royenii) is a common desert plant that is found mainly along dry riverbeds in the arid areas of the Northern Cape and Richtersveld. The stems, leaves and bracts surrounding the plant's flowers are all covered in short, white needlelike spines. The flowers are deep and cup-shaped and are lined with purple or yellow. They contain a sweet nectar – hence the Afrikaans common name, Soetdoringbos, which means 'sweet thorn bush'.*

ABOVE *Over time the rock strata have been weathered to create some very dramatic and sometimes weird shapes which add to the interest and fascination of the Augrabies area.*

LEFT *The Klipspringer is a small antelope that is capable of springing from one rock to another. Since it walks on the tips of its rounded hooves, its sturdy legs appear to be longer than they actually are. The small footprint of the Klipspringer, which measures a little over a centimetre, enables the animal to balance on extremely narrow rock ledges and footings.*
It often stands on rocks with its front and back feet close together, giving the antelope a characteristic humped posture. The muzzle of the Klipspringer is short and this gives the animal a triangular-shaped face. Below its eyes are dark glandular patches which, from a distance, make the eyes look abnormally large. Males use secretions from these glands to mark their territory.
Klipspringers vary remarkably in colour – from dull grey to golden-yellow. A remarkable feature of their coat is that, unlike all other African antelope, it is made up of thick, stiff, hollow hairs which provide the antelope with a measure of protection against injury and extremes of hot and cold. Another feature of their coat is that the coloration of individual hairs varies and this produces an overall speckled effect which provides excellent camouflage, as it mirrors the texture of finely grained boulders. Klipspringers usually occur in pairs or in small family groups comprising adults and their offspring. Males advertize their presence by standing conspicuously on prominent rocks. They are predominantly browsers and utilize the leaves, fruits and flowers of a wide variety of trees.

OPPOSITE *Above the Augrabies falls, the Orange River spreads out across some 3 kilometres (2 miles) of channels and waterways, interspersed between small islands and rocky outcrops. At the falls, the river is suddenly funnelled through this narrow chasm before dropping to the deep pool below.*

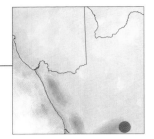

Karoo National Park

Situated some 11 kilometres (seven miles) outside the town of Beaufort West is the Karoo National Park. This 43,300-hectare (106,994-acre) park was established in 1979 to preserve the fauna and flora of the south-central Great Karoo where the average annual rainfall seldom exceeds 250 millimetres (10 inches). When the park was established Kudu, Klipspringer, Red and Grey Rhebok, Duiker, and Steenbok were already resident there. A number of other species, that were indigenous to the area, have subsequently been reintroduced, among them Springbok, Mountain Zebra, Black Wildebeest, Red Hartebeest, and Gemsbok. The vegetation is typical of the Great Karoo with hardy shrubs, herbs and annual grasses that emerge with the rain. An interesting feature in the park is a display where visitors can see an excellent exposition of typical fossils found in the Karoo as well as a model which demonstrates the region's fascinating geological history.

BELOW *The only gazelle that occurs in southern Africa is the Springbok. Some 2500 kilometres (1554 miles) of savanna and woodland separate them from the gazelles of East Africa.*

ABOVE *Springtime is flower time in the Karoo when, in many places, the plains change their dull and somewhat drab appearance through the emergence of vividly coloured vygies.*

ABOVE *The Cape Mountain Zebra belongs to the Order Perissodactyla and is thus an odd-toed ungulate, like the Hook- and Square-lipped Rhinoceros. Unlike Burchell's Zebra, the Cape Mountain Zebra is relatively rare in South Africa and is only found in the Karoo. The Cape Mountain Zebra and the Hartmann's Mountain Zebra, which is restricted to the montane regions of Namibia, are similar in appearance, except that the Hartmann's is slightly larger and there are differences in the striping around their hindquarters.*

BELOW LEFT *A close-up of the bright yellow flowers of the Wild Pomegranate reveals the species' delicate beauty.*

BELOW RIGHT *A unique feature of the* Aloe broomii *is that when the flowers are fully developed and open, they cannot be seen as they are completely hidden by their longer bracts and only the front portion of the genitals are visible.*

ABOVE *The male Cape Sparrow* (Passer melanus) *is the only sparrow in the region with a pied head and is therefore easily identifiable. The female is distinguished from other sparrows by its grey head with faint white shadow markings. It is endemic to the central, western and southern regions of South Africa, where its preferred habitat is grasslands and grain fields – often near human habitation.*

ABOVE RIGHT *The Striped Field Mouse* (Rhadomys pumilio) *is noted for the four dark stripes which run down its back. The remaining body colour ranges from dark russet-brown to almost grey-white. This mouse species occurs throughout South Africa, with the exception of the Kruger National Park. They have adapted to a wide range of habitats – from arid desert to high-rainfall montane regions. They are predominantly seed-eaters, but will also eat parts of plants and insects.*

BELOW *The Doublebanded Courser* (Rhinoptilus africanus) *is a resident of dry open and desert areas and is unmistakable because of the double bands that ring the upper breast; it has the least marked head of all the coursers.*

BELOW *The Southern Rock Agama* (Agama atra) *is found in a wide range of habitats, including semi-desert, fynbos, coastal forest and mountains. It tends to favour rocky outcrops, rocky mountain plateaus and rocky plains; it also finds shelter under the bark of dead trees. It is a large agama with a flattened body and large limbs. It feeds almost exclusively on ants and termites and along the Cape coast it forages among driftwood for various intertidal arthropods. Both males and females are territorial and form hierarchies. A dominant male displays his superiority by positioning himself on a conspicuous rock where he nods his brightly coloured head as a signal to subordinate males that he is the dominant male in the area. When threatened, he flattens himself against a rock and the bright colour of his head rapidly fades to match the colours and markings of the rock on which he is sitting.*

OPPOSITE *In spring, following good winter rains, the Karoo National Park becomes a blaze of colour.*

OVERLEAF *As the sun sets in the Karoo it lays a mantle of many colours on the often drab landscape, creating great beauty in the process.*

Richtersveld National Park

The Richtersveld National Park is partially delineated by a complex geology and resultant geomorphology made up of the Van der Sterr and Rosyntjieberg mountains in the west and south. The park's 16,445-hectare (40,636-acre) extent is bounded in the north and east by the Orange River, which forms the boundary between South Africa and Namibia. Regarded as the only true mountainous desert region within South Africa, it has a very rich diversity of succulents. These include the Halfmens, which often occurs in pairs or in small family groups. The plant's common name, which in Afrikaans means 'half-human', is derived from its uncanny resemblance to the human form when seen silhouetted against the skyline. It has a tapering, unbranched stem that is normally about two and a half metres (eight feet) in height, although specimens of four to five metres (13 to 16 feet) have been recorded in the Richtersveld. At the apex of the stem are spine-tipped, wart-like protuberances, around which obovate-oblong velvety textured leaves are densely clustered. An unusual feature of the Halfmens is that it declines towards the north at an angle varying between 20 and 30 degrees. Botanists believe the reason for this is due to the plant being phototropic, which means that in the excessive heat experienced in the Richtersveld, it turns its tips towards the sun in order to create shade for its growing shoots. The angle of declination is accounted for by the fact that it grows in areas where the sun lies to the north of it for the greater part of the year.

The Bastard Quiver Tree (*Aloe pillansii*), although similar to the Quiver Tree, is taller and has fewer branches. It is endemic to a very small, intensely hot and arid area of the Richtersveld and to a corresponding area across the Orange River in Namibia. The Richtersveld is also home to the 'Miracle', or Eight-day, Grass (*Enneapogon desyauxii*), which germinates, flowers and runs to seed within eight days after rainfall in order to ensure its survival in the unfavourable conditions.

BELOW *The Orange River cuts a verdant swathe through the tormented and barren mountains of the Richtersveld and, in so doing, it marks the South African border with Namibia as well as the northern border of the Richtersveld National Park. Moisture precipitation is lowest in the Orange River valley where it amounts to about 50 millimetres (2 inches) per annum.*

In addition to its unique range of unusual vegetation, the Richtersveld is of considerable importance from a purely geological and stratigraphic point of view. Nature has used virtually every geological process it has in its repertoire to create the unique geological character of the area. The region demonstrates an extremely varied assortment of sedimentary, volcanic and metamorphic rock formations, creating a variety of landscapes that defy description.

For 18 years the South African National Parks attempted to establish a national park in the Richtersveld in order to conserve this important natural asset. For many reasons, agreement could not be reached between the Board and the local community. However, in August 1991 agreement was eventually achieved and the park was formally proclaimed, in terms of which the South African National Parks is required to manage the park and the local community have the right to continue their traditional grazing of the land, but with a view to a voluntary reduction of stock levels in return for compensatory land elsewhere. In terms of the proclamation, the South African National Parks and the Richtersveld community are jointly responsible for determining policy and drawing up a management plan.

ABOVE AND ABOVE LEFT *The Halfmens is a succulent plant with a cylindrical stem that is usually unbranched. It is endemic to the Richtersveld and adjacent southern Namibian area and grows in dry rocky desert conditions. The stem is thickset at the base and tapers to the apex. Occasionally, spine-tipped tubercles, or warty protuberances, branch out from near the base and short branches occur near the apex. The flowers (above left), which are tubular, red inside and green outside, are produced among the leaves at the apex of the stem between July and September. According to local legend, these trees are half-human and half-plant, which is easy to understand since at a distance — and particularly when silhouetted against a low skyline — they look uncannily like human beings.*

LEFT *Although a little too far north, as well as too dry, to enjoy the full glory of the annual wildflower show that nature provides in Namaqualand, there are nevertheless a number of flower species, such as these* Dimorphotheca sp. *which make their appearance in the Richtersveld.*

ABOVE *Bibron's Gecko* (Pachydactylus bibronii) *is a large, stout gecko and probably one of the most common in South Africa. It is found throughout the country, except in the Eastern Cape, the Cape Peninsula and parts of KwaZulu-Natal. It lives on rocky outcrops, under the bark of dead trees and on the walls of houses. It is gregarious and often lives in colonies. It eats a wide variety of prey, including grasshoppers, ants, termites, lizards and beetles.*

ABOVE LEFT CENTRE *The Sand Beetle* (Physasterna sp.) *is a common beetle on the sand dunes of the Richtersveld. It is also seen along the sand banks of the Orange River. Its distribution extends all along the Namib Desert into Angola and it is active throughout the year. The smaller male is often seen following the larger female as they forage for food.*

ABOVE *In the earlier morning light the serried mountains of the Richtersveld are painted in a myriad different colours and hues, ranging from deep red to light purple. As a consequence of its varied geomorphology, the Richtersveld provides grand scenery that is unique in South Africa. The deeper you venture into its hinterland, through steep gorges and over high passes, a growing sense of awe, loneliness and wonderment prevails.*

OPPOSITE BOTTOM *The Capped Wheatear* (Oenanthe pileata) *is thinly distributed throughout South Africa, except in the eastern lowlands where it does not occur at all. Its preferred habitat is barren sandy or stony areas and short grasslands. It has a conspicuous white forehead and eyebrow, and a black cap.*

OPPOSITE TOP *The Richtersveld is important from both a geological and stratigraphic point of view. Many geological forces, active here over millions of years, have steadily created the unique character of the Richtersveld. In its long and complicated geological history virtually every geological process known has occurred. Here a wide variety of sedimentary, volcanic and metamorphic rock formations exist side by side, providing scientists with an opportunity to study petrogenesis and sedimentation under extremely variable physical conditions. As a result of the vast range of geological formations, combined with the area's broken terrain and resultant diverse microclimates, a wide variety of karroid plant species are to be found in the Richtersveld.*

OPPOSITE BOTTOM LEFT AND RIGHT *A beautiful plant resident in the Richtersveld is the Duingousblom, or Perdeblom (Didelta carnosa), which grows on sand dunes in the Western Cape and in the arid areas of Namaqualand and the Richtersveld. It is a glabrous plant with fleshy alternate leaves and brilliant yellow flowers which make their appearance between October and December. Here we see the full close-up beauty of the flower head after opening (left) and the post flowering stage (right).*

TOP RIGHT AND RIGHT *In the Knersvlakte the seemingly barren desert or semidesert landscape seems to be void of all forms of vegetation. Those who stop and get on their hands and knees will be richly rewarded when they discover the 'stone plants' of the Lithops and* Conophytum *genera. These strange succulents protect themselves by taking on the appearance of pebbles or stones lying about in the veld. It is only in the flowering season that they colourfully announce their existence, for example, the* Conophytum Bolusiae *(right). The C. obcordellum (top right) has adopted a patterning on its protective sheaths which provides almost perfect camouflage.*

BELOW *A close-up of the star-shaped flower of the* Stapelia gariepensis *reveals a very delicate beauty which is multiplied as the plant spreads out a dense maroon carpet of flowers of up to a metre or more in diameter, across the desert's floor. Incongruously, the flowers emit a nauseating fetid smell that attracts flies which then carry the flower's pollen to other plants.*

BOTTOM RIGHT *The* Aloe striata *subsp.* komaggasensis *is distinguished by the white edging along its leaves. It is only found in the Komaggas Mountains in Namaqualand, just south of the Richtersveld National Park. This subspecies is considered to be rare because of its limited distribution and gross over-exploitation by illegal plant collectors.*

Focus on
THE MOUNTAINS

When the earth was still being formed, the southern continents (as we know them today) were part of a single massive supercontinent known as Gondwana, the geological structure of which was described in the introductory chapter (*see page 18*). At this time of restless and shattering earth movements, immense isostatic readjustments occurred and parts of Africa rose in relation to others so that plateaus were formed in some places and basins in others. In the southern subcontinent a high inland plateau was created, which forms part of the great African plateau that extends from the southwestern Cape to the Red Sea. With the land's upward warping, rocks that were laid down at or near sea level were raised up to close on 2000 metres (6562 feet) and, as a result of this height above the base level, erosion was stimulated which has continued to the present day. The winds that periodically whip across the escarpment face, the storms that lash against it in anger during summer storms and the rainwater that gently trickles down to the streams and rivers draining the escarpment throughout most of the year have steadily and inexorably pushed it back from the coast. As a result, what we see as the Great Escarpment today is merely one position in a continual retreat.

The Great Escarpment extends from the Wolkberg (Cloud Mountain) just south of the Soutpansberg in Northern Province, to the northeast, and continues as a more or less continuous barrier for about 960 kilometres (597 miles). It separates the Lowveld

from the Highveld in Mpumalanga and Swaziland, before swinging to the southwest where it separates KwaZulu-Natal from the Free State. When it reaches Mont-aux-Sources, the Great Escarpment dramatically swings to the southeast to create the majesty of the High Berg, also described as the KwaZulu-Natal Drakensberg, which extends, as the Zulu people say, 'like a barrier of upturned spears' from Mont-aux-Sources in the north to the Eastern Cape border in the south. Here, at 3000 metres (9843 feet) above sea level, the Drakensberg separates KwaZulu-Natal from the kingdom of Lesotho, which stretches westward in a series of rolling mountains to create a rugged and high-lying plateau known as the 'Roof of Africa'. Along the Drakensberg escarpment there are many places of wild beauty and solitude – indeed some of the most rugged and wild mountain scenery on the African continent.

As the Great Escarpment continues beyond the KwaZulu-Natal border its character changes, becoming less rigid and discernible as an escarpment. This is due to the rise from the coastal plain to the inland plateau being spread over a number of steps, with a series of more or less parallel mountain ranges marking the beginning of each step. In the south and south-western regions of the country (mainly in the Western Cape) the mountains forming the inland plateau rim are folded. Geologists believe that towards the end of the mountain-building period there was intensive faulting and, as a result of the immense stresses to which the earth's crust was subjected, the crust buckled into enormous folds. The resulting folds were then steadily eroded by the forces of nature to create 16 different mountain ranges, which today provide many wild places in the Western Cape.

KwaZulu-Natal Drakensberg
The geological structure of the Drakensberg comprises two clearly defined areas. Rising from about 2000 to 3000 metres (6562 to 9843 feet) and more is the High Berg's mighty towering wall of basalt. Underpinning the High Berg

THE MOUNTAINS
0   50   100   150   200 km
0   25   50   75   100 miles
International Boundaries
Provincial Boundaries
Major Roads
National Parks & Reserves

Elands River →
Royal Natal National Park
Free State
Sentinel [3165m]
Mont-aux-Sources
Thukela
Eastern Buttress (Devil's Tooth) [3047m]
Bloemfontein
Maseru
Bushman's River
Giant's Castle Game Reserve
LESOTHO
Natal Drakensberg Park
D R A K E N S B E R G

SOUTH   AFRICA
Orange River

Northern Cape

Olifants River
Clanwilliam
CEDARBERG
Doring River
Citrusdal
Porterville
Groot Winterhoek Wilderness Area
Western Cape
CAPE FOLDED MOUNTAINS
Cape Town
Hottentots Holland Nature Reserve

Eastern Cape

East London

Port Elizabeth

OPPOSITE *A typical view of the High Berg, with water falling over the sedimentary cave sandstone layer. Note the imposing walls of the basalt escarpment in the background.*

ABOVE *The San were resident in the Drakensberg Mountains for hundreds of years, living in the caves and hunting in the valleys below. On the walls of many of these caves it is still possible to see the wonderful legacy of rock art they left behind, such as this example in the Giant's Castle Game Reserve.*

is the second area, made up largely of sandstone capped by cave sandstone, which is known as the Little Berg. The basalt wall, volcanic in origin, is eroded as the rivers and streams which drain water off the escarpment edge have cut deep into it and, in so doing, have hewn out heavily incised valleys and rugged buttresses which create vistas of great beauty and grandeur. This beauty changes ceaselessly with the different times of the day and the seasons of the year, as the various angles of the rising and setting sun cast changing shadows and colours upon the mountains, which in themselves turn from a lush, deep green during the wet summers to a golden brown in the dry winters. The beauty of the Little Berg is softer and more benign as the slopes are gentler, stretching from the floor of the river valleys at about 1250 to 2000 metres (4101 to 6562 feet). Rounded and richly grassed rolling mountain slopes are interlocked by riverine forests and capped by red and yellow bands of cave sandstone.

Despite their grandeur and apparent immutability, this puissant barrier has its passions and its vulnerability. Its climate is harsh, with frequent howling westerly winds, snowfalls and low temperatures in winter and sudden violent downpours in summer. Soils are thin and plants have a precarious hold on the steep slopes, while natural landslides occur from time to time, leaving deep scars that take decades to heal. It is a fragile environment that is particularly sensitive to any interference by man and this places a severe limit on its tourism-carrying capacity.

In terms of official land-use policy, four zones, each with its own distinctive characteristics and each running more or less

parallel to the escarpment ridge, have been delineated. Naming them from west to east they are: the Wilderness Heart and Landslide Zone, which together constitute the Inner Berg; and the Trail Zone and Drakensberg Threshold, which together constitute the Drakensberg Approaches.

The Wilderness Heart Zone constitutes the upper reaches of the High Berg and extends from the base of the cave sandstone westward and upwards to the Lesotho border. Due to the environmental fragility of this zone and the need to protect it against excessive use, Drakensberg land-use policy requires it to be protected as a wilderness area. It is therefore only open to hikers and, furthermore, in order to prevent degradation of the environment, it is necessary for the number of people allowed into the zone at any one time to be limited. The Landslide Zone is the narrow debris slope below the cave sandstone. Steeply angled, it has shallow soils with high rainwater run-off and sparse vegetation – all adding to the risks of landslides and erosion. For these reasons it is even more fragile and vulnerable than the Wilderness Heart Zone and therefore requires even more stringent land-use management since it is considered to be unsuited to any of mankind's occupational activities.

The Trail Zone lies immediately below the Landslide Zone and its demarcation involves the consideration of a number of factors, including slope, geological instability and altitude. The Trail Zone covers those areas which are unsuitable for intensive development on the basis of physiographic, ecological and aesthetic reasons. This is the zone that attracts most people to the Drakensberg as it is characterized by a wide range of scenic diversity. There are vistas of rocky and grass-covered terraces cut by numerous streams which are often tree- and shrub-lined; on protected slopes, patches of indigenous forest provide added interest and variation; and in the background, the jagged beauty of the High Berg brings a sense of awe and majesty to the whole scene. On the walls of the caves and overhangs that are accessible in this zone, San artists have left their paintings and in doing so have bequeathed one of the richest rock-art treasures in the world. This adds yet another dimension of interest to the Drakensberg.

The Threshold Zone stretches from the lower edge of the Trail Zone to about eight kilometres (five miles) from the foot of the Little Berg. It consists of undulating land with a more moderate climate than the zones nearer the mountains. This is where virtually all residential and tourism development has taken place.

The vegetation of the Drakensberg can be roughly divided into three distinct belts. The first of these is the Montane Belt, which extends from the valley floors to the summit of the Little Berg. Rainfall is around 1400 millimetres (55 inches) and the greater part of the area is covered by grassland, chiefly *Themeda triandra*, with various species of protea scattered on the hillsides. Most of the river valleys and the banks of the streams that come down the mountainsides are thickly forested, with Yellowwoods (*Podocarpus latifolius, P. falcatus* and *P. henkelii*) being the dominant species.

The Subalpine Belt extends from the summit of the Little Berg to just below the summit of the High Berg. Rainfall is high, averaging around 2000 millimetres (79 inches) per annum and the mountain slopes are steep. Here too, the vegetation consists mainly of grasslands with *Themeda triandra* the dominant grass, but a number of grasses typical of temperate climates also occur here. Trees do not grow in this belt and the only woody plant that occurs here is the Umtshitshi Bush (*Leucosidea sericea*).

The highest belt is the Alpine Belt which occurs from 2860 metres (9384 feet) upwards. Rainfall is less here than in the Subalpine Belt, about 1600 millimetres (63 inches) per annum, and the climate is severe. The soil is shallow and the ground is tundra-like, often boggy and swampy in summer and frozen rock-hard in winter when frequent snowfalls are common. Due to an increase in ultraviolet rays and a consequent decrease in growth-promoting hormones, many plants are dwarfed at these higher altitudes. Nevertheless, in summer, when the days can become hot and even humid, the profusion of flowering plants on the summit is remarkable.

For many years the Drakensberg has been recognized as one of the most important conservation areas in South Africa. In order to maximize the area's conservation potential, the Drakensberg Catchment Area has been established. It covers the region from Mont-aux-Sources in the north to East Griqualand in the south – an area of some 320,000 hectares (790,720 acres). The areas within the Drakensberg Catchment Area are presently managed by various agencies and each have different land-use designations.

OPPOSITE BOTTOM *In this photograph of the Bushmans River valley in the Giant's Castle Game Reserve, the zonation of the Drakensberg is clearly evident. In the background are the basalt walls of the High Berg which have been eroded over time as the rivers that flow from their summits have steadily cut back into them. In the middle distance are the rounded spurs of the Little Berg plateau which terminate in the outcrops of sedimentary cave sandstone, and in the foreground is the broadening Little Berg valley created by the river and its many tributaries.*

BELOW *Much of the Trail Zone passes through protea savanna, or woodland, which is similar to grassland. The soil is hard, shallow and fertility is limited.*

Folded Mountains of the Southwestern Cape

The southern and western Cape are the only areas in South Africa where folded mountains occur. In the western Cape these mountains strike mainly from north to south while in the southern Cape the strike is roughly from west to east. Most of the folds are relatively simple, with anticlinal mountains (the rock strata go upwards) and synclinal valleys (the rock strata go downwards), but some combine both these phenomena and are much more complex. Within each of the 16 major mountain ranges that make up the Cape Fold Mountains there are remote corners which still preserve a quality of wilderness that is little changed from primordial times. Of these, it is possibly the Cedarberg Mountains, the Groot Winterhoek Wilderness Area and the Hottentots Holland Nature Reserve where this quality of wilderness finds its most unrestricted expression.

RIGHT *The folded mountains of the southwestern Cape are covered in* fynbos, *which encompasses an extraordinary variety of plants of various shapes and sizes, in a myriad colours and textures. The mix includes proteoids, ericoids, restioids and geophytes and the result is one of the most fascinating, species-rich floral kingdoms in the world.*

BELOW *On the fynbos-clad slopes of the Kogelberg Mountains near Pringle Bay, 1417 species have been recorded in an area that covers little more than 240 square kilometres (92 square miles). This enormous species diversity results from a combination of chemical changes and different levels of moisture content in the soil. Another contributing factor is the wide variety of different locations of the same habitat occurring on the mountain slopes in the area.*

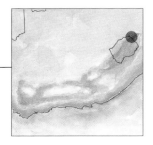

Mont-aux-Sources and Royal Natal National Park

At Mont-aux-Sources the buttresses, peaks, cut-backs and spurs so typical of most of the High Berg are strangely missing. Instead the solid basalt wall of the High Berg has been almost uniformally carved away to form a huge amphitheatre and in the broad valley that sweeps out from its base, the Thukela, KwaZulu-Natal's most important river, still clean, clear and pure bubbles over rounded rocks and pebbles on its way to the distant sea. The summit of the Amphitheatre is five kilometres (three miles) across and at each end is bracketed by prominent peaks. On the right-hand side, when viewed from the Thukela valley, is the prominent Sentinel (3165 metres; 10,384 feet) and Beacon Buttress (3121 metres; 10,240 feet) where KwaZulu-Natal, the Free State and Lesotho meet at a common point. On the left-hand side is the Eastern Buttress (3047 metres; 9997 feet) which incorporates a pinnacle, known as Devil's Tooth. Some three kilometres (two miles) from the escarpment edge is the true summit of Mont-aux-Sources, a rather nondescript hillock situated on the Lesotho plateau. But it is from this insignificant rise in the landscape that South Africa's three most important rivers rise. From its gentle eastern slopes the Thukela River springs to life and makes its way to the escarpment rim where it plunges down the face of the Amphitheatre and meanders on to the Indian Ocean in the east. From the western slopes the Western Khubedu rises and forms the upper sources of the Orange River, South Africa's largest river, which flows some 2190 kilometres (1361 miles) until eventually reaching the Atlantic Ocean in the west. And from its northern slopes, close to the source of the Thukela River, the Elands River begins its journey of life and flows north to the Wilge River, one of the main tributaries to the Vaal River which is the main source of water for Gauteng, the commercial and industrial centre of South Africa.

At the foot of the Amphitheatre the 8000-hectare (19,768-acre) Royal Natal National Park was proclaimed, and in 1950 the 794-hectare (1962-acre) Rugged Glen Nature Reserve was added to it. The park, which provides home to a variety of antelope as well as Black Wildebeest, encompasses one of South Africa's most scenic masterpieces.

BELOW *This view of the Mont-aux-Sources amphitheatre wall, Eastern Buttress, Devil's Tooth and the Inner Tower, taken from the top of the Western Buttress, clearly illustrates the drama of the weathering process that has taken place over many millions of years along the eastern escarpment edge of southern Africa. As the rivers emanating from the mountaintop have cut back into the highland plateau – aided and abetted by the erosive agents of wind, rain and temperature variations between day and night, and winter and summer – they have left behind jagged spurs which will steadily erode further until they too become isolated as tall towers. And then, as the processes of nature continue unabated, these towers will erode further into pinnacles and then into needles until, eventually, there will be nothing. In time, the line of the escarpment will move ever deeper into the highland plateau and further to the west.*

ABOVE *Over aeons of time the rivers that drain the high interior plateau have steadily cut back the escarpment face, sometimes creating pinnacles and buttresses which subsequently wither into thin needles before they disappear and sometimes grand amphitheatres – such as this one at Mont-aux-Sources.*

TOP RIGHT *Drakensberg Crag Lizards* (Pseudocordylus langi) *are usually found in large, diffuse colonies on rocky outcrops on mountain plateaus, from the Amatola Mountains in the south to the Transvaal Drakensberg in the north. It is unusual to see more than one individual in a rock crack. They prey on small beetles and flying insects.*

ABOVE CENTRE *The Jackal buzzard* (Buteo rufofuscus) *is a common resident throughout South Africa. Although the adult male is normally distinctly marked with a chestnut coloured breast and tail, this is not always so and wide variations in colouring do occur. They are normally found in montane regions and adjacent grasslands.*

ABOVE *The Orangebreasted Rockjumper* (Chaetops aurantius) *is usually found at altitudes above 2000 metres (6562 feet). Its preferred habitat is rocky mountain slopes and grassy hillsides where scattered boulders are plentiful. This species is endemic to the Drakensberg and the high mountains of Lesotho.*

LEFT *The Thukela River meanders across the highland plateau in Lesotho before making its dramatic descent over the precipitous escarpment edge into KwaZulu-Natal. The Eastern Buttress, Devil's Tooth and Inner Tower can be seen in distant silhouette against the sky. There are no trees on the summit plateau. The vegetation mainly consists of sparse, tufted temperate grassland – of which* Festuca caprina *and* Merxmuellera disticha *are the dominant species – and dwarf scrub – particularly the stunted shrubs of* Helichrysum *and* Erica. *Various herbs and shrubs, including* Athanasia, Euryops, Senecio *and* Burkheya, *are scattered among the rocks and grass tufts and, nestling low in the grass, it is possible to see the pinkish-white flowers of* Apodolirion buchananii. *In this high-altitude Alpine Zone only a few frost-resistant succulents can be found, of which various species of* Delosperma *are the most common. Growing from cracks in the rocks are* Hypoxis *and the succulent* Euphorbia clavaroides, *with its masses of tiny yellow flowers.*

BELOW *The mighty Sentinel stands guard over the Drakensberg, but even this bastion of the slowly receding escarpment is not free from nature's inevitable erosive claws as it continues to weather into an ever flatter dome.*

ABOVE *A baby Chacma Baboon is certainly very endearing, but adult baboons can become extremely aggressive when there are young in the troop. Chacma Baboons are found in almost all habitats in southern Africa, but in the Berg they are seldom seen on the summit, preferring to move below 2500 metres (8202 feet) – especially in winter when snow is a possibility. In the Berg, baboons are usually found in troops of between 15 and 20 animals, although troops of up to 40 baboons are seen from time to time.*

LEFT *A male Doublecollared Sunbird (Nectarinia afra) pauses for a moment on the flowers of the Wild Dagga (Leonotis leonorus), or Lion's Ear (also referred to as a minaret flower). This sunbird is mainly found along the escarpment and in the Southern Cape. On a clear summer's day, the Wild Dagga's tall minarets of bright-orange flowers contrast dramatically against the distant, purple-hued High Berg and the deep-blue sky. Seven species of Leonotis have been recorded in KwaZulu-Natal, of which L. leonorus is the most common. It grows in dense clumps of erect stalks that reach a height of 2 metres (6 feet). The flowers are tubular in form and velvety in texture. They are borne in successive whorls at intervals along the tall, elegant stems and have a strong aromatic scent. The plant is used for a variety of medicinal purposes, mainly as a purgative. It is also used for veterinary purposes – the whole plant, excluding the root, is boiled down and used as a tonic for calves.*

LEFT *Sloggett's Rat (Otomys sloggetti) is the only rodent that is likely to be seen on the summit of the Drakensberg, as it favours the rocky dwarf heathveld occurring there. It has longish fluffy hair, a short tail and a blunt, furry face. Sloggett's Rat is usually seen basking in the sun on low rocks during the mid-morning and early afternoon.*

Giant's Castle Game Reserve

Giant's Castle is an exposed massif situated about midway down the KwaZulu–Natal Drakensberg. Some 3314 metres (10,873 feet) high, the mountain's prominence is heightened by the fact that the main Drakensberg range swings south–west behind it. The Zulus call it *iNtabahayikonjwa* ('the mountain to which you must not point') because, according to legend, to point at it is disrespectful and as a penalty for this the mountain will bring bad weather. There must be some truth in this ancient belief, because Giant's Castle is renowned for its violent thunderstorms in summer and heavy snowfalls in winter. A game reserve of a little more than 30,000 hectares (74,130 acres) was proclaimed in 1903 and extends over the foothills and slopes of

the Giant's Castle area. Known as the Giant's Castle Game Reserve, it includes the source of the Bushman's River. The thickly grassed Low Berg and foothills in the reserve provide a natural home for a variety of antelope, including the regal Eland which breed freely here.

Birdlife is varied and includes spectacular birds of prey, such as the Martial Eagle, the rare Lammergeier, or Bearded Vulture, as well as numerous delicate sugarbirds, such as the Russet-breasted Gurney's Sugarbird (*Promerops gurneyi*) and the Malachite Sunbird (*Nectarinia famosa*).

ABOVE *A Cape Vulture, the most common vulture seen in the Drakensberg, soars freely in the Giant's Castle Game Reserve. Although the habitat of this bird is wide ranging, it only nests and breeds on cliffs. At Giant's Castle a 'vulture restaurant' has been built where visitors can get a close-up view of the Cape Vulture, Bearded Vulture or Lammergeier, and other scavengers in action.*

LEFT AND BELOW *A herd of Eland is seen on the slopes of the Little Berg in the Giant's Castle Game Reserve, with the dominating High Berg in the background. Eland are able to adapt to an amazing number of seemingly incompatible habitats, from low-lying desert scrub to well-watered montane grasslands. Although Eland are principally browsers, they will graze if they have to and are also known to dig for roots and bulbs with their front hooves and use their horns to knock down, or twist off, foliage. They are not dependent on water, as they are able to obtain all the moisture they need from their food. However, if surface water is available they will drink regularly.*

BELOW *The* Protea roupelliae, *the most common of all Drakensberg proteas, grows into a fairly large tree, reaching 4 to 5 metres (13 to 16 feet) in height. Its young leaves, which grow in whorls at the end of branches, are soft and covered with woolly down, giving them a bluey-grey to silver sheen. As the leaves grow older they turn green. The flower head is about 80 millimetres (3 inches) in diameter and the bracts are as long as, or slightly longer than, the perianth. Red in colour and paddle-shaped, with silky hairs on the outside, they curve backwards at the tip. The flowerets, which are white below and covered with pink to crimson hairs at the top, have a white style and a red stigma. They are normally pollinated by birds, such as the Malachite Sunbird, and the metallic blue* Melyris natalensis *beetle.*

BOTTOM *The Foam Grasshopper* (Dictyophorus spumans) *is common up to about 2000 metres (6562 feet) in the Drakensberg. Being a Pyrgomorphid grasshopper, it is smelly and toxic – clearly advertized by its bright colouring.*

BELOW *Evergreen forests are an important ecosystem in the Drakensberg. The climate within these forests is generally mild in comparison to that of the more open areas. Temperatures are moderate, seldom ranging beyond 3°C (37.4°F) at the coldest and 22°C (71.6°F) at the hottest, and they remain fairly constant from ground level to the canopy. There is no frost within these forests and water is normally plentiful, humidity is relatively high and evaporation is low. The soils are relatively deep and quite fertile in many places and thus productivity is comparatively high. Yellowwoods tend to dominate and, as they are very big, create a dense top canopy. Light intensity is probably the greatest limiting factor for growth within the forest – the foliage canopy reduces the light reaching the ground by as much as 90 to 95 percent and, as a result, only shade-loving plants are able to survive within the depths of the forest. Permanent shade, however, provides ideal conditions for organisms which are sensitive to ultraviolet light or dehydrate easily – these include fungi, ferns and those invertebrates that inhabit the leaf litter.*

RIGHT *The Buff-streaked Chat (Oenanathe bifasciata) is found along the eastern escarpment of South Africa as the preferred habitat of this species is rocky terrain in mountainous regions.*

FOLLOWING PAGES *The waters of the Mahai River cascade down a forested kloof in the Royal Natal National Park. The river ecosystems of the Drakensberg are characterized by very low sedimentation. As a result, light penetration is good and, since the water tumbles over many rocks and waterfalls as it descends, oxygen levels are high. Due to the low availability of phosphates and other nutrients, planktonic and attached algae are not abundant and water plants are also generally absent. Productivity is therefore low, with the main source of energy coming from plant and animal debris from adjacent ecosystems. Consumers are thus limited to detritivores and a few omnivores, the main ones being certain species of insect larvae, cladocerans, copepods and crabs.*

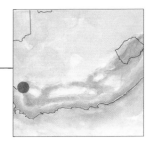

The Cedarberg

Situated in the extreme north of the Cape Floral Kingdom, with the Doring River providing its boundary in the east and the Olifants River in the west, the Cedarberg extends from Citrusdal in the south to Clanwilliam in the north. Within these natural boundaries lies a 700-square-kilometre (270-square-mile) tract of rocky mountainland. This is no ordinary mountainous region, for the quartz-sandstone which once covered the entire region has been weathered along the multiple weaknesses in its upper layers into fantastic shapes by wind and rain. Here cathedral-like structures with tall archways, carved pillars and jagged walls, such as the Stadsaal at Truitjieskraalberg, have been created by the erosive forces of nature. A mighty archway hewn out of rock crowns the Wolfberg at 1608 metres (5276 feet) and at Sanddrif not far away a 10-metre-high (33-foot) pillar of rock,

roughly resembling a Maltese cross, stands proudly on a rock-strewn rise. Also on the Wolfberg are numerous cracks, some merely centimetres wide, while others have been eroded into virtual caverns which dig deeply into the mountain's innards.

The Cedarberg falls into the winter rainfall area and annual totals range between 750 to 1270 millimetres (30 to 50 inches), with the higher slopes and mountain peaks receiving higher rainfall than the valley floors. In the drier parts a distinguishing feature is its dominance by shrubs and bushes, such as Renosterbos (*Elytropappus rhinocerotis*), Geel Magriet (*Euryops abrotanifolius*), Wild Buchu (*Diosma hirsuta*), Wild Bristle Bush (*Metalasia muricata*), various Gonna (*Passerina* sp.) and various Phylica (*Phylica* sp.). On the rocky slopes the Mountain Maytenus (*Maytenus oleoides*) and the Protea Waboom (*Protea nitida*) feature

quite prominently. On the higher slopes, where it is wetter, various ericas and leucodendrons become more common in the species mix. Of particular importance is the rare Clanwilliam Cedar (*Widdringtonia cedarbergensis*), which is an unusual tree endemic to the Cedarberg, and from which the mountain range obtained its name. It grows at an altitude of between 1000 and 1500 metres (3281 and 4922 feet) and has an average height of between five and seven metres (16 and 23 feet), but in some protected areas specimens with an estimated age of at least a thousand years have reached up to 20 metres (66 feet) or more. As the tree matures it tends to spread out and becomes gnarled, twisted and quite ungainly. Its wood is fine-grained, however, and is very beautiful when worked properly. It was heavily exploited by early woodcutters and almost became extinct as a result. Also at higher altitudes a very rare species of protea, the Snow Protea (*Protea cryophila*) can be found.

Fauna in the Cedarberg is limited to a small range of antelope, Grey Rhebok and Klipspringer being the most common. Troops of Baboon can often be heard in the kloofs and very occasion-ally Leopard will make their presence known. Black Eagles are probably the most common raptor and can be seen soaring in the updraughts above the mountains, silently searching for their prey. It is the varied and breathtaking beauty of the Cedarberg that makes this a very special wild place in South Africa.

OPPOSITE *The Maltese Cross, a silent reminder of nature's immutable forces, is a bold feature of the landscape in the Cedarberg. There was a time when this rock formation was part of a large sedimentary rock system that has since worn away, leaving just the cross and the little hill on which it stands.*

BELOW *The sandstone formations of the mountainous Cedarberg, with their extensive jointing and weaknesses, have been sculpted by nature into a variety of shapes, some grotesque, some surrealist and others sombre and monastic.*

ABOVE AND RIGHT   *The Cedarberg has relatively low rainfall and is dominated by dry fynbos, distinguished by the dominance of non-ericaceous ericoid shrubs. Notable species include* Euryops *(seen above),* Elytropappus, Diosma, Metalasia, Passerina *and* Phylica, *all of which are found on the lower slopes of the Cedarberg. Proteas are well represented and include the rare Snow Protea, endemic to a small, high altitude area of the Cedarberg stretching from Sneeuwkop in the north to Sneeuwberg in the southwest, and the glorious Bearded Sugar Bush* (Protea magnifica).

BELOW RIGHT   *The Botterboom is a thick-set, succulent dwarf tree that grows on rocky hillsides in the dry arid areas of the western Cape, including the Cedarberg. A noticeable feature of the tree is its olive-green bark, which tends to peel in thin, yellow, papery sheets. It also has fat, stubby branches, which give the tree a rather deformed look.*

OPPOSITE TOP   *The Clanwilliam Cedar is a rare tree which grows singly on rocky outcrops and on mountaintops at an altitude of between 1000 and 2000 metres (3281 and 6562 feet). Endemic to the region, it is normally 5 to 7 metres (16 and 23 feet) in height. Some Clanwilliam cedars are said to be over 1000 years old. As the tree matures, its branches become twisted and gnarled and it takes on a somewhat tormented shape. Early settlers severely exploited the tree for its fine-grained timber and many of the pews, altars and pulpits of the first churches in South Africa were carved from it. Veld fires have also taken their toll. However, attempts are being made to actively encourage plantings of the Clanwilliam Cedar and hopefully this will do much to redress the exploitation and destruction of the past.*

OPPOSITE BOTTOM LEFT   *The fruits of the Clanwilliam Cedar comprise small cones, which differ between male and female trees. In male trees the cones are very small – only about 2 millimetres (0.1 of an inch) in length. Female trees have almost spherical cones, with four rough, woody scales. The cones are usually dark brown in colour and can be seen on the tree at various stages of development throughout the year.*

OPPOSITE BOTTOM RIGHT   *The male Orangebreasted Sunbird has a dark head and throat and an orange-yellow belly and breast. This sunbird is endemic to the southwestern Cape and occurs in fynbos, flowering montane protea and aloe stands. It is the only small bird in the region that has a pointed tail.*

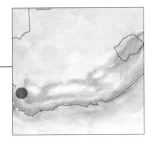

Groot Winterhoek Wilderness Area

Extending over 30,608 hectares (75,632 acres) in the Groot Winterhoek Mountains, which lie east of Porterville in the Southwestern Cape, the Groot Winterhoek Wilderness Area is spread around the Groot Winterhoek peak, which at 2099 metres (6887 feet) is the highest in the area. The mountains were broken and tortured by the tectonic forces of ancient times, but in the process intriguing beauty was created in which deep gorges laced with tumbling streams carrying cold, crystal-clear water are a prominent feature.

In some of the valleys, isolated pockets of forest have made a stand, but the dominant vegetation is montane *fynbos*. The Groot Winterhoek Mountains are well known for the abundance of ericas and disas that grow there during January and February. Although elusive Leopards are occasionally spotted in isolated parts of the reserve, they are seldom seen.

Other fauna is limited to the smaller antelope species, such as Rock Dassie (*Procavia capensis*), Klipspringer, Grey Rhebok, Common Duiker, and also Chacma Baboon. Although bird species are limited in range, a surprising number of birds of prey, such as Black Eagles, Booted Eagles (*Hieraetus pennatus*) and Jackal Buzzards (*Buteo rufofuscus*), are found. Bar-throated Apalis (*Apalis thoraciea*) and Greywing Francolin (*Francolinus africanus*) are relatively common.

RIGHT *The well-known* Disa uniflora *is one of the most beautiful of all the orchids. It is found in rocky clefts close to waterfalls and mountain streams in the mist belt of the southwestern Cape mountains. This delicate plant, endemic to South Africa, has probably been able to survive the ravages of uncontrolled plant collecting because of its highly inaccessible habitat.*

BELOW *The snow-covered peaks of the Groot Winterhoek Mountains not only reflect great beauty but also provide substantive evidence of the earth's traumatic genesis. These great mountains were created by the earth's crust buckling into gigantic folded shapes as a result of tectonic forces. Over a period of countless years, the erosive forces of nature have attacked these great folds in the earth's crust, creating a rugged landscape that loses nothing of its asperity, even when blanketed under a carpet of snow.*

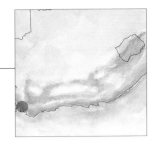

Hottentots Holland Nature Reserve

The 26,000-hectare (10,036-acre) Hottentots Holland Nature Reserve is situated within the very much larger Hottentots Holland Mountain Catchment Area at the western corner of the Cape Folded Mountain ranges where this mountain system turns to the north. Here the mighty stresses and strains the earth's crust was subjected to 200 to 300 million years ago are reflected in the region's present turbulent topography. The reserve lies in rugged and broken terrain and, as a result, notwithstanding its relative close proximity to Stellenbosch and other major urban areas of the Western Cape, it has a quality of unspoilt wildness. This is because access is by foot only, as vehicles are only able to reach the reserve's periphery. Virtually the entire reserve is covered by montane *fynbos* and many endemic species occur there. The deep valleys and gorges are forested. Wildlife is restricted to small mammals and 110 bird species have been recorded in the area.

OPPOSITE AND BELOW *Scientists have been able to establish that the origins of fynbos can be traced back to a period soon after the evolution of flowering plants, about 100 million years ago. Between two to four million years ago, after the inception of hot, dry summer climates and the widespread occurrence of fire, fynbos became the dominant vegetation type in the southwestern Cape. During the last 1.5 million years, fynbos communities have had to face periods of glacial climates which lasted for up to 100,000 years and which were about 5°C (41°F) colder than the warmer and shorter interglacial periods. During these periods of radical climatic variation, fynbos plants evolved mechanisms of survival and are thus well able to cope with the annual winter snowfalls, and the bitterly cold periods that accompany them prevailing on the higher slopes of these mountains. Fynbos also has to cope with long, hot and dry summers when rainless periods last long enough to cause complete depletion of soil moisture. While this may limit growth, the plants have adapted to the stresses imposed by the heat and drought of the summer months.*

SUMMARY OF SOUTH AFRICA'S CONSERVATION AREAS

Given below is a short summary of South Africa's most important national parks and nature reserves, many of which are dealt with more fully in the main body of the text.

KRUGER NATIONAL PARK

Situated in Mpumalanga Province along the border with Mozambique and stretching from Zimbabwe almost to Swaziland, it covers an area of 19,455km² (7510 sq miles) being some 350km (217 miles) long and, on average, 60km (37 miles) wide. It is one of the best known game reserves in the world and provides sanctuary to an extensive range of plants, trees, mammals, birds, reptiles and invertebrates.

KLASERIE–TIMBAVATI NATURE RESERVE

These are private reserves owned by more than 100 individuals, collectively covering over 60,000ha (148,260 acres) on both sides of the Klaserie River in Mpumalanga Province. The vegetation is typical Lowveld with woodland fringing the riverbanks and supports a wide range of game animals.

SABI-SANDS GAME RESERVE

The Sabi-Sands Game Reserve lies adjacent to the Kruger National Park and is made up of a number of privately owned and separately managed reserves which include some of the most exclusive game lodges in Africa.

BLYDE RIVER CANYON NATURE RESERVE

The nature reserve is situated in Mpumalanga Province and covers an area of 22,664ha (56,000 acres) of rugged and deeply incised landscape which is amazingly rich floristically and includes five of South Africa's 71 recognized veld types.

SONGIMVELO NATURE RESERVE

The reserve covers an area of 56,000ha (138,376 acres) and lies in the escarpment of eastern Mpumalanga Province. A significant feature is its rich archaeological history. The predominant vegetation includes grassland and savanna woodland, shrub forest in some areas, while in some of the higher lying areas *fynbos* elements of the Cape Floral Kingdom occur, as do three rare species of cycad.

BORAKALALO NATIONAL PARK

The Park, some 60km (37 miles) north of Brits in the North West Province, covers an area of 14,000ha (34,594 acres) of mixed bushveld, grassland and riverine forest along the Moretele River. The topography varies from rolling sandveld to rocky outcrops, deep gorges and valleys.

PILANESBERG NATIONAL PARK

Pilanesberg is located 50km (31 miles) northeast of Rustenberg in North West Province and encompasses a huge volcanic crater that rises some 600m (1970ft) above the surrounding mixed bushveld plains. It is one of South Africa's premier tourist attractions.

MADIKWE GAME RESERVE

Madikwe covers an area of 75,000ha (185, 325 acres) and is bordered in the north by the international boundary between South Africa and Botswana, the Marico River in the east, the Dwarsberg mountain range in the south and the Zeerust-Gaborone road in the west. It is a new reserve that was only proclaimed in 1990 and began operations in 1992.

SUIKERBOSRAND NATURE RESERVE

This is a small reserve covering 13,337ha (32,956 acres) situated south of Johannesburg at Heidelberg. It is intensively used for environmental education, outdoor recreation and resource management.

MARAKELE NATIONAL PARK

Situated in Northern Province in the southwestern part of the Waterberg near Thabazimbi, this park is presently 45,000ha (111,195 acres) and is due to double in size over the next five years.

GOLDEN GATE NATIONAL PARK

Golden Gate is situated in the eastern highlands of the Free State Province, southwest of Harrismith. It is principally a scenic park of some 11,630ha (28,738 acres).

KAROO NATIONAL PARK

Established in 1979, the Park is situated in the southern Karoo outside Beaufort West and covers an area of 43,300ha (106,994 acres). It is dominated by the steep cliffs and high plateaus of the Nuweveld Mountains. Most of the vegetation comprises dwarf shrubs, commonly known as Karoo bushes.

AUGRABIES FALLS NATIONAL PARK

The Augrabies Falls National Park lies in the arid Northern Cape Province. It covers an area of about 13,600ha (33,606 acres) and is primarily a scenic park, with the mighty Augrabies Falls and its deep gorge the main attractions.

KALAHARI GEMSBOK NATIONAL PARK

This is the second largest park in South Africa, covering an area of approximately 9600km² (3706 sq miles). Adjacent to it is the Gemsbok National Park in Botswana, which is considerably larger. Their combined areas exceed 36,000km² (13,896 sq miles). The international boundary between the two parks is along the Nossob River and is marked by unobtrusive markers. The animals are free to roam between the two parks and it is hoped that one day that asinine human boundary will be removed and a single park created.

RICHTERSVELD NATIONAL PARK

The Park is 16,445ha (40,636 acres) in extent and is situated along the Orange River, south of Namibia. It is South Africa's largest mountain desert park. A significant feature is that the management of the Park is shared with the adjacent local community, who still use sections of the park for grazing their animals.

WEST COAST NATIONAL PARK

The West Coast National Park is situated around the Langebaan Lagoon and includes the Postberg Nature Reserve and the offshore islands of Malgas, Jutten, Marcus and Schaapen. It covers an area of a little more than 25,000ha (61,775 acres).

GOOD HOPE NATURE RESERVE

This reserve is situated at the southern tip of the Cape Peninsula and has a coastline of 40km (25 miles), which is washed by the Atlantic Ocean on its western flank and the Indian on its eastern flank. The reserve covers a total area of 7750ha (19,150 acres).

DE HOOP NATURE RESERVE

This reserve combines both terrestrial and marine reserves which together cover more than 60,000ha (148,260 acres). It incorporates about 50km (31 miles) of coastline and extends up to 10km (6 miles) inland. The reserve is noted for its pristine dunes, extensive *fynbos* and wetlands. It has seven distinct ecosystems which support a wide variety of plant, mammal, bird and reptile species.

BONTEBOK NATIONAL PARK

The Park was proclaimed in 1931 near Bredasdorp as a means of preserving the last 22 Bontebok left on earth, after centuries of ruthless slaughter. The antelope today are descendants of those remaining 22 animals. In 1960 a larger park of 2786ha (6884 acres) was established near Swellendam in one of the few areas left with natural *fynbos*.

WILDERNESS NATIONAL PARK

The Park is interlaced by a number of lakes and wetlands and covers an area of about 10,000ha (24,710 acres). It is well known for its sedge and reedbeds which provide excellent breeding habitats for some 80 waterbird species. In the surrounding grasslands there are a variety of antelope.

KNYSNA LAKES PARK

The Knysna Lake area covers 15,000ha (37,065 acres) of which about 1800ha (4448 acres) is taken up by the lagoon. It is one of South Africa's largest estuaries and is rich in invertebrate organisms and fish, which in turn provide food for a wide variety of waterbirds. Knysna is rapidly becoming one of South Africa's premier resort destinations and as a result, inevitable tensions exist between conservation and development.

TSITSIKAMMA NATIONAL PARK

The Park comprises a narrow coastal strip of land situated along the southern Cape coast stretching some 80km (50 miles) – from the Groot River at Nature's Valley in the west to another Groot River in the east. A marine reserve extends 5km (3 miles) out to sea along the entire length of the park. The Park is characterized by two types of vegetation: indigenous evergreen forest and *fynbos*. It is particularly well known for its outstanding hiking trails.

ZUURBERG NATIONAL PARK

This was formerly a state forest which was proclaimed a national park in 1985. It is situated near Port Elizabeth in the Winterberg mountains. The Park is of particular interest to botanists because it combines three totally different vegetation types: Valley Bushveld which is characterized by low, thorny bushes and includes various tree euphorbias; False Heathland, which contains elements of *fynbos*; and evergreen coastal forest.

ADDO ELEPHANT PARK

The Addo Elephant Park, situated near Port Elizabeth, was proclaimed in 1931 to protect a remnant population of 11 Eastern Cape Elephants and a few remaining Buffalo which had managed to evade the hunters' bullets. Today the Park has an Elephant population that runs into hundreds. It presently covers an area of 12,000ha (29,652 acres), virtually all of which is covered in various species of dense woody bush.

MOUNTAIN ZEBRA NATIONAL PARK

The Park was specifically proclaimed to protect one of the last remaining populations of the Cape Mountain Zebra, which today numbers some 200 animals. The Park covers an area of 6536ha (16,150 acres) and is situated in a vast amphitheatre on the northern slopes of the Bankberg mountains. The vegetation reflects its transitional nature, between the arid Karoo scrub of the west and the temperate sweet grasslands of the east. The area in which the Park is situated experiences climatic extremes: heavy frost and snow in winter and very hot days in summer.

DWESA NATURE RESERVE

Situated in the Eastern Province, east of Idutywa are the Dwesa and Cwebe Nature Reserves which are only separated by the Mbashe River and a narrow corridor that runs to a small coastal resort hotel located between them. They share similar habitats and vegetation types

MKAMBATI NATURE RESERVE

The Mkambati Nature Reserve lies between the Msikaba and Mtentu rivers in the Eastern Province. The Reserve has mainly grassland vegetation, but because of its close proximity to subtropical KwaZulu-Natal there are important subtropical influences. As a result a wide variety of plants are found within the reserve, of which the Pondoland Coconut or 'Mkambati Coconut' (*Jubaeopsis caffra*) is endemic.

THE GREATER ST LUCIA WETLAND PARK

The Greater St Lucia Wetland Park is a combination of a number parks and reserves which have already been proclaimed, they include: St Lucia Reserve, St Lucia Park, False Bay Park, the St Lucia Marine Reserve, the Sodwana Bay National Park, the Cape Vidal State Forest and various interlinking areas in between. The Greater St Lucia Wetland Park covers five distinctly different ecosystems ranging from a marine ecosystem to dry savanna and thornveld. This rich diversity gives the Park a unique quality and status in conservation in Africa.

TEMBE ELEPHANT PARK

The Park is 29,000ha (71,659 acres) in extent and lies on the border between KwaZulu-Natal and Mozambique. It consists of dense woodland and sand forest, with various areas of shrub veld and wetlands. It was established to provide a sanctuary for the last free ranging elephants in South Africa.

NDUMO GAME RESERVE

This is a small game reserve, being a mere 10,000ha (24,710 acres) in size, but despite this it has widely ranging ecosystems which support an abundant birdlife, with 416 species recorded.

MKUZI GAME RESERVE

This Reserve, which has an area of 36,000ha (88,956 acres), has a rich variety of vegetation types, ranging from open savanna woodland to dense forests of large sycamore fig trees. The reserve also contains an open pan system which supports a wealth of waterbirds.

PHINDA RESOURCE RESERVE

This is a private reserve which has become an up-market ecotourism showpiece in South Africa. The reserve is some 15,000ha (37,065 acres) in extent, but it has traversing rights over additional surrounding land. It incorporates both hilly terrain and flat undulating acacia-covered plains which support over 10,000 head of game, including Lion, Elephant, Buffalo and both Black and White Rhino.

HLUHLUWE–UMFOLOZI GAME RESERVE

The Hluhluwe and Umfolozi Game Reserves, which have recently been combined into a single large complex of some 96,453ha (238,335 acres), are amongst the oldest conservation areas in Africa having been proclaimed in 1895. The reserve is one of great beauty and because of its diverse nature offers a variety of ecosystems which support a rich diversity of wildlife.

ITALA GAME RESERVE

Itala is some 32,000ha in extent (79,072 acres) and consists of rolling grasslands dotted with numerous aloes, steep valleys, open woodlands and bushveld. The reserve lies on the south bank of the Pongolo River in northern KwaZulu-Natal and has some 75 mammal species, most of which have been long extinct in the region and which have been re-introduced from other areas.

ROYAL NATAL NATIONAL PARK

The Park, which is 8794ha (21,730 acres) in extent, is situated in the northern Drakensberg in KwaZulu-Natal. It is dominated by a giant amphitheatre, a crescent-shaped basalt ridge which is 5km (3 miles) wide and towers some 1500m (4922ft) above the surrounding valleys.

GIANT'S CASTLE GAME RESERVE

The reserve is situated in the central Drakensberg and is named after the 3314m (10,873ft) peak which provides a magnificent backdrop to its setting on the slopes and valleys of the Drakensberg mountains. Giant's Castle was proclaimed a game reserve in 1903 as a measure to protect the fast dwindling number of Eland in South Africa and covers an area of 34,638ha (85,590 acres).

BIBLIOGRAPHY

Adams J, *Wild Flowers of the Northern Cape*, 1976, Department of Nature and Environmental Conservation of the Provincial Administration of the Cape of Good Hope, Cape Town

Berjak P, Campbell GK, Huckett B, Pammenter N.W, *In the Mangroves of Southern Africa*, 1982, Natal Branch of the Wildlife Society of Southern Africa

Botanical Society of South Africa, Veld & Flora: June 1996, Sept 1995, Dec 1993, Sept 1987, Dec 1988, Dec 1987, Kirstenbosch, Cape Town

Braack L, *A Visitor's Guide to Kruger National Park*, 1996, Struik Publishing Group (Pty) Ltd, Cape Town

Braack L, *Field Guide to Insects of the Kruger National Park*, 1991, Struik Publishers, Cape Town

Branch B, *Field Guide to the Snakes and other Reptiles of Southern Africa*, 1990, Struik Publishers, Cape Town

Branch M and G, *The Living Shores of Southern Africa*, 1981, C. Struik (Pty) Ltd, Cape Town

Brett MR, *Pilanesberg, Jewel of Bophuthatswana*, 1989, Frandsen Publishers, Johannesburg

Brett MR, Mountain AG, *Touring Atlas of Southern Africa*, 1997, Struik Publishers (Pty) Ltd, Cape Town

Felix J, *Animals of Africa*, 1981, The Hamlyn Publishing Group Ltd, London

Gibson J, *Wild Flowers of Natal (Coastal Region)*, 1975, The Trustees of the Natal Publishing Trust Fund

Hilliard OM, *Trees and Shrubs of the Natal Drakensburg*, 1985, Department of Botany, University of Natal, Pietermaritzburg

Jackson WPU, *Wild Flowers of Table Mountain*, 1977, Howard Timmins (Pty) Ltd, Cape Town

Kidd MM, *Cape Peninsula South African Wild Flower Guide No. 3,* Botanical Society of South Africa

King D, *Reef Fishes and Corals East Coast of Southern Africa*, 1996, Struik Publishers (Pty) Ltd, Cape Town

Le Roux A, Schelpe E.A.C.L.E, *Namaqualand and Clanwilliam, South African Wild Flower Guide No. 1.* Cape Department of Nature and Environmental Conservation of the Cape of Good Hope

Lighton C, *Cape Floral Kingdom*, 1973, Juta & Co Ltd, Cape Town

Mason H, *Western Cape Sandveld Flowers*, 1972, C.Struik (Pty) Ltd Cape Town

Migdoll I, *Field Guide to the Butterflies of Southern Africa*, 1994, Struik Publishers (Pty) Ltd, Cape Town

Moll E, Scott L, *Trees and Shrubs of the Cape Peninsula,* 1981, Eco-Lab Trust Fund, University of Cape Town

Mountain AG, *Paradise Under Pressure*, 1990, Southern Book Publishers, Johannesburg

Natal Parks Board, St Lucia, undated, Natal Parks, Game and Fish Preservation Board, Pietermartizburg

National Botanic Gardens, Karoo Botanic Garden, undated, National Botanic Gardens of South Africa

Newman K, *Birds of Southern Africa*, 1983, MacMillan S.A. (Publishers) (Pty) Ltd, Johannesburg

Palgraves KL, *Trees of Southern Africa,* 1981, C. Struik Publishers, Cape Town

Passmore NI, Carruthers WC, *South African Frogs, A Complete Guide,* 1995, Southern Book Publishers, Johannesburg

Pienaar U de V, Joubert SCJ, Hall-Martin A, De Graaff G, Rautenbach IL, *Field Guide to the Mammals of the Kruger National Park*, 1993 Struik Publishers (Pty) Ltd, Cape Town

Pooley E, *The Complete Field Guide to Trees of Natal Zululand and Transkei*, 1993, Natal Flora Publications Trust, Durban

Pringle J, *The Conservationists and the Killers*, 1982, TV Bulpin and Books of Africa (Pty) Ltd

Reynolds GW, *The Aloes of South Africa*, 1969, AA Balkema, Cape Town

Robinson H, *Morphology and Landscape*, 1975, University Tutorial Press Ltd, London

Rourke JP, *Wild Flowers of South Africa*, 1996, Struik Publishers (Pty) Ltd, Cape Town

Seagrief SC, *The Seaweeds of the Tsitsikamma Coastal National Park*, 1967, Botany Department, Rhodes University, Grahamstown

Sinclair I, *Field Guide to the Birds of Southern Africa,* 1994, Struik Publishers (Pty) Ltd, Cape Town

Skaife SH, *African Insect Life*, 1979, Struik Publishers (Pty) Ltd, Cape Town

Strahler AN and AH, Environmental Geoscience: *Interaction Between Natural Systems and Man,* 1973, Hamilton Publishing Co, Santa Barbara

Stuart C and T, *Guide to Southern African Game and Nature Reserves,* 1989, Struik Publishers, Cape Town

Field Guide to the Mammals of Southern Africa, 1995, Struik Publishers (Pty) Ltd, Cape Town

Tietz RM, Robinson GA, *Tsitsikama Shore,* 1977, National Parks Board of Trustees of the Republic of South Africa

Van der Westhuizen GCA, Eicker A, *Field Guide to the Mushrooms of Southern Africa*, 1994, Struik Publishers (Pty) Ltd, Cape Town

Van Rensburg TFJ, *An Introduction to Fynbos*, undated, Issued by the Department of Environmental Affairs, Pretoria

Wager VA, *Dwindling Forests of the Natal Coast*, 1976, Umhlanga Centre of the Natal Branch of the Wildlife Society of South Africa

OPPOSITE *The mighty lion has always been considered Africa's primeval monarch. Few animals challenge its right to be king and few humans fail to admire its awesome magnificence and regal supremacy in the continent's remaining wild places.*

INDEX